A ALMA AMORTALHADA
MÁRIO DE SÁ-CARNEIRO'S USE
OF METAPHOR AND IMAGE

PAMELA BACARISSE

A ALMA AMORTALHADA
MÁRIO DE SÁ-CARNEIRO'S USE
OF METAPHOR AND IMAGE

TAMESIS BOOKS LIMITED
LONDON

Colección Támesis
SERIE A - MONOGRAFIAS, CV

Depósito legal: M. 32845-1984

Printed in Spain by Talleres Gráficos de SELECCIONES GRÁFICAS
Carretera de Irún, km. 11,500 - Madrid-34

for
TAMESIS BOOKS LIMITED
LONDON

For my husband,
Salvador

ACKNOWLEDGMENTS

I should like to express my thanks for support and advice to Professor Frank Pierce, Sr. Alexandre Pinheiro Torres, Dr. I. R. Macdonald, Professor John Varey, Sr. Luís de Sousa Rebelo and Dr. Jacinto do Prado Coelho. I am grateful, too, for the help I received from Dr. John Parker's pioneering work on Mário de Sá-Carneiro and from the late Professor Jorge de Sena. I received grants from the Sir Ernest Cassel Educational Trust and the University of Aberdeen Travel Fund towards research periods in France and Portugal, and I am glad to acknowledge the help of the Gulbenkian Foundation towards the publication of this book. My greatest debt, however, is to my husband; without his judgment, erudition and loving patience it would not have been written.

CONTENTS

Page references are given in parentheses after each Sá-Carneiro quotation. The abbreviations are:

P =*Princípio*, Lisbon, 1912.
CL =*A Confissão de Lúcio* (1914), Lisbon, 1968.
CF =*Céu em Fogo* (1915), Lisbon, s.d. (1956?).
Po =*Poesias*, Lisbon, s.d. (1946?).
C I =*Cartas a Fernando Pessoa*, vol. I, Lisbon, 1958.
C II=*Cartas a Fernando Pessoa*, vol. II, Lisbon, 1959.

The pagination for the short stories in *Princípio* is:

The pagination for the short stories in *Céu em Fogo* is:

All italics are mine unless otherwise stated.
Part of the following material has been published as follows:

«*A Confissão de Lúcio*: Decadentism *après la lettre*», in *Forum for Modern Language Studies*, X (1974), 156-74.
«Sá-Carneiro and the *conte fantastique*», in *Luso-Brazilian Review*, XII, no. 1 (Summer, 1975), 65-79.
«Mário de Sá-Carneiro: A Imagem da Arte», in *Colóquio. Letras*, 75 (1983), 40-53.
«The '*Provincianismo*' of Mário de Sá-Carneiro», in *Neophilologus*, 68 (1984), 72-80.

INTRODUCTION

The study of a writer's language can shed light on the writer himself, and the knowledge acquired in this way may then reflect back on to the original field of study. The dissection and classification of the component parts in a work of literature should clear up misapprehensions, and at the same time reveal tendencies, fully-fledged attitudes, emotions, perspectives, prejudices, weaknesses, aims and inhibitions, helping the reader to achieve a better grasp of the work. In some cases this may well be considered a metaphor for the artist; as a symbol conveys a concept, so a piece of writing can convey a personality more profoundly and accurately than any amount of biographical detail or even personal acquaintance with the author could do. Once this personality is understood, the writings may take on a new dimension. At best, we may acquire more understanding of life through art; at the very least, we will know how previously unconsidered effects were created by the author.

Metaphor and image involve symbolic representation, though much less the representation of meaning than that of import.[1] They are both symbolic elements, but this is not to say that there is a code in which a given sign denotes a fixed concept, quality, attitude or emotion, or indeed that the works of an author could be successfully analysed in an inflexible, mechanical way. In this investigation, the language of Sá-Carneiro will be considered as symbolic in a fairly loose sense, and although most of the elements we shall study are obviously metaphors or images, there are, in fact, some which are not. Instead of being what Charles Mauron has called *métaphores obsédantes*,[2] they are, rather, «mots obsédants» or «expressions obsédantes», and it is because of their frequency and the author's obsessive concern with them that their suggestive nature becomes apparent. Using frequency as a criterion, we can justify our inclusion of certain words and phrases which perhaps would not normally be thought of as images or metaphors. And yet it must be added that even these are undeniably metaphorical, in the sense that they point to and include something beyond themselves, and it is this something —meta-

---

[1] «Works of art, which I am sure have *import,* but not genuine *meaning,* are symbols of a sort...» SUSANNE K. LANGER, «On a New Definition of 'Symbol'», in *Philosophical Sketches* (New York, 1964), p. 60. (First edition: 1962.) Author's italics.

[2] CHARLES MAURON, *Des Métaphores obsédantes au mythe personnel* (Paris, 1962).

phorical import rather than the metaphorical meaning usually sought—
that this study will attempt to point out.

Behind any investigation of this sort is the premise that works of
literature consist of more than is immediately obvious from the surface
meaning of their language, that images are images because they suggest
other things, that metaphors have at least two levels and that «mots
obsédants» have a symbolic function which is testified by the author's
obsessive interest in them. As Ortega once put it:

> Harto conocida es la importancia que para aprehender y fijar la indi-
> vidualidad de un artista literario tiene la determinación de su vocabulario
> predilecto. Como esas flechas que marcan en los mapamundis las grandes
> corrientes oceánicas, nos sirven sus palabras preferidas para descubrir los
> torbellinos mayores de ideación que componen el alma del poeta.[3]

Sá-Carneiro's «vocabulario predilecto» is a fruitful field of study since
it is relatively restricted and very repetitious. Some of his imagery points
to the fact that his writings echo certain well-established schools or literary movements, rather than indicating great originality, but this is revealing
too: the very fact that he feels more sympathy for one type of art than
another is significant. That Decadentism, for example, was a vital influence
is a key fact, and again, the close connections between his prose and the
nineteenth-century *conte fantastique* are equally interesting. The starting-
point of our investigation will consist of two things: the nature of the
component factors in Sá-Carneiro's work as established by his choice of
vocabulary, and their proportion to one another.

Although it is my contention that as much, if not more, can be
learned about an author from the written word as from biographical
detail, we do not need to depend entirely on Sá-Carneiro's writings to
find out about the man. What will become clear is the extent to which his
prose and poetry «betrayed» him: he was very much a confessional
writer and a writer whose emotions and tastes dominated his work.
Nevertheless, knowledge of his background and the main events of his
short life is helpful.

When he commited suicide by taking five bottles of strychnine in the
hotel room where he was living at the Hôtel de Nice, 29 rue Victor Mas-
sé, Paris, on April 26, 1916, Sá-Carneiro had yet to reach his twenty-
sixth birthday. He had been born, in Lisbon, on May 19, 1890,[4] and his
truly productive period was limited to just three years, between 1913
and 1916. Although he had, in fact, been co-author of a play, *Amizade,*[5]

---

[3] José ORTEGA Y GASSET, *El espectador,* I (Madrid, 1968), p. 203.
[4] He was born at 93 Rua da Conceição, in the Lisbon *Baixa.* At the time of
his birth his father was still a student. Both his parents came from comfortably-off
Lisbon families.
[5] His co-author was a schoolfriend, Tomás Cabreira Júnior. The play, in three

which was performed in March, 1912 and published two months later, and sole author of a book of short stories, *Princípio,* written between 1908 and 1912 and published at his own expense in the latter year, both these works are usually considered little more than juvenilia, albeit revealing juvenilia, and his reputation stands or falls on his novella *A Confissão de Lúcio,* which came out in 1914, the collection of short stories that goes under the title of *Céu em Fogo* (1915) and, perhaps more than either of these, on his poetry, nearly all of which is now available in an edition called simply *Poesias* (Lisbon, 1946) and which was written sporadically in his last three years of life.[6]

It is hard to avoid the conclusion that some, at least, of Sá-Carneiro's later tormented sensibility and emotional instability was the outcome of his mother's death when he was two and a half and she herself only twenty-three. His friend, the poet Fernando Pessoa, certainly thought so, as we shall see (below, p. 90). Although it could be argued that really Pessoa was talking about himself when he referred to the trauma of losing a mother (his own mother remarried when he was six, and he saw this as a betrayal of him), there is no doubt that for him the theory that being deprived of love results in an inability to love found a living example in Mário de Sá-Carneiro. But at least his childhood could not be described as deprived from a material point of view. Long periods were spent in the country, at the Quinta da Vitória, at Camarate, which was owned by his paternal grandfather, and in Lisbon the family lived comfortably in the Calçada do Carmo. From all accounts we gather that he was not short of money or of creature comforts and entertainment. It was he, for example, who financed a school magazine, *O Chinó,* produced in collaboration with a group of schoolfriends who were all interested in the theatre. Then we know that his father took him to Paris every year, that he was invariably well dressed and that he bought all the new books that appealed to him. He turned into a frequent and enthusiastic theatregoer as he grew older (though the standard of the theatre in Lisbon as the time was not impressive), brought out —as we have seen— a private edition of his first book and, perhaps most glamorous of all, enjoyed being a member of the family that owned the first motor car to be seen in the streets of the Portuguese capital. And he was not, as he might have been under the circumstances, totally isolated: he was surrounded by family and servants and cared for by a devoted *ama* whom he loved dearly. Yet the loss of his mother should certainly not be ignored. Though it would be absurd to see it as the principal cause of the malaise that ultimately led to his death,

acts, was given at the Teatro Clube da Estefânia in Lisbon by an amateur company. It was published by Arnaldo Bordalo.
    [6] The Ática edition of 1946 (which in fact does not carry a date) is Volume II of the *Obras Completas de Mário de Sá-Carneiro.* A new edition appeared in 1953. See too the Aguilar *Todos os Poemas* (Rio de Janeiro, 1974).

we do know from those who have undertaken research into suicide that domestic instability in childhood, whether caused by the death of a parent or the dissolution of the parents' marriage, can be a contributory factor (see below, p. 90).

The suicide of his friend and co-author of *Amizade,* Tomás Cabreira Júnior, was another profound blow. Tomás, the illegitimate son of a well-known and influential Lisbon town councillor, also lost his mother at an early age; his father showed little interest in him, for some years he lived separately, cared for by a servant, and it is said that he was ever conscious of his lack of family life. Things improved somewhat when he moved into his father's house and started school at the Liceu de São Domingos in 1905. There this shortsighted, effeminate, small and incredibly shy boy found a friend in the almost equally sensitive Mário de Sá-Carneiro, who had come to the school after a period in the Liceu do Carmo. The two boys, together with a third, Gilberto Rola, talked art and literature all the time, and Mário and Gilberto were allowed to read the manuscript of a play, *Musmé,* that Tomás had written in a school exercise book. He was determined to become an actor and an author, but these ambitions were not those that his father would have wished for his son, and there was bad feeling and, ultimately, a heated argument which also, apparently, was sparked off by Tomás' amorous exploits, strongly censured at home. The day after the row he went to school and shot himself. It was Sá-Carneiro who went around the school announcing to each group in each classroom that Tomás was dead. Before he committed suicide he burned everything that he had written, but the play *Amizade* survived since Sá-Carneiro himself had a copy of it. A few months after Tomás' death, Sá-Carneiro wrote one of his earliest poems «A um suicida» (October, 1911).[7]

It is not, perhaps, going too far to see this suicide as an event that influenced his outlook on life and death; at the very least, it opened his eyes to the fact that some people do kill themselves and it made him think about their motivation. What is obvious, it seems to me, from his poem «A um suicida» is the emphasis he places on the courage required to perform such an act: «Tu crias em ti mesmo e eras corajoso», it begins, and goes on to refer to having ideas, confidence and hope. Although it is clear that he is not advocating suicide as common practice, it is not without significance that the poem ends:

[7] For details of the Tomás Cabreira Júnior affair, see FRANÇOIS CASTEX, *Mário de Sá-Carneiro e a Génese de «Amizade»* (Coimbra, 1971). The poem «A um suicida» is reproduced on p. 341; it was first published in *Acto,* Fascículo de Cultura 1, October 1, 1951. See too ANTÓNIO CABREIRA, *Tomás Cabreira, Através da Vida e Através da Morte* (Coimbra, 1920).

... Mas tu inda alcançaste alguma coisa: a morte,
E há tantos como eu que não alcançam nada...

One other area of investigation in his life and attitudes which may well have been affected by the traumatic experiences of his early life is that of homosexuality. As we shall see in Chapter One, any judgment of Sá-Carneiro's own sexual orientation can never be more than speculation, and we do know that at the very end of his life he lived through a brief, but almost certainly consummated, affair with a woman. Nevertheless, his writings are undeniably ambivalent, and include explicit homosexual references as well as implicit indications of the latent orientation of the author. Could his abandonment by his mother, involuntary and tragic though it may have been, have contributed towards an unconscious bitter renunciation of women? Could his close fellowship with a delicate, hyper-sensitive young boy, a relationship which was highlighted by the sensa-tional, even melodramatic, way in which it came to an end, have influenced him? Could, indeed, his later friendship with another alienated poet, Pessoa, a relationship dramatised this time by their both seeing them-selves as particularly aware and vulnerable and isolated, be considered a homosexual one? This is one of the areas in which the writings illum-inate the author's life and, as we have suggested, the insight thus gained re-reflects back onto the written word.

Like so many youths in Portugal whose interests led them away from any scientific training and whose social position presumed the essential nature of a university education, Sá-Carneiro elected to study law, and enrolled in the University of Coimbra. The fact that he spent less than one academic year there, together with a total absence of any reference to this period in his writings, suggests that he found neither the place nor his companions congenial. When we consider his later record in Paris, where again he was supposed to be a law student, and which displays a total lack of interest for the subject, it is easy to see that there was never any real intention on his part to attend classes, to say nothing of completing any course successfully. There is, we are told, no record of his ever having attended lectures, not even in his first term.[8] But the very fact that he went, «permanently» this time, to Paris is a vital one. Indeed, 1912 was a key year in a number of ways. He decided to give up the idea of a period in Coimbra; his —and Tomás'— *Amizade* was per-formed and published; he published *Princípio* and acquired a certain fame (though critical reactions were mixed); he got to know most of the young men who would later form part of the Modernist Generation that came together with the shortlived journal *Orpheu;* he became part of Lisbon café society, and he spent many a long hour discussing art and

---

[8] See MARIA ALIETE GALHOZ, *Mário de Sá-Carneiro* (Lisbon, 1963), p. 15.

life with his newfound friend Fernando Pessoa. Then, on October 13, with an escort of wellwishers which included his father and his grandfather, he went to Santa Apolónia Station in Lisbon and took the train for Paris.

Once installed in the Grand Hôtel du Globe, 50 rue des Écoles, he dedicated himself to writing, spending hours and hours in cafés, often with other Portuguese artists, for whom —as we shall see— Paris was the centre of the world, and, significantly, writing home to friends in Portugal, particularly Pessoa. His favourite form of entertainment was still the theatre, but now he also had the possibility of going to the famous Paris Music Halls, and these certainly had a noticeable influence on his work. He started to write poetry, interspersed with a couple of short stories that were to become part of *Céu em Fogo,* he got to know Paris better and he established a sort of lifestyle, which did not include the study of law. In June 1913, he returned to Lisbon and met up with his friends and fellow aesthetes. In the time he spent there he went on writing: in addition to poetry and more short stories, he started *A Confissão de Lúcio,* and then prepared it, together with the collection of poems that bore the title *Dispersão,* for publication. Both *A Confissão de Lúcio* and *Dispersão* were to come out in 1914, but both were ready by the end of the previous year.

It was not until the summer of 1914 that he went back to Paris, and now, for the first time, we hear of financial difficulties in his life. His father had just gone to Africa, to what was then called Lourenço Marques, in Mozambique, and with the excuse that it took a long time to get money out of his father, given the distance involved, he sent urgent pleas to Pessoa for the cash that the sale of the remaining copies of *Princípio* in Lisbon had produced. Although he had written to Pessoa with frequency during his previous sojourn in Paris, it was now that his letters became more and more intense and personal. It was an interesting relationship, made all the more intriguing by the fact that Pessoa's replies have been lost. The obvious interpretation of the correspondence is that it merely reveals the admiration, liking, and even affection the two men felt for each other («Gosto tanto de si!» says Sá-Carneiro to Pessoa on one occasion, and his letters are full of friendship, praise and intimate revelations). But there is surely more to it than that. João Gaspar Simões was one of the first critics to see the flow of letters from Pessoa's point of view, and to hint at a certain onesidedness in their relationship. Pessoa himself was going through a difficult and worrying period in his life and his circumstances were anything but comfortable. «Pobre Fernando Pessoa!» says Gaspar Simões. «É a ele que Sá-Carneiro vai recorrer nos últimos dramáticos meses de Paris, implorando-lhe que corra, aqui e ali, em busca de dinheiro com que saciar as suas extravagâncias.» And he goes on: «Era a Fernando Pessoa, completamente desamparado em Lisboa, sem pai nem mãe a quem pedir dinheiro para alugar um quarto, que Sá-Carneiro fazia estas confidências egoístas de filho-família.»[9] Maria Aliete Galhoz sees Pessoa as Sá-Carneiro's «amigo fiel e quase predestinado, que o acompanhará e ajudará sempre com o seu devotamento e amizade»,[10] but others have wondered at the apparent ambivalence of Pessoa's reaction in the face of repeated suicide threats from his friend in Paris in the last months, especially as there was, in fact, one actual suicide attempt before he finally killed himself. In any case, Sá-Carneiro's letters are of profound importance and can, and should, in my opinion, be taken as one with his fiction and poetry for the purpose of the exercise. The critic Arnaldo Saraiva agrees: in his preface to Sá-Carneiro's letters to Luís de Montalvor, Cândida Ramos, Alfredo Guisado and José Pacheco, he claims that letters from the Portuguese author express his «complexidade psicológica», and he professes astonishment that «estudos de carácter geral dedicados ao escritor esqueçam o epistológrafo».[11]

His correspondence undeniably sheds light on the last two years of his life, whatever else it may not do, and this period —actually just a year and ten months after his return to Paris— can be seen as one of crises and decline. To add to his problems, the Great War broke out shortly after he had returned to the Grand Hôtel du Globe, and in the autumn he went home to Portugal. Strangely, he begs Pessoa in an anguished letter to keep secret the news of his imminent return, and once back home he retires to the Quinta da Vitória, making occasional trips into Lisbon, and spending his time writing short stories and poems.

When he did go back to Lisbon, at the end of October, 1914, he went to his father's address in the Praça dos Restauradores, but he obviously did not stay there. This last period of his life was clouded by ill feeling between him and his father — who was, of course, in Mozambique. The situation was complicated by the father's remarriage to a woman of —for his son at least— doubtful reputation. Indeed, it is usually thought that his precipitate flight from Lisbon in July, 1915 had something to do with his relationship with his stepmother.

But before this, he was involved with the preparation and publication of the literary journal *Orpheu,* as well as finishing and bringing out *Céu*

[9] João Gaspar Simões, *Vida e Obra de Fernando Pessoa,* II (Lisbon, s. d.), pp. 33 and 34.
[10] *Mário de Sá-Carneiro,* p. 14.
[11] Arnaldo Saraiva, *Cartas de Mário de Sá-Carneiro a Luís de Montalvor/Cândida Ramos/Alfredo Guisado/José Pacheco* (Oporto, 1977), p. 14. For further correspondence with Pessoa, see the same editor's *Correspondência Inédita de Mário de Sá-Carneiro a Fernando Pessoa* (Oporto, 1980). These are letters that were not included in the two volumes used for this study, but as Saraiva himself points out, the letters published in his later editions «não dão uma imagem diferente da que já davam as outras cartas conhecidas, e em especial as endereçadas a Fernando Pessoa» (*Cartas,* p. 11).

em Fogo and writing poetry. *Orpheu* came about as the result of the enthusiasm of Sá-Carneiro and his friends for new poetry and, indeed, new art, and it was Pessoa's poem «Paúis», written in 1913 and published in 1914, that gave its name to the first of the «-isms» espoused by the group: *Paùlismo*. Sá-Carneiro was thrilled and overwhelmed by the new style, and wrote to Pessoa about the possibility of a «volume 'paulico'» (C I, p. 137) from Paris; in Lisbon, there were plans for a «sarau páulico»,[12] but Pessoa was already thinking of a new «-ism», and the *páulico* phase was shortlived. *Interseccionismo, Sensacionismo* and Portuguese Futurism followed it, and Sá-Carneiro and Pessoa began to consider the possibility of a new journal that would be the mouthpiece of *Interseccionismo*. Pessoa was not without reservations: he was going through a spell of artistic introspection, he was undecided as to the best way for *Interseccionismo* to be «explicado aos inferiores», and at one point was convinced that the answer was a definitive book, an anthology of *interseccionista* poems. In fact, Pessoa tired of *Interseccionismo* as quickly as he had of *Paùlismo;* it was Luís da Silva Ramos, the poet Luís de Montalvor, who on his return from a spell in the Portuguese Embassy in Rio de Janeiro actually suggested that a literary magazine called *Orpheu* should be produced, for the *cognoscenti* of both Portugal and Brazil.[13] And when the first edition did come out, in March 1915, there was no explanation of any of the new poetic theories, the new «-isms», in it, despite the original intention. Perhaps it was because Pessoa was now less than enthusiastic, perhaps plans were changed because of problems created by the outbreak of war in Europe, but it was the war that made the production of the journal a real possibility, since it brought back to Portugal virtually all the potential contributors. In February 1915, everything had been decided: it was to be a quarterly *revista,* with Luís de Montalvor the Portuguese editor and Ronald de Carvalho the Brazilian. The group guaranteed four issues with their own finances, and the first number came out according to plan. It contained a dozen poems by Sá-Carneiro, headed «Para os 'Indícios de Oiro'», as well as poetry by Ronald de Carvalho, Alfredo Pedro Guisado and Armando Côrtes-Rodrigues, «Opiário» and the «Ode Triunfal» of Pessoa/Álvaro de Campos, some short «Frizos» by José de Almada Negreiros and the Pessoa play *O Marinheiro*. It was received, as its authors expected (and, indeed, hoped, though Pessoa him-

---

[12] See MARIA ALIETE GALHOZ's introduction, «Génese e história da revista *Orpheu*», in the re-edition of the journal, 2nd edition (Lisbon, 1971), p. XIV.

[13] The élitist orientation of the journal is quite clear in, for example, Luís de Montalvor's introduction to the first issue: «Nossa pretenção», he says, «é formar, em grupo ou ideia, um número escolhido de revelações em pensamento ou arte, que sobre este princípio aristocrático tenham em ORPHEU o seu ideal esotérico e *bem nosso* de nos *sentirmos* e *conhecermo-nos*», *ibid.*, p. 11. In her introduction, MARIA ALIETE GALHOZ refers to Luís de Montalvor's proposal as being for «uma revista literária para o escol intelectual dos dois países» (p. XV).

self flatly denied this)[14] with a mixture of scorn and horror. *Épater le bourgeois* was undeniably their aim, and they succeeded very well indeed: «Literatura de manicómio», said one review, and there is evidence that the volume caused a stir in literary circles — in the famous *espólio* of Fernando Pessoa were found two notebooks in which Sá-Carneiro had listed sixty-eight references to it. Volume Two came out in June 1915, and the notebooks record twenty-four mentions of it. There had been some changes. Gone were the names of Luís de Montalvor and Ronald de Carvalho, and these were replaced by those of Fernando Pessoa and Mário de Sá-Carneiro,[15] and the largely symbolist orientation of the contributions was modified so as to be predominantly *interseccionista*. The new contributors were Ângelo de Lima, who had been in a mental hospital since 1901 (and who was to die there in 1921),[16] Eduardo Guimarães, Raul Leal and an «anónimo ou anónima que diz chamar-se Violante de Cysneiros», who was actually Armando Côrtes-Rodrigues. There were illustrations by Santa Rita Pintor, with whom Sá-Carneiro spent much time in Paris in his early days there, in spite of the fact that he irritated him and infuriated him, and Sá-Carneiro's own contribution —dedicated, incidentally, to Santa Rita Pintor— consisted of the poems «Elegia», «Manucure» and «Apoteose», with the heading: «Poemas sem Suporte».[17] Again, the reaction of press and public was hostile, and political issues were increasingly involved. There were differences of opinion and tensions between the members of the group,[18] the journal made a loss, and suddenly Sá-Carneiro disappeared.

No-one really knows what prompted this unexpected departure. Was it something to do with his stepmother? Or, as Dieter Woll suggests, were there suspicions and accusations regarding his handling of the finances of *Orpheu?*[19] It is certainly true that he was not likely to be the ideal choice for the position of financial secretary to the group; what he actually did was to take upon himself —or, more accurately, on his father's name— the debts incurred by the venture. Since his father was also responsible for the cost of publishing *Céu em Fogo* and was less than pleased by the way affairs were progressing, he tried to persuade Mário

---

[14] See Fernando Pessoa's claim that he no longer harboured the «ambição grosseira de brilhar por brilhar» or «essa outra grosseiríssima e de um plebeísmo artístico insuportável, de querer *épater*» in his letter dated January 19, 1915. *Cartas a Armando Côrtes-Rodrigues* (Lisbon, s. d.).

[15] Luís de Montalvor did, however, contribute a poem, «Narciso», to this issue.

[16] See ÂNGELO DE LIMA, *Poesias Completas,* ed. Fernando Guimarães (Oporto, 1971).

[17] MARIA ALIETE GALHOZ has edited a re-edition of *Orpheu 2* (Lisbon, 1976).

[18] Nearly all of them wrote to the Editor of *A Capital,* for example, dissociating themselves from a provocative letter which had been sent by Pessoa, using the heteronym Álvaro de Campos, and which the newspaper had published.

[19] DIETER WOLL, *Realidade e Idealidade na Lírica de Sá-Carneiro* (Lisbon, 1968), p. 41.

to go to Mozambique, a move that did not appeal to his son. He fled back to Paris in such a rush that he had to obtain a passport *en route,* in San Sebastián. Only Pessoa knew he was going; only Pessoa knew his new address which, after some weeks during which letters had to be sent Poste Restante, was the Hôtel de Nice, where, nine months later, he killed himself.

His financial situation was not comfortable. Admittedly, he still received his allowance from his father, but this often arrived late, and was less than he needed to pay for all his many extravagances. The planned third volume of *Orpheu* was abandoned when his father refused to provide any more money, and there is little doubt that his financial problems contributed greatly to his unhappiness. It would be wrong, though, to attribute too much importance to lack of money when we come to consider his suicide. His *estado de alma,* to use a favourite phrase, is such that no amount of money could do anything to help; his letters and the poems he wrote in this period show this only too clearly —the «Sete Canções de Declínio», «Escala», «Desquite» and «Ápice», then «Abrigo», «Cinco Horas», «Serradura», «O Lord», «O Recreio», «Campainhada», «Torniquete», «Pied-de-nez», «O Pajem», «Caranguejola» and the «Último Soneto». Though he went on writing poetry («Crise Lamentável», «O Fantasma», «El-rei», «Aqueloutro» and «Fim» all date from 1916), he seems to have lost enthusiasm for it— and this was the one thing that had never failed before. He did write to Pessoa about a proposed *Novela Romântica,* and he did start a poem called «Feminina», but the first, of course, never materialised, and the second, of which each verse begins: «Eu queria ser mulher...» was never finished.[20]

His last months were as terrible as his ultimate death. He wrote continually to friends, particularly Pessoa, begging them for letters. «Escreva-me muito», he implored, in a letter dated April 18, «de joelhos lhe suplico» (C II, p. 183). His financial problems increased, possibly as the result of the influence of his stepmother, and when he died there was no sign of his new overcoat, his watch and a new pair of boots; it was thought that he had sold them in order to keep going. He was obviously preoccupied by his relationship with his father, horrified by news of the fall into complete insanity of Raul Leal, who had been one of the contributors to *Orpheu* (yet another instance of a kind of self-annihilation: «Raul Leal e Ângelo de Lima suicidaram-se simbolicamente na loucura», as Eugénio Lisboa has claimed),[21] convinced that he was going mad («... creia, meu pobre Amigo», he wrote to Pessoa on January 13, *«eu estou doido.* Agora

---

[20] See his letter to Pessoa dated February 16, 1916 (C II, p. 159).
[21] EUGÉNIO LISBOA, *O Segundo Modernismo em Portugal,* 9th edition (Lisbon, 1977), p. 24.

é que não há dúvidas. [...] O Sá-Carneiro está doido»), and living constantly with the thought of suicide in his mind.

His liaison with a girl of somewhat dubious morals apparently did
nothing to alleviate his condition, though she did, in fact, thwart his
attempt to throw himself under a Metro train on April 3. He had met
her, according to a confidant of his last months, José Araújo, in March
in a Montmartre café. To be precise, Araújo, in a letter sent to Fernando
Pessoa after Sá-Carneiro's death,[22] goes as far as to say that he had the
«infelicidade» to make her acquaintance. He refers to the poet's «interesse» in the girl, and adds: «digo interesse porque ainda hoje não sei se
era amor, simpatia, ou ódio, não sei». Sá-Carneiro, he says, told him that
he could not go on as they were: «impossível, impossível, aquela mulher;
um mistério, um horror», and he tells Pessoa that when he asked Sá-
Carneiro if he really loved her, the invariable reply was: «Não gosto
dessa mulher, juro-lhe que não gosto dessa mulher.» In a subsequent
letter, Araújo gives more details: «Tenho dela», he says, «as piores infor-
mações, ela tinha sobre o nosso pobre amigo uma grande influência. Já
ouvi mesmo dizer que ela lhe fazia barbaridades, entre outras a de o
obrigar a tomar *éter*.»[23] Needless to say, the relationship also cost much
more than he could afford; he spent «quantias enormes» on her in his
last two months. On the other hand, he himself claimed that he was now
living the kind of life he had always dreamed about, that he had experienced all there was to experience in the previous weeks, «realizada a
parte sexual, enfim, da minha obra».[24] If only he had some money, he
says, he could be happy for much longer, since psychologically everything is going very well. This last statement is far from convincing.

On the morning of April 26, he went to see José Araújo and asked
him to come to his hotel room at eight o'clock «em ponto» and «sem
falta». When Araújo arrived, he found that the poet had put on formal
dress and had taken a massive dose of strychnine. By the time help
arrived, he was dying. There are conflicting reports of the details of his
death,[25] about the number of farewell letters he wrote and as to whether
or not he repented of his action before he died,[26] but if we are to believe
Araújo's horrifying eye-witness account, there can be no doubt that he
suffered dreadfully. Four people attended his funeral at the Pantin ceme-
tery in Paris: three male friends, who included Araújo, and his mistress.
It was as recently as 1949 when another of those present at the funeral,
Sá-Carneiro's friend Carlos Ferreira, revealed that he had made an offer

[22] The letter is reproduced in MARIA ALIETE GALHOZ, *Mário de Sá-Carneiro*,
pp. 187-91. It is dated May 10, 1916.
[23] MARIA ALIETE GALHOZ, p. 191. This letter is not dated.
[24] Letter dated March 31, 1916.
[25] See DIETER WOLL, *Realidade*, pp. 43 and 44.
[26] Almada Negreiros claimed that he did, but Araújo fails to mention this.

of his own family burial plot in Paris to the poèt's father, so that his remains could be re-interred, or, as an alternative, had offered to buy a plot in Lisbon in conjunction with other friends. The offer, he said, was rejected, and the remains were thrown into the *vala comum*.[27]

After the funeral, Araújo and Ferreira collected his belongings together and put them in a trunk; these included many hundreds of letters, from his family, from Pessoa, from friends and from his mistress, as well as literary manuscripts. The trunk was to be sent on to Sá-Carneiro's grand-father. It was not until 1918 that any more was heard of the trunk: Sá-Carneiro's father said that it had been found, still in the hotel, but that when he opened it it contained only moth-eaten clothing.[28]

It goes without saying that the loss of Sá-Carneiro's effects is of con-siderable importance to students of Fernando Pessoa's life and works, but it is a sad loss for students of Sá-Carneiro too: the documents would have added important data to his biography. But it is what he wrote that really counts, his fiction, his poetry and his correspondence, all of them clear indications of his personality and his suffering.

Any introduction should, perhaps, attempt to sum up the orientation of a writer's output. As we shall see in this study, many influences are clearly visible in Sá-Carneiro's writings, there are many glances in a back-ward direction and much that has its roots in earlier generations of writers, in other countries —and this is important— rather than in Por-tugal. At the same time, there is originality, particularly in the poetry.

The early play, *Amizade*,[29] has more historical than intrinsic value. Indeed, when listing the «complete works», many years after the author's death, Fernando Pessoa disregarded both *Amizade* and *Princípio*.[30] *Ami-zade* has, in fact, been reprinted fairly recently, as part of François Castex's painstaking investigation of the circumstances of its creation (v. note 7), but is probably true to say that Pessoa ignored it because he considered it inferior, and therefore unrepresentative of Sá-Carneiro.[31] Even Castex refers to it as «secundária».[32] It is clearly the work of immature writers, a sentimental tale with the emphasis on plot, and with cliché situations acted out by cardboard characters. Its atmosphere is romantic — even, indeed, Romantic, with one of the male protagonists contemplating sui-cide and falling prey to a cerebral fever as the result of an anonymous letter, with paroxysms of passion, injured perfect innocence and, ultimate-

[27] This is found in a letter sent to João Gaspar Simões. See DIETER WOLL, *Realidade*, p. 45, and MARIA ALIETE GALHOZ, *Mário de Sá-Carneiro*, p. 23.
[28] JOÃO GASPAR SIMÕES, *Vida e Obra de Fernando Pessoa*, I, p. 11.
[29] Other theatrical pieces were promised but never materialised. See DIETER WOLL, *Realidade*, p. 23, and the various letters in which plans for new dramas are mentioned, e.g. the letter to Pessoa dated April 1, 1913 (C I, p. 99).
[30] See the Sá-Carneiro bibliography in *Presença* 16, November, 1928.
[31] FRANÇOIS CASTEX, *Mário de Sá-Carneiro e a Génese*, pp. 20-1.
[32] CASTEX, *Mário de Sá-Carneiro*, p. 20.

ly, the clear conviction that love is all. Nevertheless, and in spite of its weaknesses, it is relevant to any understanding of the author's later works, and it should be remembered, too, that only four years separate its presentation from his death; this is a remarkably brief period for any writer to develop into anything like full maturity in his work. In *Amizade* we find for the first time characters and themes very soon to become obsessive: the unconventional artist who is critical of bourgeois hypocrisy; the urbane man-about-town, who lives in Paris and sprinkles his conversation with French phrases; incest; suicide; a character with a mysterious background; eroticism. And, of course, friendship, since the theory behind the action is that from this love will be born.

The short stories that constitute *Princípio* are precursors of the far more successful *Confissão de Lúcio,* itself a long short story, and *Céu em Fogo,* and their quality is such that I feel they should be considered in this study, unlike *Amizade.* Furthermore, of course, they were not written in collaboration with another author, and in them almost all Sá-Carneiro's preoccupations are given full rein. All the prose, as we shall see in Chapter Two, has its origins in Hoffmann, Edgar Allan Poe's *Tales of Mystery and Imagination* and the French *conte fantastique;* emphasis is on plot and «explanation», mysteries that are solved without really resolving their underlying uncertainties and confusion, and on the repetitive surface elements of the author's concerns: the world of art and artists, love and uncritical admiration for Paris, freethinking, intelligent, clearsighted —but tormented— characters, uncontrolled excitement and uncontrollable fear. The *Princípio* stories confirm our impression of their author's preoccupation with suicide (six of the seven protagonists kill themselves at the end of the day), with incest and with mystery, and of his revulsion in the face of mediocrity and the pedestrian monotony of life which is typified by growing old. The earliest stories are those that constitute the section entitled «Diários» («Em Pleno Romantismo», «Felicidade Perdida», «A Profecia» and «Página dum Suicida»); these were written between November 1908 and September 1909, when the author was 18 and 19, and already, as Maria Aliete Galhoz has claimed, the myth of *o Outro,* a sort of counterpoint to the author's *eu,* is evident.[33] This projection is found throughout his later work: *o Outro* reveals Sá-Carneiro's inner turmoil in *A Confissão de Lúcio* (where it is *sexualizado* in the character of Ricardo), in *Céu em Fogo* (where one of the stories is actually called «Eu-próprio o Outro»), and in many of the poems; many years later, José Régio wrote a perceptive one-act play called *Mário ou Eu-propio — o Outro.*[34] It is, I think, true to say that Sá-Carneiro's neuro-

---

[33] CASTEX, *Mário de Sá-Carneiro,* p. 76.
[34] Lisbon, 1957.

sis did not change between the publication of *Princípio* and his death; it merely became more intense.

A Confissão de Lúcio has been seen as Sá-Carneiro's «principal obra em prosa»,[35] and although this may well be true, it is equally true that there is no difference *in kind* between it and *Princípio* or the later *Céu em Fogo* collection. It is sustained and organic, unlike the flashes of excitement that some of the short stories resemble. It is mysterious, but carefully worked out, so that there *is* an answer, even though the answer takes us no further. It is indeed superior to much of the prose, though not all (several of the *Céu em Fogo* pieces are equally successful). Ultimately, though, it is no more important than anything else written by the author for purposes of comprehension. And if the poetry does, as I believe it does, represent the best of Sá-Carneiro, if it is, as I have suggested, on the later works —especially the poetry— that his reputation stands or falls, this does not mean that any of his work can be ignored. It is all equally typical, and —in the end— equally tragic. It is undeniable that the writings reveal the man, and in this case at least, knowing the man is all-important. As José Régio has put it:

> De Mário de Sá-Carneiro claro que só há um retrato completo e justo: o seu auto-retrato, magnìficamente pincelado a cores alucinantes nas suas páginas mais pessoais.[36]

On every page, in fact.

---

[35] MARIA DA GRAÇA CARPINTEIRO, *A Novela Poética de Mário de Sá-Carneiro* (Lisbon, 1960), p. 15.
[36] *Pequena História da Moderna Poesia Portuguesa* (Oporto, 1976), p. 115. (First edition: 1941.)

PART ONE

"NATURAL" IMAGES

CHAPTER 1

PHYSICAL AND SPIRITUAL APPETITES

SEX

Sexual imagery and terminology are excellent sources of information regarding Sá-Carneiro's attitudes and inhibitions, some of which may well have contributed to the problems he encountered in coming to terms with himself and with other people. In spite of a quantitative emphasis on heterosexual relationships, there is no lack of reference to homosexuality, either in explicit terms or implicitly, and perhaps sometimes even unconsciously.

The traditional image of the innocent young virgin is one of the heterosexual images frequently found. It is so refined and exaggerated by the author that it is not only de-sexualised but also dehumanised and irrelevant, a symbol now of the inaccessible and, more important, the unwanted. It is a Romantic literary convention totally unrelated to what the author knows and certainly unconnected to what excites him. A creature of this sort is almost entirely spirit, but in any case belongs to the bourgeois world of marriage and conventional courtship that Sá-Carneiro found distasteful. She has to be «redeemed» — through death, disappearance, or by a revelation that she never, in fact, existed. The protagonist of the *Céu em Fogo* story «Mistério», for example, dreams of «uma companheira... Uma noiva talvez...», with «mãos brancas», «uma boca húmida» and «tranças louras» (CF, p. 135), then imagines «raparigas louras lendo livros de versos» with, significantly, children playing nearby (CF, p. 140). But when, unusually, he does find a «pequenina esposa» with «mãos brancas, sadias» and «lábios dourados» (CF, p. 147), their happiness is shortlived. In *A Confissão de Lúcio*, Ricardo de Loureiro —one of the protagonists— gives his version of the image:

> Para mim, o que pode haver de sensível no amor é uma saia branca a sacudir o ar, um laço de cetim que mãos esguias enastram, uma cintura que se verga, uma madeixa perdida que o vento desfez, uma canção ciciada em lábios de ouro e de vinte anos, a flor que a boca de uma mulher trincou... (CL, p. 63)

3

A relationship with such a woman would correspond to love, involving the spirit as well as the body and, with very few exceptions, Sá-Carneiro's characters have no experience of this. Ricardo lies in bed at night «entressonhando [...] o amor» (CL, p. 47), no more. He tells of a past encounter with two young girls; although one of them attracted him deeply, he quite deliberately decided against prolonging the acquaintance. Now he claims that «essa tarde foi a mais bela recordação» of his life, and he goes on to protest that he loves the unknown, unremembered creature (CL, p. 65). The hero of «Em Pleno Romantismo» does in fact find true love, but it is «amor *sem esperança*» (P, p. 150). Then again, in «O Incesto», a griefstricken widower looks back on his «amor *aniquilado*» (P, p. 185). Love either belongs to the past — the «ternura feita saudade» of «Dispersão» (Po, p. 64), — or is inaccesible — «quase o amor» (from «Quase», Po, p. 68), — or is the property of other people — «Olho em volta de mim. Todos possuem — /Um afecto, um sorriso, um abraço» («Como eu não possuo», Po, p. 70). And yet the loss, the «ternura perdida» (C II, p. 7), or its permanent absence are either caused deliberately or at least are rationalised. What is conventional is distasteful, especially the tedium of married love. Raul and Marcela in «Loucura» are married but manage to avoid this: «não eram dois esposos, eram dois amantes» (P, p. 48), for «os esposos que se amam como esposos, se não amam» (P, p. 49). Ricardo's unexpected marriage in *A Confissão de Lúcio* shocks the narrator, Lúcio: «o prosaico, vulgar casamento» is a phrase in «Loucura» (P, p. 44), while we are told that Raul himself often used to say: «O *matrimónio...* Ah! como eu abomino essa palavra!» (P, p. 44, author's italics). This reflects Sá-Carneiro's real-life attitude: in a letter to Pessoa dated February 26, 1913, he refers to «os que têm família e amor *banalmente*» (C I, p. 72). Sundays are seen as typical of family life and therefore outside the experience of the Sá-Carneiro *persona,* a fact about which the author reveals himself not altogether unhappy since the compensations are transcendental: «Porque um domingo é família / [...] *E os que olham a beleza* / Não têm bem-estar nem família» («Dispersão», Po, p. 62).

Those who fit into the conventional pattern, who have taken on «essa banalidade» which is marriage («Loucura», P, p. 45), are among those whom Sá-Carneiro and Fernando Pessoa called *lepidópteros.* And the term is not confined to people: Barcelona is a «terra de província, *lepidóptera*» (C II, p. 9) says Sá-Carneiro, and he writes a letter to Pessoa one day in «um Café *lepidóptero*» (C I, p. 149). The contempt shown for *lepidopterismo* in the sexual sphere is as evident from the infrequency of references to conventional amorous relationships as it is from their inaccessible unreality when they are mentioned. Conversely, the only other heterosexual female type in Sá-Carneiro appears with significant frequency and is patently accessible: this is the predatory *femme fatale* figure, whose lovers are victims not conquerors, and whose sexual tastes often invite conflict and violence and consequently give rise to fear.

The aggressive female who flaunts her irresistible sexuality is in fact a common image: virtually all heterosexual activity in the prose and the poetry involves women of this type. The *grande cobra* in «O Fixador de Instantes» is a good example: she is a veiled dancer, a latter-day Salome, «a sua voz a enclavinhar-se em luxúria» (CF, p. 265). Her erotic gyrations are graphically described:

> As pernas vibravam, perniciosas, uma friagem húmida, esguia; o ventre frutificava. Só as pontas dos seios prosseguiam o seu mistério...
>
> Ebânicas, as tranças tinham-se-lhe desprendido; e era já só perversão e loucura a grande viciosa, quando, ao arquear-se sobre a cisterna aluci-nante, morta num êxtase — os próprios seios lhe golfaram nus, espectrais de roxidão, heráldicos de crime... (CF, p. 265)

In the poem «Bárbaro» we find more irresistible dancing: «Mima a luxúria nua — Salomé asiática» (Po, p. 106), while in «Loucura» Raul quite deliberately turns his wife into «uma cortesã grega, uma prostitu-ta romana, uma cócóte parisiense» (P, p. 55). Then, in the same story, we find a «viciosa garota» (P, p. 98) not unrelated to the *grande fera* of «O Fixador de Instantes». There are many descriptions of these *femmes fatales* — one has a «cara provocante» (CL, p. 39), another has «cabelos soltos, loucamente» (CF, p. 41); there is a mysterious woman with «ca-belos torrenciais», who is «alta» and «escultural» and who wears a bizarre costume which reveals one nipple (CF, p. 76) and there are dancers with «carne esplêndida de sol» (CL, p. 39) or «carne luminosa» (CF, p. 286) and «dedos esguios, maquilhados, perturbantes» (CF, p. 288); in the poem «Manucure», we speculate on the possible effect if the «dançarina russa, / Meia-nua, agita as mãos pintadas da Salomé» (Po, p. 171); in *A Confissão de Lúcio,* there are references to the «pernas nuas» of the dancers (CL, p. 39), the «linha escultural das pernas» of the heroine (CL, p. 93) and the «bicos dos seios [...] dourados» of the *mulher fulva* (CL, p. 42); in the «Bailado» section of «Asas» and in «O Incesto» we find «seios dourados» again (CF, p. 203, and P, p. 326). Paint and make-up are frequently mentioned by Sá-Carneiro: «a ponta ma-quilhada do [...] seio» (CF, p. 77), «seios *pintados*» (P, p. 327) and «o seu sexo *maquilhado*» (CL, p. 95) are but a few instances of the painting of erogenous parts of the body, and there are also numerous references to «unhas pintadas». The excitement provoked by make-up is clear when Vitorino Bragança, in «Resurreição», talks about the «carnes *maquilha-das*» of his adolescent dreams and adds that he has always wanted to «possuir [...] a maquilhagem» (CF, p. 330). There are two conditions to sexual relationships with this kind of female: they must be extra-mari-tal, and there must be conflict, violence and fear. There will be «segredos

5

de adultérios» («Sete Canções de Declínio», Po, p. 126). Interestingly, in a letter dated August 23, 1915 to Pessoa, Sá-Carneiro outlines a new novel, and we discover that one of its most exciting elements is to be «a posse *no adultério*» (C II, p. 66). Then the love affair between Lúcio and Marta in *A Confissão de Lúcio* is adulterous, and almost all the sexual encounters in *Céu em Fogo* are, if not adulterous, casual. Violence is ever present: there are «amplexos *brutais*» (CL, p. 26), a dancer is «esbraseada e *feroz*» (CL, p. 42) and even a woman's breasts are described as «agressivos» (CF, p. 89). In retaliation for feminine brutality, the protagonist in «Ressurreição» dreams of how he would make love to a *mulher dourada:* «havia de a *morder,* de a *ferir* —sim, de a *ferir!*— com os seus beijos» (CF, p. 289), and we also find masculine violence associated with sexual excitement in «A Grande Sombra» and in «O Fixador de Instantes». Sex always involves conflict: in «Ressurreição», for example, the dancer's half-naked body is referred to as «o corpo *triunfal* de Salomé» (CF, p. 286), and the *mulher fulva* of *A Confissão de Lúcio* finishes her erotic dance a *vencedora* (CL, p. 42). The aggressive nature of the *femme fatale* is often complemented by a certain hardness and masculinity in her physical characteristics and by emphasis on her dominant rôle. Her strength and ability to inspire fear are frequently underlined: Lúcio, for example, tells of his habitual response to Marta: «ao possuí-la *eu era todo medo*» (CL, p. 101). Then, while Salome dances, we find «a luz a virgular-se *em medo*» («Salomé», Po, p. 86), and Caesar says to the dancer in «Bárbaro»: «*tenho medo de ti* num calafrio de espadas» (Po, p. 107). The narrator's meeting with the mysterious woman in «A Grande Sombra» is attended by «um *pavor* oculto» (CF, p. 79), while in «O Incesto», «no leito vasto [...] muitas vezes tivera [Luís] *medo*» (P, p. 192). As for masculine characteristics, the second *bailadeira* in *A Confissão* has «pernas [...] escalavradas de músculos, de durezas — *masculinamente*» (CL, p. 74) and the adjectives *esguia, magra* and *esbelta* are found with great frequency in descriptions of seductive women, though usually they have «seios bem visíveis» (CL, p. 39, for example). Male passivity —or, in some cases the desire for a passive rôle— suggests a homosexual temperament even in supposedly heterosexual characters: in Inácio de Gouveia's case, in «Ressurreição», «a sua primeira amante não a buscara ele; ela própria viera ao seu encontro — nem a possuíra ele; *ela só o possuíra*» (CF, p. 287), while Lúcio, in *A Confissão,* says: «não fui eu que a possuí — ela, toda nua, *ela sim, é que me possuíu*» (CL, p. 96). And Marta had, in fact, initiated their physical relationship: «as suas mãos, naturalmente, pela primeira vez encontraram as minhas» (CL, p. 94), he admits, while another night, «sem me dizer coisa alguma, ela pegou nos meus dedos e com eles acariciou as pontas dos seios» (CL, p. 95). The hero of «A Grande Sombra» reveals that he has recently been conscious of «a sensação esguia de ser insidiosamente uma rapariguinha suave e loira que viesse de se entregar ao seu amante» (CF, p. 61), and his brief relationship with the self-styled «Princesa velada» is initiated by her, not him. She is, incidentally, described as «alta» and «escultural» (CF, p. 76), and her fancy-dress for the masked ball is that of a pageboy. Furthermore, she carries a dangerous-looking dagger.

Homosexuality is found both in practice and in theory. «Ressurreição» ends with an act of intercourse between the male protagonists in which the dead woman they have both loved is, as it were, resurrected:

> ... os seus corpos nus, masculinos, se entrelaçaram... E então foi a Vitória, nesse abraço limpo, unisexuado — o triunfo impossível que *um deles* entressonhara outrora [...]
> ... a força sexual de ambos, astralmente, lograsse, conjugada, resuscitar entre os seus corpos — para A esvaír — Paulette, ela-própria, toda nua e subtil, arfando luar... (CF, p. 352, author's italics),

and before this, Inácio has felt «simpatia» (CF, p. 318) for his man friend and «um desejo subtil de o beijar na boca» (CF, p. 319). Xavière Gauthier, in her book *Surréalisme et sexualité,* comments on this type of situation:

> Les rapports de plusieurs hommes qui désirent la même femme sont de nature homosexuelle. La femme, objet de circulation entre hommes, n'est souvent qu'un prétexte. Ici [in a particular work she is discussing] le phénomène est encore plus apparent, puisque la femme est absente. [cf. Ressurreição»]. [...] leur vie amoureuse [that of the men] se déroule *entre hommes*.[1] (author's italics)

There is, too, lesbian dancing in the *Confissão* «orgy» and the hostess herself is described by Gervásio Vila-Nova as «uma grande sáfica» (CL, p. 31). In «Eu-próprio o Outro», the narrator says of *o Outro:* «Só então pude medir bem o que me liga a ele. Não é afecto, *embora chegue a ter desejos de o beijar*» (CF, p. 214). Characters sometimes theorize on the subject. «Se eu fosse mulher», admits Ricardo de Loureiro (CL, p. 66), «nunca me deixaria possuir pela carne dos homens — tristonha, seca, amarela: sem brilho e sem luz...». And he adds, «sou todo admiração, todo ternura, pelas grandes debochadas que só emaranham os corpos de mármore com outros iguais aos seus — femininos também» (CL, p. 67). Then Gervásio Vila-Nova confesses: «Sinto tantas afinidades com essas criaturas... [Lesbians] como também os sinto com os pederastas...» (CL, p. 28). In real life, the subject was occasionally mentioned. For example, in a letter to Pessoa dated October 6, 1914, Sá-Carneiro says, «quero mesmo escrever as ASAS neste volume [*Céu em Fogo*] por causa do ALÉM e BAILADO, ultra-*pederasta* assim o volume»

---

[1] Xavière Gauthier, *Surréalisme et Sexualité* (Paris, 1970), p. 240.

7

(C II, p. 19, author's italics). But most revealing of all are the implicit references the author makes to attitudes and relationships which are, to say the least, ambiguous. The sexual relationship between Marta and Lúcio in *A Confissão de Lúcio* is ostensibly a heterosexual one. Yet the *dénouement* of the book reveals that Ricardo de Loureiro had quite deliberately fabricated Marta in order that his physical desire for Lúcio could be satisfied: a heterosexual relationship serves to disguise and facilitate homosexual love. Lúcio himself enjoys this in a vicarious fashion: «Ao estrebuchá-la [Marta] agora», he says, «era como se, em beijos monstruosos, eu possuísse também todos os corpos masculinos que resvalam pelo seu» (he has discovered that he is not her only lover) (CL, p. 119). Interesting, too, is the wish to be, or even the consciousness of being of the opposite sex: Ricardo in *A Confissão de Lúcio* considers how he would behave if he were a woman (CL, p. 66), while later the solution to his incapacity for friendship and affection is seen as a change of sex: «*só poderia ser amigo de uma criatura do meu sexo, se essa criatura ou eu mudássemos de sexo*» (CL, p. 69, author's italics), after he has recalled his «desejo perdido de ser mulher» (CL, p. 67). Sá-Carneiro's unpublished poem, «Eu queria ser mulher pra me poder estender», quoted in his letter to Pessoa dated February 16, 1916, is yet another instance of this wish. Then the *alma* is often seen as belonging to the opposite sex like the Jungian «anima»; in «Não», we find: «Se a minha alma fosse uma Princes nua / E debochada e linda...» (Po, p. 91), while Ricardo explains the seemingly inexplicable presence of his «wife» in *A Confissão* by saying: «Marta é como se fora a minha própria alma», and he goes on: «foi como se a minha alma, sendo sexualizada, se tivesse materializado» (CL, p. 150). There is, too, an implied parallel in the poem «Bárbaro»:

> —Não sei quem tenho aos pés: se a dançarina morta,
> Ou a minha Alma só que me explodiu de cor... (Po, p. 107)

Many of Sá-Carneiro's men do have feminine characteristics. Gervásio Vila-Nova, in *A Confissão,* is not without a certain «feminilismo histérico» (CL, p. 19); then there is «o inquietante viscondezinho de Naudières, louro, diáfano maquilado» (CL, p. 24), and in the time that Lúcio and Ricardo are separated, Ricardo begins to look more feminine (CL, p. 72). Of Sérgio Warginsky, the narrator says: «enfim, se alguma mulher havia entre nós, parecia-me mais ser ele do que Marta» (CL, p. 76). On more than one occasion we find characters complaining of the tedium of there being only two sexes: «*conhece alguma coisa mais desoladora do que isto de só haver dois sexos?*» asks the dream man in «O Homem dos Sonhos» (CF, p. 158, author's italics), and in «Ressurreição», in a moment of ecstasy, there are «auréolas nimbadas de carnes irreais *doutros sexos»* (CF, p. 292). The protagonist is delighted by the idea of sexual *desdobramento,* «noutros corpos *doutros sexos»* (CF, p. 331). This dissatisfaction with the sexual conditions of life is reflected in two other ways; first, in the changing and «defusing» of these conditions, often attributing sexual characteristics to non-sexual elements and seeking escape from «normal» sex in «voluptuosidades novas» (CF, p. 163), and second, in sporadic periods of revulsion in the face of sexuality. In *A Confissão de Lúcio,* the American woman who maintains that «a voluptuosidade é uma arte» (CL, p. 26) reveals that her reaction to «o fogo e a luz, os perfumes e os sons [...] [the] perversidade da água, [the] requintes viciosos da luz» is «uma verdadeira excitação sexual» (CL, pp. 26-27). Ricardo refers to *«uma ânsia sexual* de possuir vozes, gestos, sorrisos, aromas e cores» (CL, p. 63, author's italics), while in «A Grande Sombra», the narrator confesses that in his love of mystery «freme qualquer coisa de sexual» (CF, p. 49). Bizarre, too, are «curvas pederastas!» (Po, p. 178), «misticismo sexual» (CF, p. 317), «beijos de água, carícias de espuma» (CF, p. 330), «voluptuosidades de água e sol» (CF, p. 285), «visões luxuriosas de cores intensas» (CL, p. 40) and «desejos espiritualizados» (CL, p. 27). The *homem dos sonhos* eulogises the alternative reality of «visual» sex: «como é delicioso possuir com a vista...» (CF, p. 164). Nausea in the face of sex is found in *A Confissão de Lúcio:* we read about «carícias repugnantes, viscosas» (CL, p. 26), «incompreensíveis náuseas» (CL, p. 101) and physical revulsion at the thought of lovemaking:

> Possuí-la, então, seria o mesmo que banhar-me num mar sujo, de espumas amarelas, onde boiassem palhas, pedaços de cortiça e cascas de melões... (CL, pp. 123-4)

It is significant that Lúcio's «repugnâncias incompreensíveis» (CL, p. 122) are physical, and experienced «mesmo até no momento dourado da posse» (CL, p. 101). He admits (CL, p. 122): «Tive sempre grandes antipatias *físicas»,* and the same is true for the hero of «Mistério», who «não tinha repugnâncias morais — só tinha repugnâncias *físicas»* (CF, p. 139). For Inácio, in «Resurreição», *all* sexual intercourse is disgusting:

> A Náusea Maior — pelo menos o vómito negro sucedendo ao espasmo dourado. Coisas peganhentas e húmidas, mal cheirosas, repugnantes... Onde encontrar beleza nos contactos do cio? Beleza... Mas haverá ridículo mais torpe?... Ah! o horror dos sexos — cartilagens imundas, crespas, hilariantes... E os suspiros da cópula; as contracções picarescas, suadas... Infâmia sem nome! Infâmia sem nome! Como resistir a tudo isto um alma sensível? (CF, p. 286)

Sadly, he cannot turn his back entirely on this area of life: «não lograra ainda renunciar definitivamente aquilo que os outros possuíam» (CF, p. 287). This problem is developed in many examples of sexual Narcissism and leads to a search for temporary relief in onanism and voyeurism. Inácio himself is one of the characters who, in a «grande piedade cariciosa por si próprio» (CF, p. 347), suffers «um desejo infinito de se beijar sobre os lábios, nos espelhos» (CF, p. 347). Another is Zagoriansky, «beijando-se nos espelhos» in «Asas» (CF, p. 191). There are many other cases of this attitude and sometimes it goes further. In «Resurreição», there are references to onanism — for example, *dançarinas nuas,* consigned to the flames in the erotic dreams of Vitorino's adolescence, who «corriam para as chamas, friccionando os sexos...» (CF, p. 330). And there is frequent theorizing, such as when Inácio talks of «uma arte de masturbação» (CF, p. 331), and asks, «não será a masturbação a voluptuosidade máxima de Alma?» (CF, p. 331). As for voyeurism, we find that consciousness of other people's sexual relationships is often enough to excite or even satisfy: Lúcio, for example («sabê-la possuída por outro amante [...] só me excitava», CL, p. 119). And characters may be described in terms of other people's desires; Sérgio Warginsky, in *A Confissão de Lúcio,* has «lábios vermelhos [...] [which] guardavam uns dentes que as mulheres deveriam querer beijar» (CL, p. 76). Sá-Carneiro's characters do tend, in fact, to speculate on the subject of other people's sexual relationships: «ai, como deviam ser grandiosos aqueles beijos profundos», says the *homem dos sonhos* (CF, p. 161); in «Resurreição», Inácio, on discovering that Étienne is having an affaire with the girl he desired, «chegou a desejar que Étienne possuísse a rapariguinha, já, nessa mesma hora, ali, na sua frente» (CF, p. 319). Again suggesting homosexuality, we find evidence of disappointment with heterosexual relationships: in *Princípio,* there are phrases such as «pobres amantes desiludidos, cansados» (P, p. 203) and «o amor é uma ilusão» (P, p. 300); Inácio, who «desde a infância, tinha ideado corpos nus, ruivos amplexos, êxtases de íris — mil voluptuosidades mágicas», finds that when he can eventually put his fantasies into practice, he returns «desiludido» (CF, p. 285); in «O Incesto», disappointment is clearly expressed: «beijava então livremente [...] Mas esses beijos reais, deliciosos, valeram menos do que os grandes amplexos sonhados» (P, p. 288). The *homem dos sonhos' tédio* is caused partly by the limitations of heterosexual relationships:

> Por fim sempre os dois sexos se acariciarão, se entrelaçarão, se devorarão. (CF, p. 164)

And we have the impotence/disillusion of «Como eu não possuo»: «não possuo mesmo quando enlaço» and «eu não logro nunca possuir» (Po, pp. 70-1). Fantasised sex, as in the case of the protagonist of «O Incesto» who «puro ainda, sabia fantasiar no entanto todas as volúpias, todos os êxtases» (P, p. 287) is, in many cases, infinitely more rewarding than the real thing.

10

Sá-Carneiro's preoccupation with sex may well be judged disproportionate. His writings seem to be a manifestation of the complete freedom of his erotic imagination, perhaps the result of «une très grande énergie vitale inoccupée», as Baudelaire once said of Edgar Allan Poe,[2] or of what Mario Praz has called «mental erethism».[3] There is, in any case, a distinctive and revealing feature in his eroticism, and that is his habit of attributing sexuality to non-sexual elements or objects. Many of these —water, fire, voices, light, etc.— are, of course, traditional erotic symbols, but Sá-Carneiro exaggerates their qualities and rôle. Sexuality is found absolutely everywhere; Maria Aliete Galhoz calls it «sensualismo obsessivo»,[4] and it seems undeniable that we are dealing with sexual immaturity accompanied by a sense of inadequacy. The evidence for this accusation is obvious. It comprises firstly, the use of violence in sex (though this is by no means the only reason for its presence) and secondly, the frequent emphasis on onanism. In his «Perfil de Mário de Sá-Carneiro»,[5] Joel Serrão speculates on this, on Sá-Carneiro's «ambivalência sexual» [which] «teria sido acentuada por uma imaginação fertil e refinada, suscitadora de práticas onanistas, e excitada por estas» (pp. 138-9). He adds:

> A verdade, porém, é que [...] Mário de Sá-Carneiro vai tentar, quase no fim, um último esforço para trocar os «vícios de marfim» pelo amor adulto normal. (p. 140)[6]

Onanism results in controlled, undemanding ecstasy, easily accessible, if ultimately unsatisfying. Thirdly, the theory of sexual immaturity is supported by voyeurism and speculation on the nature of other people's sexual relationships. Indeed, we sometimes have the impression that the narrator himself, in recounting a story, is indulging in a kind of literary voyeurism. His sense of inadequacy leads to a desire to escape to an area where no demands are made. Therefore, sexuality outside sex is titillating but safe, and «unreal» sex («possuir com a vista», etc.) is yet another outlet. No proof of either sexual potency or, indeed, social charm, is required. Ricardo's refusal to pursue his acquaintance with the *costureira* who attracts him so much means that he has no need to put himself to the test. Nevertheless, he can suffer for love in an acceptable, non-shameful way — «Como lhe quero... Como lhe quero... Como a abençôo... Meu amor! meu amor!» (CL, p. 65).

---

[2] CHARLES BAUDELAIRE, «Edgar Poe, sa Vie et ses oeuvres», in *Curiosités Esthétiques. L'Art romantique* (Paris, 1962), p. 617. (First edition: 1868-69.)
[3] MARIO PRAZ, *The Romantic Agony* (London, 1962), p. 352. (First edition: 1933.)
[4] *Mário de Sá-Carneiro*, p. 71.
[5] JOEL SERRÃO, «Perfil de Mário de Sá-Carneiro», in *Temas de Cultura Portuguesa* (Lisbon, 1960), pp. 127-44.
[6] «Vícios de marfim» is a phrase found in the poem «Certa Voz na Noite Ruivante...» (Po, p. 93).

Disappointment with sex, which often develops into strong revulsion, may come about in three ways. Immaturity and a sense of inadequacy may spring from, or lead to impotence, with violence as a compensatory reaction. (The reaction of the powerless man in the face of a dominating *femme fatale* is often one of violence in the writings of Sá-Carneiro. Violence in this context may also be seen as a means of generating the excitement which is missing from the relationship.) Then this reaction to the flesh may well be that of the fastidious, aesthetic artist. The basic conflict is between the Ideal, which is Art, and the real, or Nature, and this would appear to be an insoluble problem if «natural» desires are still present in spite of the intellectual and emotional rejection of what they signify and lead to. Art is structured, beautiful, planned, balanced, and it is in this way that sex is imagined too, until the bubble is burst by cruel experience. The *femme fatale* is no more than an artistic creation, animality in jewels, the essence of powerful sex; she is a *safe* creation, for the key feature of sophistication is its remoteness, and of artificial decoration, its impersonality. There is evidence of the contrast between the fantasised sex of Sá-Carneiro's writings and imagination and the real thing from the letters that he wrote to Pessoa. As John Parker has pointed out,[7] Sá-Carneiro never mentions the opposite sex in his letters, but as we know, in a letter dated March 31, 1916, he announces:

> Vivo há 15 dias uma vida como sempre sonhei: tive tudo durante eles: realizada a parte sexual, enfim, da minha obra — vivido o histerismo do seu ópio, as luas zebradas, os mosqueiros roxos da sua ilusão. (C II, p. 174)

Yet this is the very letter in which he announces his forthcoming suicide. He insists that his reason for killing himself is lack of money, but this is surely not his only motive: it seems reasonable to assume that disillusionment with his personal relationships was at least one factor which contributed towards his death. It may even have been a major cause. All his life he had fed on an image of ideal feminine sexuality and extreme, intense, tempestuous relationships, continuous ecstasy, violence and climactic glimpses of the transcendental. But as de Quéant, a character in Péladan's *Le Vice suprême*[8] points out, «à tout chercheur d'impossible, la déception est due». The third possible explanation for the problem of disappointment and revulsion in the face of sexual experience (and it should be emphasised that these three theories are not mutually exclusive) is that these constitute the natural antipathy of someone with homosexual tendencies, however latent, in contact with a heterosexual

[7] JOHN PARKER, *The Life and Works of Mário de Sá-Carneiro*, unpublished Ph.D. dissertation, University of Cambridge, 1959, p. 41. I am grateful to Dr. Parker for permission to quote from his thesis.
[8] JOSEPH (SÂR) PÉLADAN, *Le Vice suprême* (Paris, 1884).

situation. With this answer we find yet another explanation of the «unreal» sexual situations we have already noted: that they serve to symbolise the abolition of limitations. The superficial limitations of the stories may well act as a metaphor for the physical and social limitations imposed on homosexuals.

We shall never know if Sá-Carneiro was homosexual or not, but the quantitative emphasis on heterosexuality in his work is misleading. The heterosexual orientation of so many of the stories and poems is part of a socio-literary convention, but may also result from a lack of awareness in the author of the extent of his own tendencies. Let us consider the evidence. The complete inaccessibility of «marriageable females» may be seen as an excuse. The literary tradition of unrealizable love lies behind this attitude, but the fact that Sá-Carneiro chooses to use this particular tradition is itself revealing. His distaste for the institution of marriage may be seen as a form of rationalisation in the face of uncontrollable circumstances. We may add to this the association of marriageable females with coldness; they are incapable of arousing real passion. Conversely, the predominance of women with whom it is impossible for the man to play the dominant rôle is significant. His only source of power is unanswerable violence, yet another *raison d'être* for this latter element. The explicit opposition of repulsive heterosexual desire and clean homosexuality in «Ressurreição», while obviously intended to shock, may also be seen as significant, and via homosexual intercourse the torment of frustration is ultimately removed. It is impossible to ignore Sá-Carneiro's consciousness of the feminine part of human duality. The personalised form of the *alma* is both part of him and at the same time autonomous and uncontrollable. Then there is the element of Narcissism: a love for the part of him that he would like to be. The desire to actually *be* a woman suggests several hypotheses. It may be a wish to become the elusive woman with whom no satisfactory relationship has been achieved;[9] it may even be an early symptom of schizophrenia;[10] it may also, we are told, be a way of acquiring masculinity:

> For a man to identify himself with a woman may [...] be a process in which he does not deprive himself of masculinity [...] but rather gains possession of it; since the woman with whom he identifies can be [a] primitive type of powerful mother-figure, who is masculine as well as feminine.[11]

We are of course in no position to pass judgement regarding the second theory, but there is convincing evidence for the validity of the first and third. That the woman with whom he wishes to identify is a *mother-*

---

[9] ANTHONY STORR, *Sexual Deviation* (Harmondsworth, 1968), p. 61. (First edition: 1964.)

[10] STORR, p. 67.

[11] STORR, p. 63.

13

figure is not acceptable, but that this woman exercises the sort of power normally found in men is. The irresistibility of the *femme fatale* is curiously important: in the face of her power the victim is helpless and all responsibility for the relationship is taken from him. She is incapable of failure and the male has no option but to be successfully seduced. The ambiguity of several of the heterosexual relationships reveals, at the very least, an awareness of sexual ambivalence in the author. The desire for more than two sexes is certainly an expression of dissatisfaction with sexual conditions as normally enjoyed. There is no ridicule in the description of sexually ambivalent characters: dandies and androgynes are described reverently and taken seriously. Again, this attitude is based on an area of literature already well established, but it cannot be overemphasised that it is one that Sá-Carneiro chooses to continue.

All this contributes to an ambivalent picture, suggesting either ignorance of the presence of homosexuality on the part of the author or a refusal to face up to it. Either of these hypotheses presupposes the fear of (further) social hostility, even from the despised *lepidópteros* who represent sexual normality.

Sá-Carneiro's works reflect three literary areas: Romanticism, Decadentism and the various movements of the twentieth century. He himself is perfectly well aware that his writings are largely neo-Romantic, but at the same time he is convinced that they represent something quite new. In two letters to Pessoa, dated August 22 and 23, 1915, he gives the outline of a projected work, *Novela Romântica,* and says that the protagonist will be «um Lúcio, um Inácio de Gouveia — enfim um dos meus personagens-padrões lançado em pleno período romântico, vivendo um enredo ultra-romântico» (C II, p. 61), and the implication is clearly that to place «um Lúcio» or «um Inácio de Gouveia» in this setting would be an anachronism. Of course, Sá-Carneiro is right in a way: it is impossible to disregard the literary and social influences of the best part of a hundred years. It will be «um romantismo outro» (C II, pp. 63-64), of which one important characteristic will be its modern and individualistic style: «*o estilo será o meu* — e daqui virá o principal anacronismo» (C II, p. 64, author's italics). He sees the result as «uma intersecção» of the «alma e estilo romântico: com a alma e estilo interseccionistas» (C II, p. 64). And in all his works, we often do see the evidence of the author's manipulation of some of the characteristics of Romantic writing and thought. He often uses the word «romantic» in a knowing fashion, though not at all —it seems— cynically; when he refers to «jardins *românticos* a amor e tradição» (CF, p. 281), for instance. Accusations of self-dramatisation in the characters can also be found: in «A Grande Sombra», an acquaintance is possessed of an «ingénuo capricho de *se romantizar*» (CF, p. 68), while in «Loucura», Raul talks about dying «*românticamente,* numa noite de luar» (P, p. 81). But in spite of all this awareness, Sá-Carneiro was far more of a Romantic than he ever supposed: he revealed many symptoms of Romanticism proper, and even more of what Croce called «Later Romanticism», or Decadentism,[12] especially with regard to sex, and the associated realms of love and violence. One of his most obvious Romantic characteristics is exaggeration, inevitably resulting in strong contrasts and extremes, uncontrollable emotions, melodrama, sentimentality, suffering and all-powerful passion. The many definitions of Romanticism given by F. L. Lucas in his well-known book [13] are all apt when discussing Sá-Carneiro's works, especially George Sand's assertion that «everything excessive is poetic» and Brunetière's vision of the movement as «a blind wave of literary egotism». Lucas remembers, too, that it has been called «Emotion against Reason» and he quotes Abercrombie's assertion that it is «a withdrawal from outer experience to concentrate on inner experience». Sá-Carneiro's imagery reflects his ideology: his inaccessible, innocent virgin image is obviously Romantic, fundamentally not all that far removed from a *princesse lointaine* figure.[14] His obsessive preoccupation with sex, too, may be partly an echo of the Romantics: Praz refers to them as «these sex-obsessed romantic artists».[15] And his distaste for the bourgeois, his contempt for marriage, are also Romantic attitudes: the Romantics, with the concept of the fatal lover, the Byronic Fatal Man, the «dogma that the intense, true life of feeling does not and cannot survive into middle-age», as Alvarez has put it,[16] had a *Weltanschauung* incompatible with the pedestrian nature of any lasting relationship, of any conventional institution. Relationships between the sexes will of necessity be extra-marital: Denis de Rougemont has referred to «romantic morality, holding the claims of love to be indefeasible and implying a superiority from a 'spiritual' standpoint of mistress over wife»,[17] while the Bohemian *poète maudit* is clearly not to be restrained by petty rules from the direction in which he must go.

[12] Quoted by PRAZ, p. xvi.
[13] F. L. LUCAS, *The Decline and Fall of the Romantic Ideal* (Cambridge, 1963), p. 9 et seq. (First edition: 1936.)
[14] EDMOND ROSTAND: «Moi, j'aime la lointaine/Princesse.» See too his play, *La Princesse lointaine* (Paris, 1895), and for a good example of the Romantic attitude in this area, GUSTAVO ADOLFO BÉCQUER, «El rayo de luna» (1862), in *Obras*, vol. I (Madrid, 1915), one of the «leyendas». The hero, Manrique, «el loco soñador de quimeras o imposibles» (p. 176), pursues a once-glimpsed flash of white which he assumes to be a «mujer misteriosa» (p. 176), with a beauty from his adolescent dreams. Manrique, Bécquer claims, «había nacido para soñar el amor, no para sentirlo» (p. 173) and the search ends, as it must, in disillusion when he discovers that all he had seen was a ray of moonlight: «el amor es un rayo de luna», «la gloria es un rayo de luna» (p. 186).
[15] PRAZ, p. 205.
[16] A. ALVAREZ, *The Savage God* (London, 1971), p. 172.
[17] DENIS DE ROUGEMONT, *Passion and Society*, trans. Montgomery Belgion (London, 1962), p. 234. (First edition: 1940.)

Sá-Carneiro's most striking affinity is with Decadentism, and a great many of his favourite images can be found in the literature of the *fin de siècle.* One of the most important of these is the *femme fatale,* and we must not lose sight of the fact that this image was popular among other young Portuguese writers of the period. As John Parker rightly says:

> The disdain for woman common to Sá-Carneiro's generation was a fashionable pose based on a literary education nourished on decades of decadent novels in which impotent iconoclasts brought toppling from its pedestal the idealised statue raised to the universal mother. «La femme est naturelle, c'est à dire abominable», wrote Baudelaire, and a host of competent idlers hastened to sacrifice themselves to the ubiquitous sadism of the monster, the vampire who sucked the blood of her lovers, like a spider devouring her mate after coitus. Lorrain, d'Aurevilly, Borel, Sue, Mirbeau, Janin, Péladan, Schwob, Huysmans — these and others provided the sentimental education of Sá-Carneiro's generation, and since their experience with women was almost entirely limited to intercourse with prostitutes they substituted for real woman a distorted image of this monstrous creature of fable.[18]

The *femme fatale* was part of the vogue for «fatal sex» which, as Alvarez has pointed out, was the substitute for the Fatalism of the Romantics, being «an enhancement rather than a contradiction of a life dedicated to art».[19] She was found as frequently in the visual arts as in literature and there are countless representations of Salome, for example, in Symbolist paintings —by Moreau (in *The Apparition,* 1876), by Aubrey Beardsley (c. 1894), by Vittorio Zecchin (*Salome Triptych,* 1909-1912), by Gustav Klimt (1909), by Picasso (*Salome Dancing before Herod,* 1905) among others— and Edward Lucie-Smith has commented that «Moreau's women [...] even if not active destroyers, like Salome, are beings whom it would be unwise to offend».[20] In literature, Salome was a stock figure. In his *Rimes dorées,*[21] Théodore de Banville wrote:

> Comme c'est votre joie, ô fragiles poupées!
> Car vous avez toujours aimé naïvement
> Les joujoux flamboyants et les têtes coupées.

while in 1887, Jules Laforgue was writing on the same subject:

> Or là, sur un coussin, parmi les débris de la lyre d'ébène,
> la tête de Jean (comme jadis celle d'Orphée) brillait,
> enduite de phosphore, lavée, fardée, frisée, faisant rictus
> à ces vingt-quatre millions d'astres.[22]

---

[18] PARKER, p. 41.
[19] ALVAREZ, p. 179.
[20] EDWARD LUCIE-SMITH, *Symbolist Art* (London, 1972), p. 69.
[21] THÉODORE DE BANVILLE, «Rimes dorées», in *Poésies Complètes,* vol. II (Paris, 1878-79).
[22] JULES LAFORGUE, «Moralités légendaires» (1887); in *Oeuvres Complètes* (Paris, 1902).

In Oscar Milosz we read:

> La vie d'un sage ne vaut pas, ma Salomé,
> Ta danse d'orient sauvage comme la chair,
> Et ta bouche couleur de meurtre,
> Et tes seins couleur de désert,
> O Salomé de mes Hontes,
> Salomé! [23]

and Cansinos-Assens, in his *Salomé en la literatura*,[24] talks about Flaubert's *Hérodias* (1877), Oscar Wilde's *Salomé* (first performance, Paris, 1896), Stéphane Mallarmé's *Hérodiade* (1898), a short poem, *Salomé,* of Apollinaire (1913) and, nearer home, the *Salomé* of Eugénio de Castro (1896).[25] It was not only in the visual and literary arts that this figure held sway: on November 28, 1906, Vienna saw the first performance of the opera *Salomé* which Richard Strauss had based on Wilde's work. Praz has noted that the Romantic «Fatal Man» became the Decadent «Fatal Woman» as the century wore on,[26] and gives many more examples, not only of Salome, but of «Fatal Women» in general: in Baudelaire, Barbey d'Aurévilly, Rachilde, Huysmans and Mirbeau among others.[27] This was the period of the powerful woman and the passive, even timid man, and this artistic heritage was one which suited Sá-Carneiro's ambivalent sexual make-up. The *fin de siècle* was, too, a period in which homosexuality was a fashionably literary subject, though it was often euphemistically disguised as the power of personality. It is interesting to compare the first meetings of, for example, Basil Hallward and Dorian Gray in Oscar Wilde's *The Picture of Dorian Gray,*[28] M. de Phocas and the narrator in Jean Lorrain's *M. de Phocas.Astarté*[29] and Lúcio and Ricardo in *A Confissão de Lúcio.* In the English novel, we read:

> I turned half-way round, and saw Dorian Gray for the first time. When our eyes met, I felt I was growing pale. A curious sensation of terror came over me. I knew that I had come face to face with someone whose mere personality was so fascinating that, if I allowed it to do so, it would absorb my whole nature, my whole soul, my very art itself.[30]

---

[23] OSCAR MILOSZ, *Le Poème des décadences* (Paris, 1899).
[24] R. CANSINOS-ASSENS, *Salomé en la literatura* (Madrid, 1920).
[25] EUGÉNIO DE CASTRO, *Salomé e Outros Poemas,* 1896.
[26] PRAZ, p. 170.
[27] PRAZ, p. 295.
[28] OSCAR WILDE, *The Picture of Dorian Gray* (London, 1891) (first appearance in book form). Quotations are taken from *Complete Works of Oscar Wilde* (London, 1970).
[29] JEAN LORRAIN, *M. de Phocas.Astarté* (Paris, 1901). (Quotations are taken from an undated edition [1929?].)
[30] WILDE, p. 21.

In *M. de Phocas.Astarté*, Lorrain's protagonist explains why he has chosen to unburden himself to the narrator, rather than to anyone else (for he hardly knows him):

> Vous seul pouviez me comprendre, vous seul pouviez accueillir avec indulgence les affinités qui m'attirent vers vous.[31]

In *A Confissão de Lúcio*, Lúcio says:

> Pela primeira vez eu encontrara efectivamente alguém que sabia descer um pouco aos recantos ignorados do meu espírito — os mais sensíveis, os mais dolorosos para mim. E com ele o mesmo acontecera — havia de mo contar mais tarde. (CL, p. 46)

(Cf. Dorian Gray's reaction to Basil Hallward: «He too», says Hallward later, «felt that we were destined to know each other».[32]) Philippe Jullian has described *The Picture of Dorian Gray* as «an overtly pederastic novel»,[33] and it is Jullian, too, who refers to Lorrain's *Histoires de masques* (1900) as «histoires homosexuelles facilitées par l'incognito».[34] An interesting characteristic of the homosexual Lorrain's attitude to heterosexual intercourse has some bearing on the element of violence we have noted in Sá-Carneiro: Jullian writes:

> Dure contrainte pour un sodomiste que de louer les courtisanes! Il s'en consolait par la férocité. Toutes payèrent pour celle qui n'avait pas su le mener dans le droit chemin: «Je l'avoue, cette chair *que je venais de posséder brutalement* me fit horreur.» [cf. Sá-Carneiro's characters' revulsion in the face of sex]

and he is left with «un goût de viande morte dans la bouche»,[35] again a phrase revealing a familiar attitude. Explicit references to homosexuality were, on the whole, not yet accepted, but it was certainly a talking point in Paris, and in 1891 Léo Taxil's *La Corruption fin-de-siècle,* with its condemnation of Paris society, had an interested and shocked reception. There was a fashion too for beings of indeterminate sex, a plethora of literary and plastic androgynes or hermaphrodites: the creature seen on the Sphinx in Lorrain's *M. de Phocas,* the ambiguius *déesse/dieu* of Gautier's «Contralto», in Balzac's *Séraphita* and *La Fille aux yeux d'or,* in Latouche's *Fragoletta*, in Moreau's paintings and in those of Toorop and many others. The immediate literary source may well have been *Mademoiselle de Maupin;*[36] as for painting, Edward Lucie-Smith claims that the originator of this fashion was Moreau:

[31] LORRAIN, p. 16.
[32] WILDE, p. 22.
[33] PHILIPPE JULLIAN, *Oscar Wilde*, trans. Violet Wyndham (London, 1971), p. 190.
[34] PHILIPPE JULLIAN, *Jean Lorrain ou le Satiricon 1900* (Paris, 1974), p. 190.
[35] JULLIAN, *Jean Lorrain,* p. 111.
[36] THÉOPHILE GAUTIER, *Mademoiselle de Maupin* (Paris, 1835), referred to by Praz, pp. 199-200.

The Neoplatonic idea of the androgyne was to exercise a powerful fascination over late nineteenth-century critics and aestheticians, but it was Moreau who gave form to this idea in paint upon canvas.[37]

Sá-Carneiro was influenced by the nineteenth-century cult of the dandy and exquisite, led by such characters as Robert de Montesquiou and Jean Lorrain, but it is his preoccupation with dancers which is most apparent in his work; this vogue too originated in the Decadent period. Perhaps Loie Fuller, the American ex-actress who «had invented her own extremely original style of dancing in which her graceful, whirling movements were enhanced by the soft, floating fabrics of her costumes and a constant change of coloured lighting effects»[38] was the main source of artistic inspiration. (Mallarmé and Rodenbach, among others, wrote about her, while Kolo Moser, of the Vienna Secession, made her the subject of one of his most famous paintings.) For readers of the works of Sá-Carneiro, Jean Lorrain's description of one of her dances takes on a new significance:

Modelée dans la braise ardente, la Loïe Fuller ne brûle pas; elle filtre et suinte de la clarté, elle est la flamme elle-même. Debout dans un brasier, elle sourit, et son sourire a l'air d'un rictus de masque sous le voile rouge dont elle s'enveloppe, ce voile qu'elle agite et fait onduler comme une fumée d'incendie le long de sa nudité de lave.[39]

But this «poetical» dancing of Loie Fuller was not the only *fin-de-siècle* form of the art which excited the Portuguese author: many of his women are taken from the world of the Music Hall (e.g. Paulette, in «Ressurreição»), and he shows an immature and sentimental attitude towards them. Unlike Jean Lorrain, who saw these girls as real people, Sá-Carneiro sees them as both intensely erotic and intensely sordid, a stimulating combination.

Emphasis on the influence of Romanticism and Decadentism may tend to suggest that Sá-Carneiro had no awareness at all of the current scene in Paris. This is not true, but where the relationship between the sexes is concerned he had certainly not broken free from his heritage, either artistic or social. His choice of background and style for his female protagonists shows very little advance on those found in Decadent literature, though some of his women may be a little more emancipated socially. His actresses and dancers with their bizarre dress and make-up, Bohemian lives and sexual libertinism reveal the stamp of the *fin de siècle,* and where sexual matters are concerned it is only infrequently that there is any evidence that the stories and poems were written in 1915 and not in 1895.

---

[37] LUCIE-SMITH, p. 68.
[38] RAYMOND RUDORFF, *Belle Époque. Paris in the Nineties* (London, 1972), pp. 314-15.
[39] Quoted by JULLIAN, *Jean Lorrain,* p. 140.

FOOD, DRINK, DRUGS

Sá-Carneiro's contempt for the everyday, the pedestrian and the *lepidóptero* is reflected in his attitude towards food: such an inelegant subject must be either ignored, glamorised or form images of distaste and revulsion. The infrequency of references to food, eating or appetite is easily explained: the Sá-Carneiro character is concerned with his *estado de alma,* the mysteries of the Beyond, the problems of human contact and the difficulties of sexual fulfillment, not with the commonplace necessities of life. When food is mentioned with positive connotations, it is invariably sophisticated and expensive or fantastic. In real life even, the few food images the author mentions are luxurious and expensive. But in the prose and poetry, the majority of references are metaphors or similes employed to heighten expressions of revulsion or boredom: the «restaurante onde os pratos sejam sempre os mesmos, com o mesmo aspecto, o mesmo sabor» (CF, p. 160), for example, or the repellent young man, «esculpido em *manteiga*», who is a «*criatura açucarada*» and provokes the same nausea in Lúcio as «uma mistura de *toucinho* rançoso, enxúndia de galinha, *mel, leite* e *erva-doce...*» (CL, p. 123). In «Ressurreição», one of the repulsive thoughts that occur to Inácio de Gouveia and sully the purity of his masturbatory *oiro* consists of «*doçuras* gordurosas» (CF, p. 192). Finally, the sense of taste itself is used in several ways: in entirely or partly metaphorical references to, for example, «um *além-gosto* a doença, a monstruosidade» of which Lúcio is ever conscious after sexual intercourse with Marta (CL, p. 101), or in the taste of a kiss in «Em Pleno Romantismo»: «que *sabor* encontrei nesse beijo ardente... um *sabor* acre, estranho... o *sabor* da paixão!» (P, p. 151). Specific areas of taste, in particular, acidity, are treated partly metaphorically: «seios loiros, de pontas trigueiras e *ácidas*» (P, p. 318), for example. There are occasional cases of metaphorical usage in set phrases, but more interesting are the almost Baudelairean *correspondances* involving taste: «um frio *ácido*» (CF, p. 95), «o giro *ácido* das rodas» (CF, p. 176), «um ar que *sabia* a luz» (CF, p. 197), «*acidez* toda nua» (CF, p. 50), «luz *insípida*» (CF, p. 63) and a «ruído *acre*» (CF, p. 127).

Alcohol represents the halfway mark between food and drugs. Whether provoked by another person or self-induced, sexual excitement is the commonest area in which the metaphor of alcohol is found. Lovers are «*bêbados* de beijos» (P, p. 56) and suffer a «*bebedeira* roxa após uma noite de amor e estrangulamentos» (CF, p. 265); passion may well be «singular e *capitosa*» (CF, p. 345). Sex and luxury go together and champagne is frequently mentioned: the mysterious Marta intoxicates Lúcio «de *champanhe*» for example (CL, p. 91), and an apotheosis will be «*à espuma loira do champanhe*» (CF, p. 259). Paris is seen as «golfando seios entornando *Champanhe*» (CF, p. 282), and «como um *álcool* de êxtase» is the phrase used in the description of «agitação urbana» (CF, p. 138). Intoxication also implies confusion or vertigo, either conventionally or in an image such as «Luas de oiro se *embebedam*» («Rodopio», Po, p. 76). In real life, Sá-Carneiro claimed to dislike alcohol, and the imagery of intoxication is no more than a literary convention for him. Like conventional, heterosexual, bourgeois love, it is something with no real relevance, and he transfers his own attitudes to his characters. In the January 21, 1913 letter to Pessoa, he says:

> Os vícios são *hábitos,* apenas são maus-hábitos.
> [...] Nunca poderei ser um vicioso, da mesma forma que nunca serei um homem regrado. (C I, p. 52)

Compare Inácio de Gouveia, in «Ressurreição»:

> o álcool apenas o adormecia, o tabaco o enfastiava; as drogas — além de lhe repugnarem numa sensação gordurosa — só o abatiam, sem o fazer vibrar, nem sonhar, nem esvaír...
> O seu *álcool,* em verdade, era-se ele próprio — e o seu éter, a sua cocaína...
> ... Depois, um vício não é mais do que um mau hábito... Ora Inácio nunca pudera ter um hábito. (CF, p. 296)

Sá-Carneiro is equally disgusted by drugs but makes occasional use of them as images in his work. Associated words such as *alucinante, capitoso, anestesiar* and *veneno* are also found. «Que *droga* foi a que me inoculei? / Ópio de inferno em vez de paraíso?» (Po, p. 59) we find in «Álcool», while in «A Inigualável» is the line: *Ruiva de éteres e morfinas...* (Po, p. 111). The author is also concerned with the therapeutic effects of drugs: in madness, claims the foreigner in «Mistério», one would at least go on living, «embora morto na ânsia, tranquilo, *morfinizado*» (CF, p. 142). Happiness and enthusiasm are seen as a kind of lack of awareness in «Ressurreição»: a *«morfinização* em excelso» (CF, p. 323). Ricardo de Loureiro sees Paris as «o único *ópio* louro para a minha dor» (CL, p. 56). The Decadent atmosphere of drug-taking is evident in the «voz, *opiada*» of a dancing Princess (Po, p. 92) and the «domínio inexprimível de *ópio* e lume» (Po, p. 99). But it is in images conveying euphoria, excitement and apotheosis that drugs are most often used: «Como nunca o mundo inteiro se me centralizou no punhal... Pairava todo *um sonho de ópio*...» (CF, p. 83); then: «Fixá-la, sim, encerrá-la em jade — *ópio coleante*... profética volúpia...» (CF, p. 122); or: «uma nova Arte — diademada e última, excessiva e secreta, *opiante,* inconvertível» (CF, p. 189). Even in real life, in the letter to Fernando Pessoa of March 31, 1916 about his sex life, Sá-Carneiro refers to the *«histerismo do seu ópio»* (C II, p. 174). As for *alucinante, capitoso, anestesiar* and even *veneno,* it is the

21

first, together with such forms as *alucinador* and *alucinação,* that is found with most frequency. *Alucinação* is a key element in Sá-Carneiro's «vocabulario predilecto», and the source may well be internal; this is fascinating for the egocentric writer or character. Furthermore, it involves a step into the Unknown, the mysterious, the areas of experience which are both exciting and incomprehensible. Reaction to hallucinatory elements is not always one of fear or revulsion but rather one in which fear and revulsion are mixed with a sense of attraction, or even of pleasure. At the one extreme we find, for example, the «martírio *alucinante*» of Ricardo's suffering and alienation in *A Confissão de Lúcio* (CL, p. 54), the «pesadelo *alucinante*» of Lúcio's terrible experience when Ricardo shoots Marta (CL, p. 154) and the *«alucinação* de tortura» of «Eu-próprio o Outro» (CF, p. 217), all of which reveal unadulterated suffering. At the other end of the scale there may be entirely positive connotations. The American woman in *A Confissão de Lúcio* has «cabelos fantásticos, de um ruivo incendiado, *alucinante*» (CL, p. 22); in the «orgy» at her house, «o mais grandioso, o mais *alucinador,* era a iluminação» (CL, p. 37) and the impression the guests are left with is «alucinadora» (CL, p. 43). Typical of the love/hate relationship of the author with certain areas of life are the examples which involve both fascination *and* revulsion; for example, in «O Fixador de Instantes», «um pavor me *alucina*» (CF, p. 267), and in a letter to Fernando Pessoa dated February 26, 1913, we find the admission that a poem made him «tremer num calafrio *alucinador*» (C I, p. 77).

The three clearcut treatments of food and drink in Sá-Carneiro's writings are significant in both obvious and slightly less obvious ways. It is obvious that the glamorising of food, at one end of the scale, and its absence from the scene at the other both point to the conclusion that the author sees himself as an artist, a man of intense sensibility. We are made aware of an attitude of superiority, isolation and snobbery, and this may well have been, at least in part, caused by Sá-Carneiro's sense of being a «country cousin». The luxury and sophistication of Paris life never ceased to delight him, especially in comparison with what to him was the backwardness of Lisbon, and this is echoed in the attitude of his character Inácio in «Ressurreição» (CF, p. 281). Sá-Carneiro was anxious to present a particular image of himself, that of a connoisseur and epicure, gourmet and (would-be) aristocrat. Less obvious and more interesting is his use of food imagery to represent objects or causes of revulsion. Some of these images are conventional enough, but he finds some surprising areas of food imagery distasteful, and in any case is excessively fastidious. It is revealing that the common qualities of those foods he finds revolting are sweetness and softness: qualities usually seen as feminine ones, and which, in fact, he does apply on one occasion to an effeminate-looking young man whom he finds nauseating (CL, pp. 122-123). His fastidiousness, it seems, is parallel to that felt with regard to sex, and these images are actually used to represent revulsion with sex from time to time: in both cases we are dealing with the needs of the flesh. And in addition to revulsion in the face of the rotten or the dirty, we are also made aware of the negative qualities of the raw or the spoiled, the first suggesting the author's immaturity yet again, while the second echoes his disappointment with sex. As for the sense of taste itself, this is seldom used entirely metaphorically: we are often dealing with real physical revulsion, as the author explicitly states on more than one occasion, *repugnâncias físicas,* a genuine inability to stomach the things of the flesh in spite of the demands of the appetite.

There are two important conclusions that can be reached regarding the treatment of alcohol and drugs in Sá-Carneiro: the first is that unlike sexual references, their importance is in proportion to the infrequency of their appearance; the second, that in spite of this, their intoxicating, even hallucinatory, qualities make them a key image in the works of a man for whom «only the unknown is worth knowing».[40] The locutions are often commonplaces —«drunk with pride», «the alcohol of her lips»— and the narrative references are unoriginal — the fallen woman ruined by drugs («Ressurreição») — but the value of words such as *alucinante* lies in the indication they give for the need for some sort of change from the present condition, a need that is both artificial and, for Sá-Carneiro, genuine. It is artificial in the sense that it is associated with a previous literary movement, in this case Decadentism. The desire for new experiences is a key element of the literature of the period, and would appear to be in part an extension of the Romantic ethos: the Decadents were plagued by *ennui,* and the usual remedy is made up of new sexual, artistic and social experiences, new places, even attempts at a new life. The protagonists of the fiction of Decadentism and Aestheticism are constantly disillusioned and bored by the dullness of what they find around them —Dorian Gray, in Oscar Wilde's story, finds life «a great disappointment»,[41] for example—, and the search for the Ideal and the fascination with mystery are two of the results. As in his treatment of sexual relationships —which themselves may be a metaphor for the relationship of the individual with those around him and life in general— Sá-Carneiro's use of the concept of intoxication/hallucination is important because it involves fear, revulsion and pleasure at the same time. It is therefore the door to the only form of excitement available to the disillusioned and unfulfilled: the Unknown. For Sá-Carneiro this is a genuine need more than the mere echo of a literary convention. The juxtaposition of a preoc-

---

[40] PARKER, p. 392.
[41] WILDE, p. 137.

23

cupation with intoxication and a real-life total abstinence from this state indicates the same dichotomy between imagination and experience as was suggested by his treatment of sex: we have here more «mental erethism».

RELIGION

Although it has been said on more than one occasion that in Sá-Carneiro religion is significant by its absence,[42] there is certainly no lack of images taken from two areas of religious experience: the traditional ritual and decoration of the Church, and metaphysics in general. Then there a plethora of references to the soul, its condition and even its destiny.

Traditional ritual and adornments obviously hold a great fascination for the author, but their interest is aesthetic rather than religious. The images conjured up by the dancer in the «Bailado» section of «Asas» are clearly so: «em jorros de asas a crescer, alteia-se *o órgão santo... O altar-mor vibra de lindo... [...] — Nossa Senhora da Cor! A nave sagra-se* em ânsia... Ergue-se *o cálice-Auréola...*» (CF, p. 202), while in the poem «Nossa Senhora de Paris», we find «Fico *sepulto* sob *círios*», «*Altares e velas*» and «*As grandes naves a sagrarem-se*» (Po, p. 85); there are many more examples. In saying this we are not, of course, denying the existence of emotion on the part of the spectator: sometimes there is no reaction, but «fujo tambén ao luar» (Po, p. 84), for example, is the result of the sight of the cross.

Sá-Carneiro sometimes uses religious and metaphysical images and metaphors in an entirely conventional way (*ídolo* and *demónio* for example), but of course, it is in their less conventional use that he is most interesting, and connotations here too are those of beauty and art. In *A Confissão de Lúcio,* Gervásio Vila-Nova is seen as having a *sacerdotal* look about him, and the author uses expressions such as «*ascetismo* amarelo» and «*abstenções* roxas» to describe his physical appearance (CL, p. 19). Zagoriansky, in «Asas», is said to have a «rosto *litúrgico*», and later convinces the narrator of his sincerity solely because his expression is «tão dolorida e *flagelada*» (CF, p. 181); Vila-Nova looks «*hierático*» (CL, p. 34) and the author adds that «em redor da sua figura havia *uma auréola*» (CL, p. 20) in which «tudo se cifrava» (CL, p. 21). Ricardo, in *A Confissão de Lúcio,* even describes Paris as having «*uma auréola* [...] que a envolve e a constitui *em alma*» (CL, p. 57).

It is, in fact, mainly in the communication of atmosphere, the portrayal of attitudes, moods and reactions in the characters, and as aids to the

---

[42] See, for example, MARIA DE GRAÇA CARPINTEIRO, *A Novela.*

narrative line that we find religious terminology. There are «*Áureos templos* de *ritos* de cetim» («Distante Melodia», Po, p. 99), and in another poem, «Taciturno», we find the image: «*Cibório* triangular *de ritos infernais*» (Po, p. 101); in *A Confissão de Lúcio,* there is a «tristeza *maceradamente* vaga» (CL, p. 74). As for the attitudes and ideology of the characters, we find that, in a way, Gervásio Vila-Nova lives up to his priestly image when he discusses voluptuosity: «não era uma arte. Falassem-lhe do *ascetismo, da renúncia.* Isso sim!» (CL, p. 27). In «Ressurreição», Inácio feels «uma ânsia *religiosa* de se humilhar... e *ungir-se* de Saudade...» (CF, p. 325), whereas in «A Grande Sombra», the narrator confesses: «Nunca me *ciliciaram* pesadelos de remorso» (CF, p. 101). Ricardo de Loureiro's passion for the cosmopolitan, modern world epitomised by Europe in general and Paris in particular is typical: «Europa! Europa! Encapela-te dentro de mim [...] *unge*-me da minha época!» (CL, p. 58). It is interesting that Sá-Carneiro uses this phrase in real life too: in a letter to Fernando Pessoa dated September 4, 1914, he refers to the Visconde de Vila-Moura:[43] «agora o Vila-Moura também se quer *ungir* de Europa — de Paris!» (C II, p. 14). As his correspondence reveals, Sá-Carneiro is not unconscious that he is choosing a religious vocabulary, but whether he is as conscious of it as he believes he is is another matter. Religious terminology as an aid to the narrative line of the stories or poems is not frequent: much of it is largely descriptive, even though it does help to move the action forward. On a purely narrative level, renunciation and sacrifice are sometimes considered (though seldom carried out), while semi-descriptive phrases are more often found: «batem asas *de auréola* aos meus ouvidos» (Po, p. 58), for example, or «*a hóstia da comunhão, comunga* nos seios dourados...» (CF, p. 203), or «moços e velhos torturam *num misticismo* as suas pobres almas» (P, p. 202).

The use of the word *alma* (and less frequently, *espírito*) is complex: it is used occasionally in a loose, conventional way — for example, to mean «person» («em face das grandes angústias as *almas* mais superiores valem tanto como as outras», P, p. 311), or «being» («um júbilo infinito lhe envolvera toda a *alma*», P, p. 317), and the word can sometimes mean «personality» (Ricardo and Lúcio enjoy each other's company and conversation, and their friendship goes on «na mesma harmonia, no mesmo convívio de *alma*», CL, p. 71; later, Lúcio has a long *tête-a-tête* with Marta, Ricardo's wife, but, he says, «não apareciam as nossas *almas*», CL, p. 79, and we know from this that the conversation was a superficial one). Furthermore, the word sometimes incorporates connotations of completeness, and, of course, there are set expressions such as «com

---

[43] Is it interesting to remember that the Visconde de Vila-Moura (1877-1935), an important exponent of Decadentism in his novels, short stories and criticism, wrote a novel called *Nova Safo* which caused a scandal in 1912.

25

todas as forças da minha *alma*» (P, pp. 252-3), and «estados de *alma*» (passim). The frequency even of conventional usage is interesting. But somewhat less conventionally, the soul is seen as an autonomous entity over which the protagonist or poetic *persona* has no control (e.g. «sentia a sua *alma* prestes a voar», P, p. 315), and this autonomous entity, with physical characteristics of its own, is nevertheless a part of a man's whole being. It is treated as if it were another person. The fact that two «people» can live together, is important. The soul is autonomous — «*a minha alma anda estremunhada*», «a minha *alma* chega muitas vezes a pegar no sono, *a fechar os olhos*» (CL, pp. 53 and 54-5, author's italics) — feeling *ânsias,* suffering *espasmos,* tiredness and cold, bleeding, growing hard, drying up, seeing, fearing, thinking and understanding. It is even described as slim on one occasion. It acts and reacts independently. But its «indepen- dent» existence can be the source of conflict, even in real life, for in a letter to Fernando Pessoa, dated December 31, 1912, Sá-Carneiro des- cribes his current state of *anestesiamento* in this way: «Outros obtêm essa beatitude morfinizando-se, ingerindo álcool. Eu não; [...] Consigo expulsar a *alma*. E a vida não me dói.» (C I, p. 43, his italics.) Much later, in another letter (dated August 30, 1915), he tries to define the madness from which he is sure he is suffering: «Eu actualmente ando *sempre com a Alma de estômago vazio mas sem apetite*» (C II, p. 73, author's italics). In November of the same year, he elaborates on this to Pessoa: «A vida corre vazia, *de alma* e de corpo — mas vazia *de alma* porque não estou para a encher» (C II, p. 116). This idea is frequently echoed in his writings: the soul's suffering is the man's suffering, and with the exception of the moments when he «expels» it, it is part of him. At best he is affected by the state of his soul and at worst he is its impotent victim. There are innumerable examples of both conditions, from the lights, perfumes and colours which penetrate the soul (CL, p. 41) and the nostalgia the soul feels for the Beyond («Partida», Po, p. 51) to «o martírio inconcebível» of the soul (P, p. 277), its decline («põe-se-me a *Alma*», «Asas», CF, p. 201) and «a *alma* amortalhada» («Dispersão», Po, p. 63). Body and soul are compatible for they *do* live together, but are incompatible in the sense that this cohabitation is intolerable for one of them; the only relief lies in the form of *vita minima* that Sá-Carneiro calls *anestesiamento,* in which the soul is «discarded», if only for a short period. The usual boundaries of the soul/body opposition are quite deliberately blurred from the point of view of standard Christian teaching, but the very fact that the soul is seen as (almost) a separate literary character in some cases, and actually materialises in others («Eu-próprio o Outro», «A Grande Sombra» —in a way,[44]— and *A Confissão de Lúcio*) is evidence

---

[44] Strictly speaking, it is the actual death of the murdered woman that is seen as materialising in this story, but there are grounds for including this as an

not only that the author is consciously manipulating the concept, but also that he owes something to the more bizarre quasi-religious movements of the late nineteenth and early twentieth centuries. The possibility of the materialisation of the spirit was, after all, a subject much discussed for many years: photographs and «proof» of the presence of etheric bodies were fairly common, there were many investigations into the so-called projection of the double (usually brought about by an emotional crisis) and there was no shortage of cases of people —some of them, like Goethe, Alfred de Musset and Guy de Maupassant, famous— who claimed to have seen themselves.[45] Even though the double is *not* the spirit, according to Occult teachings, and will eventually be discarded in the same way as the physical body is, there is little doubt that Sá-Carneiro was influenced by the vogue for the Occult. The reader's acceptance of the conventional spiritual/carnal opposition is often challenged: in the assertion that the excitement of the erotic dancing in *A Confissão de Lúcio* is felt by the soul, for instance. The soul can dictate to the body, and Sá-Carneiro takes great delight in turning the accepted relationship upside down. He creates people with visible souls and invisible bodies in one story, but it is the attribution of sexual characteristics to the soul that is most striking, with masturbation being considered the «voluptuosidade máxima de Alma» (CF, p. 331) and expressions such as «*em Alma* copulada...» (Po, p. 92) and «orgia de carne *espiritualizada*» (CL, p. 36). In *A Confissão de Lúcio,* Marta herself is the sexual projection of Ricardo's soul. The few cases of the conventional use of the image are found either in the early works (i.e. *Princípio*) or in «A Estranha Morte do Prof. Antena», which is somewhat different from Sá-Carneiro's other writings. In the later writings there is, of course, the traditional assumption of the close relationship between the soul and the Absolute or the *Além*. The line in «Partida», «A minh'*alma* nostálgica de além» (Po, p. 51), is reminiscent of the Augustinian viewpoint found in a thousand other poets from Camões to Wordsworth, while the «morte da minha *alma*» of the poem «Dispersão» is not the welcome peace found in the *vita minima,* but the complete annihilation *without oblivion* which the poet's life has become.

In the more unusual treatment that Sá-Carneiro affords to the words «soul» and «spirit», he betrays a consciousness of the duality that is explicitly revealed on a narrative level in several of his works: he has within him someone else —o *Outro*/the soul— and this love/hate cohabitation is often insupportable to him. It is interesting to compare this relationship as seen on a narrative level (in «Eu-próprio o Outro») and as

---

example: the incarnation of an integral, but metaphysical component circumstance of a human being shows the direction of the author's fantasies.

[45] See NANDOR FODOR, *Encyclopaedia of Psychic Science* (London, s/d) (1933?).

seen by means of the image of the soul. In the *Céu em Fogo* short story we find:

> Compreendemo-nos mal. Nunca estamos de acordo. Instante a instante ele me vexa, me sacode. Enfim, *me coloca no meu lugar.*
> Não pensa em coisa alguma como eu penso. (author's italics)
> [...]
> A sua companhia tortura-me. Mas busco-o por toda a parte. (p. 213)
> [...] só *vivo* em face dele. (author's italics) (p. 214)
> Decididamente vou-lhe fugir. (p. 216)
> O que eu digo, é ele quem o pensa... (p. 217)
> Ele não me deixa nunca... (p. 220)
> Como libertar-me?... (p. 222)

Elsewhere we come across: «A cada passo a minha alma é outra cruz» («16», Po, p. 96), «Como eu quisera, enfim de alma esquecida, Dormir em paz...» («Além-Tédio», Po, p. 73), «existiria liberto e solitário de Alma, vivendo só a Arte» (Inácio in «Ressurreição», CF, p. 293), «Acabarei talvez em corpo exilado da minha alma» (C I, p. 174), «Os homens que estragaram tudo [...] inventaram a alma» («Loucura», P, p, 116) and «uma perna não sofre. Não tem alma» (CL, p. 55). The inevitable outcome of this incompatibility is death, either physical or metaphysical. The solution to the «Eu-próprio o Outro» dilemma is greeted joyfully by the narrator:

> Enfim — o triunfo!
> Decidi-me!
> Mata-*lo*-ei esta noite... quando *Ele* dormir... (CF, p. 22) (author's italics)

and in killing *o Outro,* he will kill himself. There are numerous literary precedents for this, many of which are referred to in Dr. Otto Rank's *Don Juan. Une étude sur le Double,* Paris, 1932. For example, there is the French film *L'Étudiant de Prague* (1912), a version of the Paul Wegener original, in which a young man, haunted by his double, shoots it and in so doing, commits suicide. Then, of course, there is Oscar Wilde's *The Picture of Dorian Gray,* where Gray kills himself by attacking his own portrait, and Edgar Allan Poe's *William Wilson,* in which the death of the double which persecutes the protagonist virtually constitutes his own death, since his double is his good half. W. B. Yeats, in his *Ideas of Good and Evil* (1903), tells the tale of a man who created what he calls an «image», «like the image of a man made by somebody who could not model» (p. 35); when, as a sick man, he tries to destroy it, he himself falls «as if he had given himself a mortal wound, for he had filled it with his own life» (p. 37). In *A Confissão de Lúcio,* the link between the narrative and metaphorical levels is abundantly clear: Ricardo states that Marta exists «como se fora a minha própria *alma*», adding: «foi como se a minha *alma,* sendo sexualizada, se tivesse materializado» (CL, p. 150).

Ricardo's killing of Marta is a form of self-destruction; Lúcio recounts that:

> *Quem jazia estiraçado junto da janela, não era Marta — não! — era o meu amigo, era Ricardo...* (CL, pp. 153-4, author's italics)

In the same story, it is possible to see the two men, Ricardo and Lúcio, as two halves of the same person, as Cleonice Berardinelli has suggested so convincingly,[46] the prose writer and the poet fused together by fire the night of the «orgy». If we take this further, we see that by getting rid of one half, both halves die. Ricardo commits a «murder» and dies himself, while Lúcio «dies» metaphorically: a careful reading of the last section of the novel confirms this:

> «A minha vida ruíra toda no instante em que o revólver de Ricardo tombara aos meus pés. Em face a tão fantástico segredo, eu abismara-me. ¿Que me fazia pois o que volteava à superfície?... Hoje a prisão surgia-me como um descanso, *um termo...*» (author's italics) [...] «As longas horas [...] eu só as vi em bruma» [...] «coisa alguma me *animaria.*» (author's italics) [...] (pp. 155-6).

> «Passaram velozes os meus dez anos de cárcere» [...] Os meses corriam serenamente iguais» [...] O prazer maior de certos detidos, era de se debruçarem do alto do grande muro, e olharem para a rua; isto é: para a vida. [...] Eu poucas vezes me acercava do muro [...] pois nada me podia interessar do que havia para lá dele.» [...] «eu com raros dos outros prisioneiros me misturava» [...] (pp. 157-8). «Para ele [another prisoner] como para mim, também a vida parara — ele vivera também o *momento culminante*» (author's italics) «a minha vida no cárcere [...] nada tem de interessante para os outros, nem mesmo para mim» [...] [On coming out of prison] «Morto, sem olhar um instante em redor de mim, logo me afastei para esta vivenda rural, isolada e perdida, donde nunca mais arredarei pé» (p. 159). «Acho-me tranquilo — sem desejos, sem esperanças. Não me preocupa o futuro [...] *permaneci mas já não me sou*» (author's italics, p. 160)

Sá-Carneiro's reshaping of the image betrays a complete disregard for Christian teachings. The only time that the soul's destiny is ever mentioned is in the fairly frivolous context of a Science Fiction mystery, and in any case, it is a negative reference. Furthermore, as Octavio Paz has said of Luis Cernuda, Sá-Carneiro is a completely unchristian writer since he lacks a sense of sin;[47] no remorse is ever felt by any character in the prose or by the poetic *persona*. Any passing regrets are selfish reactions to uncomfortable circumstances. If someone wants to go back, it is so that life may be better, so that he may feel as he wants to:

---

[46] CLEONICE BERARDINELLI, «*A Confissão de Lúcio*», in *Colóquio*, no. 26 (December 1963), 52-4.
[47] OCTAVIO PAZ, «La palabra edificante», in *Los signos en rotación* (Madrid, 1971), p. 143.

> Oh! regressar a mim profundamente
> E ser o que já fui no meu delírio... («Escala», Po, p. 116)

Furthermore, there is never any question of the poet's own responsibility: if things have changed for the worse, he regrets this, but the cause was beyond his control. Where some emotion stronger than selfish regrets may well be expected (in *A Confissão de Lúcio*, «O Fixador de Instantes» or «A Grande Sombra») there is nothing. There is no apparent moral to any of Sá-Carneiro's works, no homiletic aim, and a guilty conscience is as noticeably absent as are any manifestations of the power and influence of organised religion or Christian ethics, or the need for either. If Ricardo, in *A Confissão de Lúcio,* shows signs of remorse, he is merely deploring his own suffering, his own *tédio.* If Lúcio is at all preoccupied about deceiving his friend, he consoles himself by pointing out that he bears him no malice:

> ainda que o meu procedimento fosse na verdade um crime, eu não praticava esse crime por mal, *criminosamente.* Eis pelo que me era impossível ter remorsos. (CL, p. 100, author's italics)

Unlike many of his predecessors in the literature of Decadentism and Aestheticism, Sá-Carneiro is not concerned with sin. The majority of examples of imagery drawn from religion are aesthetic and the rest are psychological. They are certainly not religious.

Here again we are confronted by the author's vision of himself as aesthete and artist, and it is partly true to say that his real interest was in the decorative, as Mario Praz said of Oscar Wilde.[48] That his religious images appeal to the senses rather than the emotions is also significant: they *are* moving, but the emotion is of a different kind. There is no sense of the purpose of any liturgical element, no sense of the presence or the existence of God, and, furthermore, the imagery is frequently used in connection with sex. So we have an aesthetic artist, unaffected by the values of the *lepidópteros,* aware of beauty, which is inextricably linked with sensuality and, by extension, with sex. And all these characteristics are found in Romantic and Decadent/Aesthetic artists.[49] They see more and are aware of more, than ordinary men; as Bécquer said:

---

[48] PRAZ, p. 378.

[49] The boundaries between (French) Decadentism and (English) Aestheticism are somewhat vague. PHILIPPE JULLIAN, in *Esthètes et Magiciens* (Paris, 1969), helps to clarify the confusion (pp. 32-3), pointing out, among other things, exclusive characteristics of one or other movement. For example, in England, «l'esthète, par une perversité qu'il appelle humour, s'amuse parfois de ce qu'il admire le plus» (p. 32); then there is the fact that in France, «tous les thèmes des Fleurs du mal furent repris par les artistes [of the Decadence]» (p. 32). He adds, «Si l'Angleterre donc était esthète la France fut décadente. Il n'y eut que peu de décadents en Angleterre, à part certains disciples de Wilde, et peu d'esthètes en France, qui pourtant peut revendiquer le plus exquis de tous, Robert de Mon-

En la mar de la duda en que bogo
ni aún sé lo que creo;
sin embargo estas ansias me dicen
que yo llevo algo
divino aquí dentro [50]

and that *algo divino* that is ironically not religious leads to heightened perception, increased sensibility, and at the same time to unconcealed scorn for those who are not the same. The resulting sense of alienation and superiority is enough in many cases for the artist to dismiss all bourgeois values, especially the moral code, and sometimes religious practices. And yet the ritual and the decoration of the Church are beautiful, fascinating in their links with the Unknown and, for Sá-Carneiro, ever present in art and literature. Robin Spencer has pointed out that «the theory behind the art of the Aesthetic Movement was that it could be enjoyed for its own sake, *and need impart nothing more than its own decorative existence to the beholder*».[51] Aesthetic preoccupation with liturgical imagery was more connected with Romantic and Decadent fashion than creed, and there are countless examples of the popularity of the external trappings of Catholicism among earlier artists. Stendhal is said to have been fascinated by Gilles de Rais' love for «liturgical ceremonial and sacred music».[52] John Parker reminds us that «Baudelaire had made considerable use of religious symbols and imagery in the expression of his satanism, and for a generation without faith the exotic aspects of the religion held considerable aesthetic attractions».[53] In the paintings of Moreau, the jewel-like colours of the detailed backgrounds, the Baroque adornments, the archways and pillars have an ecclesiastical air (e.g. *The Apparition*, 1896; *Jupiter and Semele*, 1896; *The Suitors*, 1852, among others), even though the atmosphere is Byzantine rather than Christian. Jullian, in his discussion of «The Mystical Chimera» in Symbolist art, says: «Decorators such as Tiffany and Grasset [...] deliberately imitated stained-glass windows when they did not actually make them»,[54] and later, he describes the Moreau painting *The Unicorns* as containing «femmes coiffées de hennin, à demi recouvertes d'ornaments *quasi sacerdotaux*».[55]

tesquiou» (p. 33). He indicates, too, the different political and social backgrounds in the two countries, making for different artistic reactions, especially the pessimism so noticeable in France, but obviously the Aesthetes and Decadents had a great deal in common.

[50] GUSTAVO ADOLFO BÉCQUER, Rima VIII, in *Rimas* (Madrid, 1963), p. 27.
[51] ROBIN SPENCER, *The Aesthetic Movement* (London, 1972), p. 10.
[52] STENDHAL, *Mémoires d'un touriste* (Paris, 1927), vol. i, pp. 318 et seq. Quoted in PRAZ, p. 345.
[53] PARKER, p. 456.
[54] PHILIPPE JULLIAN, *Dreamers of Decadence* (London, 1971), p. 73. This is a greatly-improved version of *Esthèthes et magiciens*, not just a translation.
[55] JULLIAN, *Jean Lorrain*, p. 34.

On another occasion, describing the writer Jean Lorrain, the same critic refers to his «bagues *épiscopales*».[56] The ritual of the Church is often found in Decadent novels: M. de Phocas, in Lorrain's book, attends Mass on Good Friday, 1895, for example, and later he refers to ecclesiastical ornaments:

> Il y a aussi des yeux dans les transparences des gemmes, les anciennes gemmes surtout, les cabochons troubles et laiteux dont sont ornés certains ciboires et certaines châsses aussi de saintes embaumées, comme on en voit dans les trésors des cathédrales de Sicile et d'Allemagne.[57]

Joséphin Péladan —the self-styled Sâr Péladan— uses liturgical imagery too, especially in *Le Vice suprême;* he himself was an example of the vogue for assuming priestly garb and he even claimed to be some sort of priest. His own appearance, as the well-known portrait of him by Marcellin Desboutin (1891) shows, was eccentric in the extreme, and, as Jullian has pointed out, his costume was «reminiscent of Lohengrin and Nebuchadnezzar».[58] This type of dress did not lack its imitators: José Rebelo de Bettencourt, in his «O Café Martinho do meu tempo»,[59] talks of his conversations with Santa Rita Pintor, Sá-Carneiro's daily companion in his early days in Paris, who is obviously the model for Gervásio Vila-Nova; Santa Rita revealed to him one day: «É para parecer mais velho que eu me visto assim, *com estes fatos quasi eclesiásticos,* com este colarinho duro e esta gravata preta». But it is in Symbolist painting, even more than in Decadent literature, that religion is converted into art, for in the literature of the period the interest in the external trappings of the Church was in fact often linked to a certain religious faith, however unorthodox (such as the Sâr Péladan's resuscitation of the Order of the Rosicrucians, the *mage* of *Le Vice suprême,* and M. de Phocas' sense of sacrilege and attacks of remorse). Even in the field of the visual arts, a great deal of, at the very least, introspection and metaphysical consideration was going on; in 1893, Maurice Denis wrote to Odilon Redon, «Nous sommes tous préoccupés de Dieu. Aujourd'hui le Christ est vivant. Il n'y a pas eu depuis longtemps d'époque plus passionnée que la nôtre pour la Beauté religieuse».[60] This is where the Portuguese author parts company with many of these artists. Maria da Graça Carpinteiro has pointed out that in his works, «o problema do Desconhecido é tratado na mais completa ausência das hipóteses religiosas».[61] He is concerned with the Unknown, though, and liturgical imagery is relevant in this con-

---

[56] JULLIAN, *Jean Lorrain,* p. 286.
[57] JULLIAN, *Jean Lorrain,* pp. 32 and 39.
[58] JULLIAN, *Dreamers of Decadence,* p. 75.
[59] JOSÉ REBELO DE BETTENCOURT, *O Mundo das Imagens* (Lisbon, 1928), p. 59.
[60] Quoted by JULLIAN, *Esthètes,* p. 93.
[61] MARIA DE GRAÇA CARPINTEIRO, *A novela,* p. 11.

nection as well as being important as a feature of beauty. As Lionel Johnson, the English Aesthetic poet, wrote:

> ...as the awed rejoicing priest
> Officiates at the feast,
> Knowing how deep within the liturgies
> Lie hid the mysteries.[62]

A large proportion of Sá-Carneiro's liturgical imagery can be classified as religion for art's sake, but some of it is there because of its emotional relevance to a man who could be described in the same terms as was «the young colossus of the decadence»,[63] Jean Lorrain: «très peu croyant mais passionné de mystère».[64] Liturgy is related to the Unknown. Then, as sex is often described in liturgical terms, it is «mystified» by being connected with religion, and this too is part of the author's Decadent heritage: Verlaine, for example, in his *Poèmes saturniens* had associated ceremony and sensuality many years previously (1866) when he wrote:

> Dans un palais soie et or, dans Ecbatane,
> De beaux démons, des satans adolescents
> Au son d'une musique mahométane,
> Font litière aux Sept Péchés de leurs cinq sens[65]

while there are countless examples of the relationship between sex and ritual within the area of the Occult and Black Magic. The «mon corps est un autel qui veut être adoré» of Liane de Pougy[66] is a commonplace of the period, typical of what Mario Praz has called «the inevitable mingling of sacred and profane».[67] As far as Sá-Carneiro is concerned, to mystify and mythify sex reveals yet again his adolescent attitude, while his obsessive interest in the Unknown springs from his consciousness of possessing an increased sensibility, together with a sense of isolation from common people. Interesting people, people who are different, people who are worthwhile have *auréolas,* are described as *nimbados* or are touched with Mystery, again revealing the influence of the Occult; but the important thing is that they are exotic, not ordinary, and this élitist attitude is ever present. They are people who are further along the path to the Ideal, who have discovered the answer to life's mysteries or who are, at least, aware of the direction they must take in order to do so.

Sá-Carneiro's preoccupation with the *alma* too, though undeniably

---

[62] LIONEL JOHNSON, «Walter Pater», in *Writing of the 'Nineties,* ed. Derek Stanford (London, 1971), p. 185.
[63] JULLIAN, *Oscar Wilde,* p. 101.
[64] JULLIAN, *Jean Lorrain,* p. 148.
[65] PAUL VERLAINE, *Poèmes saturniens* (1866).
[66] In a letter to a friend (1904), Jean Lorrain refers to this assertion made by Liane de Pougy. Quoted in JULLIAN, *Jean Lorrain,* p. 216.
[67] PRAZ, p. 394.

genuine, is part of his immediate literary and artistic background. As Jullian has pointed out, «Souls are to Symbolism what angels were to Romanticism».[68] But Sa-Carneiro does not use the image in the standard Symbolist fashion; the one characteristic that the Sá-Carneiro *alma* and the Symbolist soul share is that of belonging to another world. Jullian says of the incidence of the image in Symbolism: «this profusion of souls is not so much the result of a return to Christian belief as of a horror of materialism»,[69] while João Gaspar Simões affirms that Sá-Carneiro was a poet for whom «a arte é, fundamentalmente uma *transposição*, isto é, uma passagem para *além* da realidade quotidiana do homem» (author's italics).[70] The image of the soul represents the two conflicts that Adolfo Casais Monteiro has pointed out: Sá-Carneiro's internal conflict and the conflict that existed between him and the world.[71] But in neither case is there any connection whatsoever with religion, and the Unknown is the *além* of the Symbolists rather than any Christian eternity; God Himself is no more than an image of power, used in connection with what Gaspar Simões has called Sá-Carneiro's «admirável megalomania».[72] Sá-Carneiro is looking for himself *now;* like his character Professor Antena, he is not trying to «romper o futuro das nossas almas, além-Morte» (CF, p. 237). He is asking: «Onde existo que não existo em mim?» («Escavação», Po, p. 55). Many critics have seen this disregard of the Christian faith as contributing to his downfall and his suicide,[73] and it is indeed undeniable that he found no comfort in religious beliefs. Religion, for him, comprised aesthetic beauty —«a beleza da religião», one might say [74]— and a link with the Unknown which is both a Symbolist commonplace and a manifestation of his aristocratic vision of life, while

---

[68] JULLIAN, *Dreamers of Decadence*, p. 71.
[69] JULLIAN, *Dreamers of Decadence*, p. 71.
[70] JOÃO GASPAR SIMÕES, «Mário de Sá-Carneiro ou a Ilusão da Personalidade», in *O Mistério da Poesia* (Oporto, 1971), p. 122. (First edition: Coimbra, 1931.)
[71] ADOLFO CASAIS MONTEIRO, *Considerações Pessoais* (Coimbra, 1933), p. 126.
[72] JOÃO GASPAR SIMÕES, «A Ilusão», p. 143.
[73] For example, JOÃO R. MENDES, «Sá-Carneiro, Poeta da Soledade», in *Brotéria*, vol. XXXII, fascículo 5 (May, 1941), 507-19, refers to the author's false desire for independence and his refusal to accept God. Mendes answers Sá-Carneiro's poetic question «Onde existo que não existo em mim?» by asserting that «Nós existimos em Deus» (p. 512). The same critic, in «Crítica a *Indícios de Ouro*», also in *Brotéria*, vol. XXVI (January, 1938), 111-12, had mentioned Sá-Carneiro's «longa ausência de Deus» (p. 112). A. DE CASTRO GIL, in *Sá-Carneiro, Miguel Torga, José Régio, Três Atitudes perante a Vida* (Coimbra, 1949), attributes the author's lack of «self-control» (the words are given in English, p. 39) to the absence of God in his life. He did not, according to Castro Gil, hear the voice of conscience when contemplating suicide: «queimou-se na pira maldita das suas paixões incontroladas» (p. 53). M. A. ANTUNES, in «A Poesia Modernista. De *Orpheu* a *Altitude*», in *Brotéria*, vol. XXXI (October, 1940), is less explicit, but unless I have misread him, holds similar views: he refers to «o drama trágico do homem entregue às suas próprias forças» (p. 307).
[74] See GASPAR SIMÕES, «A Ilusão», p. 123.

at the same time providing him with an image (the soul) to help him in his struggle to investigate his own inner turmoil.

The fact that there are striking similarities between the works of Sá-Carneiro and previous literary movements in France and England in particular does not suggest that he was an unoriginal writer, though we know that he was not even the first Portuguese author to asssimilate and manipulate these earlier currents. His acquaintance with the attitudes and forms reflecting his European literary heritage may well have come largely from the influence of his compatriots, but it is probably safe to assume that he had read some of the original works. In any case, he handles these elements in an individualistic way.

CHAPTER 2

THE SUPERNATURAL

DEATH, MYSTERY, THE BEYOND

Needless to say, Sá-Carneiro often uses death imagery in an entirely conventional way: «*morto* de sono» (CL, p. 54) for example, and we find the occasional simile connected with death. But far more revealing is the author's striking association of sex with death, an association referred to explicitly in *Princípio*: «morte e amor, andam sempre juntos» («O Incesto», P, p. 299). There is no lack of death images in erotic circumstances: a climatic embrace, «*agonizando* num arqueamento de vício» (CL, p. 40); «medo inquieto e *agonia*» (CL, p. 101) and the «*agonia* fluida» (CF, p. 147) of sexual intercourse. There are also instances of the relationship within the actual narrative; for example, the stabbing of the dancer in «Bárbaro» (Po, p. 107) and the murder of the unknown woman in «O Fixador de Instantes». In «Loucura», Marcela reveals that Raul asked her if she would commit suicide with him — «*morrer* feliz nos seus braços» (P, p. 71), while in «Ressurreição», the fictional sculptor's mystic-erotic experience with the statue of Christ was to end in his attacking it, «*morrendo* sobre a estátua» (CF, p. 336). Other examples are the murder of the «rapariga mascarada» in «A Grande Sombra» and the sudden, inexplicable death of both lovers in «Mistério». In very many cases, death is a positive image, the correlative of ecstasy, the element which preserves euphoria, making it transcendental and eternal. A door is opened to the Unknown in order to find a solution for eternal puzzles. The Professor, in «A Estranha Morte do Professor Antena», sees death as a stage towards knowledge; the Sphinx, in «O Fixador de Instantes», is «saudosa a luar e *morte*» (CF, p. 265); in «Página dum Suicida», we find: «*Morte!* que mistérios encerras?» (P, p. 171), «eu, *descobrirei a Morte!*» (P, p. 172) and «a única coisa interessante que existe actualmente na vida, é a morte!» (P, p. 174, author's italics).

Suicide is the next stage — suicide, that is, as a positive act, rather than a means of escape from the intolerable. Its frequency is striking, and the author's own suicide makes this element of particular interest;

36

disapproval for this course of action is never expressed by Sá-Carneiro's characters: on the contrary, one of them says: «*Os suicidas!* Ah! com que entusiasmo os admiro, como os respeito!» (P, p. 274), and in *A Confissão de Lúcio,* we are told that Gervásio Vila-Nova «não foi um falhado, porque teve a coragem de se despedaçar» (CL, p. 21).

Death may also be seen as an image of final destruction, with connotations of impotence and insensibility: «*morto* para a vida e para os sonhos» (CL, p. 15), for example; in the poem «Epígrafe», there is a clear indication of destruction with «A cor *morreu* — a até o ar é uma ruína» (Po, p. 83); in «O Fantasma», the emphasis is again on a sort of *vita minima*: «*Morreram-me* meninos nos sentidos» (Po, p. 163). All this suggests an extension to the concept of death — a kind of metaphysical death, death-within-life. Life is clearly thought possible on two levels, and the higher of the two seems seldom to be achieved by any of Sá-Carneiro's *dramatis personae:* they have «almas *mortas*» (P, p. 203), like Lúcio who leaves prison «*morto, sem olhar um instante em redor de mim...*» (CL, p. 159), so that «*a morte real* [would be] apenas um sono mais denso» (CL, p. 160). There are «sete Princesas que *morreram*» («Ângulo», Po, p. 109) and an «Antiga quinta deserta / Em que donos *faleceram*» («Sete Canções», V, Po, p. 124), while in «O Recreio», «*Morre* a criança afogada» (Po, p. 141). In one of his letters, Sá-Carneiro talks of his own «estado de alma actual», describing it as «*morto* — mas vivo 'por velocidade adquirida'» (C I, p. 154, letter dated June 20, 1914). Expressions such as *esmagar, desmoronar-se, fender-se, destrinçar-se, desarticular-se* and *despedaçar-se* are also used, creating a somewhat less final effect: for example, Ricardo, in *A Confissão de Lúcio,* says «Como sofro *despedaçadoramente*» (CL, p. 151), while the protagonist of «O Fixador de Instantes» refers to his condition as «asas *partidas*» (CF, p. 269); Inácio, in «Ressurreição», has an «alma *quebrada*» (CF, p. 282) and the artist in «Mistério» thinks the furniture and the walls in his room «cresciam sobre ele a *esmagá-lo*» (CF, p. 131). Even his thoughts are «esmagadores» (CF, p. 131). This condition is slightly different from the *vita minima* designated by images of death in life: in many cases the state of the individual has been brought about by some particular experience known to the reader, usually one connected with conflict, or an act of violence of some sort. Unlike the condition of the *mortos-vivos,* it may well be temporary; it is marginally less serious but frequently more painful.

In the same way that the death imagery connected with sex may sometimes be exciting and sometimes repulsive, the concept of death itself can vary between the intriguing and the horrible or tragic. In «Mistério», the thought of suicide causes the protagonist no fear, only a sadness which is almost sentimental: «dilacerava-o uma ternura infinita; uma piedade ilimitada por si próprio. Pois havia de se destruir ele? [...] Que tristeza!»

(CF, p. 132). He is, in part, one of the characters referred to by Alvarez when he wrote:

> ... they [the Romantics] conceived of death and suicide childishly: not as an end of everything but as the supreme, dramatic gesture of contempt towards a dull bourgeois world. [...] [The Romantic] epidemics of suicide *à la mode* had one belief in common: that the suicide himself would be present to witness the drama created by his death. «Our unconscious», said Freud, «... does not believe in its own death; it behaves as if it were immortal».[1]

In this case, we are not made explicitly aware of his concern with the drama of his own death, but of his ability to stand back from the event and see it objectively. Ricardo de Loureiro is a reflection of the quotation from Freud: «*se não fosse haver a certeza absoluta de que todos morremos*», he asserts, «*eu, não me 'vendo' morto, não acreditaria na minha morte...*» (CL, p. 50, author's italics). The hero of «Mistério» feels something stronger than sadness as the narrative progresses: «o suicídio repugnava-lhe» (CF, p. 142), while in «Loucura», the protagonist's diary contains the entry: «*só há uma coisa pior do que a vida; é a morte*» (P, p. 116, author's italics). Here there is a preoccupation with the terrors of death: «Viver *para morrer*... Ah! como é horroroso... como é horroroso» (P, p. 109).

The element of mystery is one found with frequency on both narrative and symbolic levels, serving as the pivot of the stories and the essence of the images; the «*mistério* que é meu e me seduz» («Partida», Po, p. 51) is an eternal obsession. All the short stories revolve around a mystery and its solution —how did Professor Antena die, who is Marta in *A Confissão de Lúcio,* who is the *homem dos sonhos,* who is the nobleman in «Mistério», will the death forecast in *A Profecia* come about? — and not a few of the characters owe their interest to their air of strangeness. Lúcio, in *A Confissão,* refers to himself, not without irony, as «um herói com seus laivos de *mistério*» (CL, p. 16); an exciting feature of Gervásio Vila-Nova is that «no seu corpo havia *mistério*» (CL, p. 20), while as for Marta, «O *mistério* era essa mulher» (CL, p. 92). In «Mistério» (with its obviously significant title), the protagonist describes his moment of triumph: «Projectei *Mistério*» (CF, p. 74), while of the *homem dos sonhos,* Sá-Carneiro writes: «Aquele homem parecia-me um *mistério*» (CF, p. 157). Mystery is a more or less permanent characteristic of all these individuals; less permanently, we find cases such as that of the American woman in *A Confissão de Lúcio* who fleetingly «teve um sorriso de *mistério*» (CL, p. 35) or of the «Raul sorumbático e *misterioso* doutros tempos» of «O Incesto» (P, p. 103). Mankind in general is often classified as mysterious

---

[1] ALVAREZ, p. 177.

too, or various aspects of human life are seen in this way. After all, «O *Mistério* [...] somo-nos nós em verdade», according to Professor Antena (CF, p. 237). Sex («só as pontas dos seios prosseguiam os seu *mistério*», CF, p. 265) and dreams are found in this category («o sonho é o *misterioso* mensageiro que nos vem recordar a vida», P, p. 165), while death, that «região misteriosa» (P, p. 174), is the greatest enigma of all.

If death is the ultimate future mystery, more immediate and everyday problems and puzzles are frequently somewhat overdrawn and seen as mysterious too: they provide a «*mistério* duma incerteza» («Sete Canções de Declínio», II, Po, p. 121). The outcome is suffering: «Em face do *mistério* não se pode ser calmo» (CL, p. 103). And the mysteries to be solved are sometimes universal: this is the motivation behind Professor Antena's research, since, were it not that one book is missing from his library, «a humanidade teria avançado de mil séculos — haveríamos, quem sabe, descoberto enfim o *Mistério*...» (CF, p. 229).

Sá-Carneiro uses the word *mistério* in two ways: it may denote ignorance of facts which can and probably will be remedied: in the short stories there is at least a superficial tidying up of narrative mysteries with the passage of time. But there is, on the other hand, frequent use of the concept as permanently inexplicable, at least in this world —«o inexplicável não se explica» (P, p. 228)— and in fact, we are made thoroughly aware of a greater entity, the autonomous absolute which is *o Mistério*. The «arrepios *misteriosos* das luzes» of the *Confissão de Lúcio* «orgy» are exciting for this very reason (CL, p. 26); in «A Grande Sombra», we find a «paisagem-iluminura, transtornada de *Mistério*» (CF, p. 90), and later, the protagonist says: «a minha dor enclavinhou-se em *Mistério*» (CF, p. 110); in «Ressurreição», Notre Dame is seen «a projectar *mistérios*» (CF, p. 280) and Inácio's new book has «páginas [...] sumptuosas de *mistério*» (CF, p. 338). The autonomous absolute is often referred to explicitly: in «A Grande Sombra» it has always fascinated the protagonist; the story actually begins: «—O *Mistério*... Oh! desde a infância esta obsessão me perturba — o seu encanto me esvai...» (CF, p. 39), and the author goes on to refer to «a sumptuosidade inigualável do *mistério!*» (CF, p. 40), «um mundo *misterioso*» (CF, p. 41), «o lindo *mistério*» (CF, p. 47), «minha atracção de *Mistério*» (CF, p. 49) and «o gosto roxo e macerado do *Mistério*» (CF, p. 54). And these are but a few examples of the use of the word in the one short story: in eighty-four pages (pp. 39-123), *mistério, misterioso* and *misteriosamente* are used no fewer than thirty-nine times, *segredo/secreto* twenty-seven times, *enigma* ten times, *inexplicável* three times and *desconhecido* nine times, to say nothing of related words such as *imponderável* or images such as the Sphinx. When the narrator muses:

39

«Seria com efeito tudo aquilo um enigma — ou nada mais do que uma aventura interessante, rara, inesperada; contudo bem natural?...» Ah! se enfim eu estivesse na posse dum segredo... (CF, p. 78),

the difference between mysteries that can be resolved and those which are touched by the transcendental is clear. It is obvious, too, that it is the second category which is important: the mystery that is «contudo, bem natural» can be pleasant, but does not have the power to dominate a man's life. The sort that does is frequently represented by the image of the Sphinx: Marta, in *A Confissão de Lúcio,* is fascinating and attractive, «sempre a mesma esfinge» (CL, p. 103), while the jury is intrigued by Lúcio's attitude at the end of the story: «romanesca de *esfíngica»* (CL, p. 155). The décor at the «orgy» is exciting: «um estranho palco erguido sobre *esfinges* bronzeadas» (CL, p. 34), and the appearance of Gervásio Vila-Nova is irresistible since his is a «corpo de *esfinge,* talvez, em noites de luar» (CL, p. 20). A climactic moment in the poem «Partida» includes the line «Doido de *esfinges* o horizonte arde» (Po, p. 53).

With this element, the author again reveals an ambivalent attitude, a love/hate relationship; his fascination is not very far away from at best, disillusion and at worst, intolerable dread and horror. There is a cynical reference to disillusion in «Pied-de-nez»: «O Erro sempre a rir-me em destrambelho-/Falso *mistério,* mas que não se abrange...» (Po, p. 145); in «A Grande Sombra», we see the excitement — disillusion — horror process clearly, and we find: «sou eu próprio que logo arremesso para longe o *mistério* falso [...] como se os *mistérios* não fossem sempre falsidades» (CF, p. 70). In «A Grande Sombra», the narrator wishes it would go away: «procuro às vezes persuadir-me de que tudo isto é bem simples, bem real — que não existirá *mistério* algum» (CF, p. 104). In the same story, we read about his self-disgust, as he sees himself as an «*esfinge* de papelão» (CF, p. 71), while in «Aqueloutro» the height of cynical self-contempt is reached: «O mago sem condão, o *Esfinge* Gorda» (Po, p. 167). In the poem «Ângulo», the *miragem,* an image which even in its most positive settings («saudosa de *miragens»,* CF, p. 92, and «*Miragem* roxa de nimbado encanto», «Partida», Po, p. 53) has connotations of falsehood, now becomes explicitly deceptive: «Em *miragens* de falsos horizontes» (Po, p. 108), for example. In many cases, it is a question of an incomprehensible force which cannot be resisted, and the result is pain and terror. The narrator of «O Homem dos Sonhos» is disturbed almost to the point of insanity: and Lúcio says: «sempre tive nojo [...] da gente que o *mistério* grifou» (CF, p. 124). The child in «A Grande Sombra» is terrified by mystery: «nume febre de medo, a ranger de mistério» (CF, p. 44), while later, his fear and panic increase as the mystery increases. A parallel attitude is found in «A Profecia» — «Eu tive sempre muito medo do *desconhecido»* (P, p. 164) and in *A Confissão de Lúcio,* where Lúcio says: «as nossas vidas passavam torturadas [...] de *incompreensões*» (CL, p. 46).

The author's ambivalent attitude is found, too, in his affection for adjectives suggesting haziness, evanescence, inaccessibility and incomprehensibility, which sometimes provoke fascination, sometimes fear: «beijos *subtis*» (CL, p. 19), «listas úmidas de sons [que] se vaporizabam *subtis*» (CL, p. 38), characters who are «ungidos de *Vago*» (CL, p. 62), «carne [...] *fugitiva*» (CL, p. 74), «êxtases *perdidos*» (CL, p. 95), jewels which are «brilhos *remotos* de densas pompas» (CF, p. 77), «vibrações *longínquas* de orgia imperial» (CF, p. 164), the «asas duma quimera *longìnquamente* batendo» (CF, p. 196), a «paisagem *de subtileza*» (CF, p. 89), «obras [...] ungidas *de Incerto*» (CF, p. 277), «móveis orientais *indecisos*» (CF, p. 80), «seios *perdidos*» (CF, p. 199), «sons *perdidos* de azul» (CF, p. 89) and «Janelas *incertas*» («Não», Po, p. 89). Most often we find an attitude of fascination rather than of fear, but there are a few cases with sinister connotations.

The Beyond, the search for which runs through all that Sá-Carneiro wrote, represents an alternative reality. There is no question of its being a subsequent reality in the religious sense of a life after death; it is *simultaneous,* and true artists are constantly aware of it. Almost anything can serve to provide a glimpse of this desirable region, and certain elements, such as mystery, are its earthly manifestations. Like so many other images, it may be seen as repellent and attractive at the same time: to be conscious of it gives rise to a pharisaic attitude, and in «O Incesto», the author is explicit in his expression of this credo. Although he says that «entre os artistas se enfileiram alguns dos grandes desgraçados da terra», he adds that this is better by far than the «existência vazia e desoladora» of the majority, «que é a maior e mais real miséria deste mundo» (P, p. 196). As we have seen, people can be touched with the Beyond, and the most interesting of them have some sort of indefinable aura. Furthermore, Sá-Carneiro considers that the eternal search for the *além* is aided by certain experiences, such as the appreciation and creation of works of art. In *A Confissão de Lúcio,* Ricardo and Lúcio are present at the first performance of a new *concertante* entitled *Além;* when the last notes die away Ricardo gives it high praise indeed: «São véus rasgados sobre o *além*» (CL, p. 83), he says. The actual creation of a work of art serves the same purpose, and when Inácio, in «Ressurreição», writes a new novel, he gains immeasurably from the experience: «ungira-se mais grifadamente de *Além*» (CF, p. 301). In «Asas», one of the fantastic texts is again entitled *Além,* this time by the protagonist-translator who is overwhelmed by its genius (CF, p. 196), and the dancing in the «Bailado» section also provides a glimpse of the Unknown. It is an act of creation, though staying in the imagination rather than being expressed in a work of art, that leads the strange nobleman of the story «A Grande Sombra» to use the word which is so closely connected to *além* in Sá-Carneiro — *glória*:

> já experimentou tamanha *glória?*... Dormir num grande palácio deserto... às escuras... e antes de adormecer, à força de concentração... só com a sua vontade... ah! ah!... povoar de figuras as casas vazias... na treva... (CF, p. 105)

In «Loucura», a book of short stories «foi quase uma *glória*» (P, p. 23), and in «A Estranha Morte do Professor Antena», we find:

> Com efeito um grande sábio cria — *imagina* tanto ou mais do que o Artista. A Ciência é talvez a maior das artes — erguendo-se a mais sobrenatural, a mais irreal, a mais longe em Além. (CF, p. 226, author's italics)

The Professor himself refers to man as «o Segredo-Total» and adds: «Deixemos o futuro, esqueçamos Amanhã — sonhadores heróicos de *Além*» (CF, p. 237). But it is striking how infrequently Sá-Carneiro mentions science as a means to the desired end compared with the numerous occasions on which sex is seen at the first stage: in the «Além» section of «Asas», just before the moment of disillusion, the author says that he felt «entrelaçado d'Ouro, sagrado d'*além*-Cor» (CF, p. 198); the strange *homem dos sonhos* talks about the delights of sex, including «os dentes que rangem e grifam nos espasmos de *além*» (CF, p. 164); the lovers in «O Incesto» are described as «amantes ébrios da *glória*, conquistadores do Vago!» (P, p. 202), while sex and violence are combined in «O Fixador de Instantes»: «A *glória* fora excedida!» says the narrator after his sexual encounter with *a grande fera* (CF, p. 268); then, when he kills her, he exclaims: «*Glória! Glória!* Tenho-a para sempre!» (CF, p. 269). Sometimes some unknown force will provide the stimulus, and we read of unexpected and unexplained moments of awareness: «tenho ocasiões repentinas, outros dias», says the protagonist of «O Grande Mistério», «em que me chegam grandes júbilos entusiasmados. À minha volta tudo ecoa *glória*...» (CF, p. 60). The search for the Beyond is seen as a kind of mystical journey which can be the result of sensual stimulation and over a longer period, which forms a permanent part of the artist's experience. It is found in the poem «Partida», after the poet has asked:

> A vida, a natureza,
> Que são para o artista?

What is necessary is to break away:

> ... subir *além dos céus*
> Que as nossas almas só acumularam (Po, p. 52)

In the poem «Álcool» we find: «Luto, estrebucho... Em vão! Silvo p'ra *além*...» (Po, p. 58), while in «Dispersão», death is referred to:

Vejo o meu último dia
Pintado em rolos de fumo,
E todo azul-de-agonia
Em sombra e *além* me sumo. (Po, p. 64)

In «Quase», we are clearly aware of both the effort and the failure: «um pouco mais de azul — eu era *além*» (Po, p. 68). As in religious mysticism, the appreciation of the existence of the transcendental by the senses is no more than an initial stage: the protagonist of «Mistério» is happy in his (sexual) «triumph», but «alguma coisa faltava ainda —uma pequena luz— para chegar ao fim: ao *além*» (CF, p. 147). The desired state is «*além*-realidade» (C I, p. 58), «*além*-voluptuosidade» (C I, p. 58), it is the poet's *glória* and *beleza* («Não», Po, p. 89). The journey may go back-wards in time, too, and then the implication is of a kind of Augustinian memory of paradise: «A minh'alma *nostálgica de além*» («Partida», Po, p. 51) for example. Sometimes the journey —which, more often than not, is an ascension— *is* successful, if only momentarily:

O arquiteto sublime, o grande construtor das torres, acumulara andares sobre andares, e a torre maravilhosa tocava quasi o céu. Quisera subir às cumeadas. E fôra escalando sempre triunfante a ladeira da vida. Do alto da sua torre, do alto da cupula de aço refulgente, debruçava-se para ver o seu triunfo. E via a *Gloria*. («O Incesto», P, pp. 347-8, original orthography)

In the same way as the *Além* is beyond reality, the impact of everyday words may be increased by the addition of *além* as a prefix; often this serves to intensify suffering or revulsion: in *A Confissão de Lúcio*, for example, there is a «luz de *além*-Inferno» (CL, p. 38) and an «*além*-gosto a doença» (CL, p. 101). One of Sá-Carneiro's poems is actually called «*Além*-Tédio» (Po, p. 73).

A word found more frequently than almost any other is *sombra*, and it too can be seen to have close connections with the Beyond. As with so many other images, its conventional metaphorical use can be disre-garded immediately and we are left with examples which reveal that it appears to be interchangeable with *mistério* or *além* as far as its allusive qualities are concerned, and that it represents an area that again inspires fear as well as fascination. *Sombra, mistério* and *além* stand for the alter-native reality which must be conceived of finitely but which is made insubstantial with the use of terminology that suggests vagueness, inac-cessibility and intangibility. *Sombra*, unsurprisingly, signifies a visible facet of the supernatural, so that suffering is evident in *A Confissão de Lúcio* when Lúcio states categorically that he and Ricardo were unhappy: «Não éramos felizes —oh! não... As nossas vidas passavam torturadas

43

de ânsias, de incompreensões, de agonias *de sombra...*» (CL, p. 46), but in «A Grande Sombra», the protagonist gains his objective — «Tenho o que queria», he says «*a Sombra*» (CF, p. 111). However, there is a great deal more emphasis on the positive side of the image, for example, when the protagonist of «A Grande Sombra» optimistically considers the possibility of suicide; it will not be a question of abandoning his beloved *Sombra,* «Ao contrário... Mergulhar nela indefinidamente» (CF, p. 122). Even a touch of the image is positive in «Partida»:

> A minh'alma nostálgica de além,
> Cheia de orgulho, *ensombra-se* entretanto (Po, p. 51),

while in the same poem, we see *sombra* as a stage in the quasi-mystical journey: «*Sombra,* vertigem, ascensão — Altura!» (Po, p. 53). We are inevitably reminded of the Platonic allegory of the cave, where a prisoner, released after a life-time of darkness and immobility,

> would need, then, to grow accustomed before he could see things in that upper world. At first it would be easiest to make out shadows and then the images of men and things reflected in water, and later on the things themselves.[2]

Between the everyday (unsatisfactory) world and Sá-Carneiro's version of the «upper world» is an area of shadow, the only thing he can make out. The first stages in a sexual relationship often represent this early *sombra* stage in the search for the transcendental: as the «Grande Sombra» hero becomes more and more attracted to the strange *princesa velada,* his awareness of this increases: «Como nunca, se me acentuava agora um estranho calafrio — um calafrio de *sombra*» (CF, p. 77).

> Tudo se esbateu aos meus sentidos, se nimbou de Subtil. Tudo hoje apenas advinho. Eis como venço seguir olvidado — preso por fios de *sombra* ao meu quebranto. (CF, p. 87)

He has discovered himself «*em Sombra*» (CF, p. 90), but it seems impossible to reach the ultimate stage in this world; the bizarre aristocrat is a reminder of the need for something more: «A sua voz lembra-me *uma sombra.* [...] todo aquele homem me lembra *uma sombra*» (CF, p. 108), «era tão *sombrio* o tom da sua voz», «Parecia velar-lhe a garganta *a sombra*» (CF, p. 111). Then at last the narrator is sure: «O Erro e *a Sombra* existem-Me» (CF, p. 112), and his final destination is glimpsed in the first place in the form of a shadow: «sentia-se, não se via, pressentia-se numa emanação de altura — *a sombra* dum grande edifício torreado» (CF, p. 119). His eventual suicide is less of a departure than an arrival: «O grande salto!... ao Segredo... na *Sombra...* para sempre... e a Ouro!...

---

[2] PLATO, *The Republic of Plato,* trans. F. M. Cornford (Oxford 1966), p. 224.

a Ouro!... a Ouro!...» (CF, p. 123). The ending of «O Fixador de Instantes» is similar; the protagonist has triumphed, has captured for ever the moment of ecstasy: «estilizei-me em tempo. Parei. Que delírios, o resto?... *A grande sombra! a grande sombra!...*» (CF, p. 270). As we have already seen, art can also provide the first stage: the novel Inácio writes in «Ressureição» is seen as «grifando *sombra* e Além» (CF, p. 317), and the author also tells us about «os laivos imperiais de Novo com que a sua obra hoje se timbrava, mosqueando-o de Auréola, diademando-se *de Sombra*» (CF, pp. 322-3), but there is an interesting variation when the artist is thought capable of actually projecting *sombra* into his works, leaving himself empty and, to all intents and purposes, dead. We find this in the case of the «Grande Mistério» narrator:

> Embora toda a minha Arte se fixe em Mistério, cingidamente — jamais me nimbo de Além. *Terei deixado sombra — pode ser — sombra diademada, nos meus livros: sombra de artifício, porem; sombra imóvel, sombra morta, que me não vibra:* que eu crio, mas que não me envolve; que só projecto de requinte. (CF, p. 47)

The obvious connection between *sombra* and *mistério* is confirmed if the number of times the word *sombra* is used in the short story «A Grande Sombra» is taken into account; we saw that *mistério*, together with associated words, is found at least thirty-nine times and *segredo/secreto*, twenty-seven; *sombra* appears forty-six times (this figure includes *sombrio* and *sombrear*). There are proportionately more cases of the words *mistério, segredo* and *sombra* in this story than in any other. Now this obviously does not actually prove that the words are interchangeable, much less synonymous, but it does suggest that they all belong to the same area of thought. And when we consider that on many occasions, the word *sombra* is part of a two-part expression, or forms part of a sequence of images, it is clear that though «mystery», «secret» and «shadow» represent respectively a quality, a condition and an effect, they all serve the same purpose and therefore *are,* in a sense, interchangeable. The ultimate stage in the journey is explicitly referred to in the «Bailado» section of «Asas», with art and sex acting as catalysts: it is «além-*Sombra*» (CF, p. 204). The problem is that on this earth, triumph must be shortlived and partial, like that of the hero of «Mistério» who almost reaches the desired state, and even for a time thinks that he has, seeing himself as a «conquistador iriado da *sombra*» (CF, p. 147).

   Sombra, then, is a manifestation of the ineffable and —in this world— unreal. And this «unreal» reality, is evoked by adjectives such as *imortal, infinito, irreal, quimérico, ausente* and *eterno,* together with their associated adverb, verb and noun forms; they invariably treat of art or sex: a «partitura *imortal*» (CL, p. 84), and a «pintor *imortal*» (CF, p. 128); the *homem dos sonhos'* vision of «multiple» sex («*Infinito! Infinito!* Era ruivamente era, o cântico aureoral da carne», CF, p. 162), the «espasmos *eternos*» and the «vibrações *infinitas*» of the bizarre sexual experience of Inácio in «Ressurreição» (CF, p. 292) and the «*infinito* de amor e de felicidade» of «O Incesto» (P, p. 187). Even more revealing are the references to elements touched by the transcedental: «*Quimérico* e nu, o seu corpo subtilizado...» (CL, p. 42), «Que cenário *de quimeras!*» (CF, p. 45), «campanários e cúpulas *irrealizam-se* ao longe» (CF, p. 91), «auréolas nimbadas de carnes *irreais*» (CF, p. 292), «um perfume é uma irrealidade» (CL, p. 104), «uma noite *de quimera*» (CF, p. 257), «a ascensão *infinita* da minha obra *irreal*» (CF, p. 268), «olhos *de infinito*» (P, p. 183) and «laivos *de infinito*» (CF, p. 198). Ultimately it may be possible to assert that for Sá-Carneiro there is only one basic area of obsessive interest in this world, that of art, and that art is the road to what for him is the only other area of obsessive interest — the Beyond.

The Beyond is the goal, and the search must fill an artist's life; his striving is frequently seen in terms of dreaming and, like *sombra,* dreams are halfway between two realities. Ricardo de Loureiro is very aware of the contrast: «áureos *sonhos,* cinzentas realidades», he says (CL, p. 53). The encounter between the «Grande Sombra» protagonist and the *princesa velada* is described in these terms too: we have already seen that it is a question of an enigma and a secret, mystery and shadow, all keys to another level of existence. Now we find that the dream image enters: «transmigrei-me», says the hero, «a um mundo de *sonhos*» (CF, p. 79). The possibility of preserving the moment of ecstasy is signalled by his eyes falling on a jewelled dagger: «Como nunca o mundo inteiro se me centralizou no punhal... Pairava todo um *sonho* de Ópio» (CF, p. 83). In «Mistério», artistic creation and dreams are equated as the artist creates, «ungidamente, as suas obras imortais, *acastelando sonho após sonho*» (CF, p. 135), while the narrator of «Asas» recalls a certain period of his life that was touched with splendour: the memory comes to him «em laivos de *sonho,* de beleza e pasmo — de inquietação, misteriosamente» (CF, p. 172). In some expressions *sonho* is interchangeable with *sombra,* if not with several other words. «Criaturas de *sonho/sombra/segredo/enigma/quimera/subtileza*» are all the same thing. To dream is to recognise, and to elaborate on the awareness of something beyond our earthbound existence; thus Lúcio's annihilation in *A Confissão de Lúcio* is underlined, for he claims that he is «morto para a vida *e para os sonhos*» (CL, p. 15) with *both* realities beyond his reach and his aims. When there is still life and hope, the image is a positive one — «entressonhando a glória» (CL, p. 47), «Resvalam sonhos lindos» («Nossa Senhora de Paris», Po, p. 84), «O grande sonho —ó dor— quase vivido» («Quase», Po, p. 68) and «me perdi em sonhos geniais» (CF, p. 263) are but a few examples — but of course, «quem está morto, não sonha» (P, p. 165).

46

This image, like so many others, may be good or bad, for a dream may turn into a nightmare and a vision may become an obsession. In *A Confissão de Lúcio,* Lúcio describes Ricardo's death and his own confusion as a «*pesadelo* alucinante, infernal» (CL, p. 154). In «O Incesto», the process of deterioration is evident: as the love between the two protagonists begins to acquire bizarre characteristics, the author comments: «Mas um dia o *sonho* terminou; começou o *pesadelo*» (P, p. 189). And visions, the «*Visões* de Nós-próprios» of «Asas», or the «visões luxuriosas de cores intensas» of the *Confissão de Lúcio* «orgy» (CF, p. 174, and CL, p. 40), can easily turn into «*visões* estranhas» (P, p. 296), a «*visão perturbadora*» (P. p. 296, author's italics), «*visões* [...] abomináveis» (P, p. 339) or, ultimately, into really disturbing obsessions, such as when the disintegration of the narrator in «A Grande Sombra» is accompanied by «*obsessões* de molduras» (CF, p. 112). In *A Confissão de Lúcio,* Lúcio refers to his «*obsessões* destrambelhadas» (CL, p. 111), and then seems to equate his *dores* and *angústias* with his *obsessões*» (CL, p. 128).

Synonymous with the Beyond is the Ideal. And it is the *homem dos sonhos* who actually reaches it («derrubara a realidade, condenando-o ao sonho», CF, p. 168) and is disappointed. Nevertheless, the search for it is a constant in Sá-Carneiro's writings. In «Cinco Horas» are the disillusioned lines: «Passar tempo é o meu fito, / *Ideal* que só me resta» (Po, p. 135), while in «Aqueloutro», the poet is scathing about himself:

> O sem nervos nem ânsia, o papa-açorda...
> (Seu coração talvez movido a corda...)
> Apesar de seus berros ao *Ideal*. (Po, p. 167)

In «Dispersão», he is more self-indulgent:

> Eu tenho pena de mim,
> Pobre menino *ideal*... (Po, p. 65),

and in «A Queda», we discover the cause of the fall: «Em raivas *ideais* ascendo até ao fim» (Po, p. 80). In a letter to Pessoa dated July 13, 1914, Sá-Carneiro refers to the «estados de alma, ânsias, tristezas, *ideais,* grandes torturas de que saíam os meus livros...» and assures Pessoa that «tudo isso acabou» (C I, pp. 171-172). The *homem dos sonhos* found the Ideal and was disillusioned; Sá-Carneiro cannot find it, and can no longer bear the struggle.

Any investigation into the works of Sá-Carneiro is bound to reveal the limitations of his range. This is not necessarily a denigratory statement and, indeed, many great writers have worked on an equally small scale. Furthermore, the author's problems are by no means trivialised if we say this, nor is any shadow of doubt cast on to the authenticity of his suffering. What does result is that the critic is given an inkling that there may be a relatively simple answer to his questions. Already there is clear evidence of overlapping and interchangeability in the metaphors, images and *mots obsédants;* the Beyond, or the Unknown, represents an ideal ineffable reality which is in strong contrast to the mediocrity of everyday life, and the search for it is all. It would be absurd, of course, to claim that there are never any misgivings, since Sá-Carneiro was only human: though normally scornful of the ordinary man's dull routine and lack of standards, taste, excitement and awareness, there are moments when his reason reminds him that others seem to suffer less and even appear to find happiness. He is not, of course, alone in this attitude: the Baudelairean view of the aristocratic artist has had very many adherents, and some of them have occasionally at least questioned their creed. Sá-Carneiro's regrets at being different are not strong, but they are there, right through his work. Even in real life, in fact, he admitted some misgivings on at least one occasion. In a letter to Pessoa dated February 26, 1913, he says:

> Os crepúsculos que ainda nos prendem à terra — àqueles que sonhamos — e nos fazem sentir um vago pesar pela *facilidade* — porque é fácil e quente e cariciosa: «Naquela vida faz calor e amor.» Mas logo a reacção em face do triunfo maior — a carreira ao ideal. Mais alto, sempre mais alto. Vida e arte, no artista confundem-se, indistinguem-se. [...] A minha vida «desprendida», livre, orgulhosa, «farouche», diferente muito da normal, apraz-me e envaidece-me. No entanto, em face dos que têm família e amor banalmente, simplesmente, diàriamente, em face dos que conduzem pelo braço uma companheira gentil e cavalgam os carrousséis, eu sinto muito [sic] vez uma saudade. (C I, p. 72, author's italics)

But what follows is all-important: «Mas olho para mim. Acho-me mais belo, e a minha vida continua.» He sees himself as one of the «rois de l'azur», a «prince des nuées» who is «exilé sur le sol au milieu des huées»,[3] and there is nothing that can be done about it. The interchangeable images of the earthly manifestations of the Beyond, *sonhos, mistério, enigma, segredos, sombra,* etc., are all irresistible in their fascination but contain elements that inspire fear and dread. In his ambivalent attitude towards dreams, Sá-Carneiro is echoing a Romantic preoccupation which is found in Jean-Paul, Novalis, Hoffmann, Tieck, Brentano, Kleist, Nodier, Nerval and all the Symbolists,[4] in Bécquer in Spain,[5] and in Coleridge,

---

[3] CHARLES BAUDELAIRE, «L'Albatros», in *Les Fleurs du mal,* 2nd edition (Paris, 1861).

[4] See ALBERT BÉGUIN, *L'Âme romantique et le rêve* (Paris, 1939), and PIERRE-GEORGES CASTEX, *Le Conte fantastique en France de Nodier à Maupassant* (Paris, 1951).

[5] See JORGE GUILLÉN, «Lenguaje insuficiente: Bécquer o lo inefable soñado», in *Lenguaje y poesía* (Madrid, 1962). (First edition, *Language and Poetry,* Cambridge, Mass., 1961.)

among others, in England. Almost all these authors express fear as well as an obsessive interest. It is significant that *Nodier*'s first two short stories were subtitled *La Vision* and *Les Démons · de la nuit;* [6] about the latter, Pierre-Georges Castex says: «il évoque dans *Smarra* [the main title of *Les Démons de la nuit*] notamment, des phénomènes de cauchemar»,[7] and he entitles a study of Nodier, «Nodier et ses rêves».[8] Of Hoffmann, Albert Béguin writes: «Le rêve surgit au milieu de la vie présente, très concrète pourtant; il y perce des trouées immenses qui ouvrent sur le monde invisible de l'art ou sur les obscurs domaines du cauchemar»,[9] and he adds, «on ne peut nier que le cauchemar n'ait attiré et parfois possédé l'auteur du *Vase d'or*»[10] (author's italics). Even in the case of Novalis, the night and dreams, which constitute «la porte qui s'ouvre sur le monde intemporel, la voie par où l'on atteint, hors de toute solitude, de tout désespoir, de toute existence séparée, à l'espoir infini»,[11] and which are therefore to be sought as a Christian mystic longs for union with God, are inextricably associated with death. As for Jean-Paul, Béguin describes him as:

> le maître incontesté du rêve, le poète des grands songes, cosmiques, le peintre des paysages fabuleux où l'univers se fait musique et couleur, où le moi se perd voluptueusement dans des espaces infinis, —mais aussi l'évocateur des apparitions terrifiantes, des têtes sans regards, des champs de carnage et des hommes sans mains.[12]

Then again, Nerval begins *Aurélia*:

> Le Rêve est une seconde vie. Je n'ai pu percer sans frémir ces portes d'ivoire ou de corne qui nous séparent du monde invisible. Les premiers instants du sommeil sont l'image de la mort.[13]

In Coleridge too we are aware of an ambivalent approach: an absorbing interest coupled with dread of «the fiendish dream» and «the unfathomable hell within».[14] The common denominator in these and the thousand other examples that might be given, from Balzac to Marcel Schwob, from Swedenborg to John Addington Symonds, is the unquestioning acceptance that dreams constitute another existence, another life. Nerval says: «nous ne pouvons déterminer l'instant précis où le *moi,* sous une autre

[6] CHARLES NODIER, «Une Heure ou la Vision», in *Les Tristes ou Mélanges tirés des tablettes d'un suicide* (Paris, 1806); *Smarra ou les Démons de la nuit* (Paris, 1821).
[7] PIERRE-GEORGES CASTEX, p. 9.
[8] CASTEX, pp. 121-67.
[9] BÉGUIN, p. 296.
[10] BÉGUIN, p. 297.
[11] BÉGUIN, p. 213.
[12] BÉGUIN, p. 166.
[13] GÉRARD DE NERVAL, *Aurélia* (Paris, 1855).
[14] SAMUEL TAYLOR COLERIDGE, «The Pains of Sleep» (1803).

forme, continue l'oeuvre de l'existence»[15] (author italics), but for these writers, there is no question about the fact that it does. Castex, in his book on the *conte fantastique,* maintains that for Nerval, «le songe est pour lui le moyen de passer d'un monde à l'autre».[16] Thus the journey into dreams involves the rejection not only of the oppressive limitations of this world but also of the security they afford, and the dream stage on the road to the Ideal is reached by taking the risk of being plunged into something too horrible to bear. To the Romantics, and to their successors the Symbolists, Decadents and Aesthetes, dreams were a facet of mystery; to Sá-Carneiro, dreams and mystery are the same thing. The preoccupation with both had been current among artists; though Sá-Carneiro's preoccupations are turned into original works of art by means of his individualistic treatment of them, they are not new. He did little more than appropriate the tail-end of a tradition, albeit one which had been extended and elaborated greatly since its apogee in the nineteenth century. Pierre-Georges Castex sees the passion for the exploration of mystery as coming to a head around 1830 and refers to its various aspects: animal magnetism, then «le somnambulisme, la sorcellerie, la lycanthropie, la possession, les transes et l'extase mystique», attempts to understand and account for magic by means of science, theorising about nightmares — significantly enough — and a general interest in the Occult.[17] He claims that all the writers he is concerned with in his study of nineteenth-century fantastic literature were fascinated, to a greater or lesser degree, by mystery. Of Guy de Maupassant, he writes: «Le titre [of his last short story, *Qui sait?*] résume son horreur anxieuse devant le mystère des choses».[18] Of Nerval we read: «Gérard de Nerval croit à une correspondance entre les événements de notre existence quotidienne et les mystères de l'au-delà»,[19] while for Prosper Mérimée, «l'univers lui paraît peuplé de forces redoubtables» with a «menaçante présence».[20] Théophile Gautier is no exception: «le goût du surnaturel est lié chez lui à un développement excessif de sa vie intérieure», says Castex,[21] and Balzac never stopped believing in the «interférences entre le monde visible et le monde invisible».[22] But the list is endless and could, of course, include authors from countries other than France, although it was in France in particular that the cultivation of mystery in literature was most influential. And the preoccupation with mystery was not limited to writers or

---

[15] NERVAL, *Aurélia,* p. 219 in the Paris, 1961 edition (*Les Filles du feu* and *Aurélia*).
[16] PIERRE-GEORGES CASTEX, pp. 309-10.
[17] CASTEX, pp. 57-8.
[18] CASTEX, p. 393.
[19] CASTEX, p. 309.
[20] CASTEX, p. 248.
[21] CASTEX, p. 223.
[22] CASTEX, p. 213.

quasi-scientists. As the century progressed, the fashion spread to the visual arts, and the Symbolist painters became equally interested in the Unknown. Jullian quotes Odilon Redon: «Qu'ai-je mis dans mes ouvrages pour leur [his admirers] suggérer tant de subtilités?» he asks, and answers: «*J'y ai mis une petite porte ouverte sur le mystère*»,[23] while Lucie-Smith refers to a further Redon reflection which is equally revealing: «the sense of mystery», said Redon, «is a matter of being all the time amid the equivocal, in double and triple aspects, and hints of aspects (images within images), forms which are coming to birth, or which will come to birth according to the state of mind of the observer».[24] This attitude too is ambivalent and a great number of his paintings involve death and menace — *Head of a Martyr, The Green Death, The Red Death* and *The Grinning Spider,* for example. The same love of mystery is found in countless other painters — indeed it is a key element in Symbolist art. There are hundreds of representations of its most popular symbol, the Sphinx (for example Franz von Stuck, *The Kiss of the Sphinx* and *The Sphinx,* Fernand Khnopff, *The Caresses of the Sphinx* and Jan Toorop, *The Sphinx*); it is the ideal amalgam of all that interested the Symbolists, the Decadents and the Aesthetes, comprising mystery («enigma por excelencia, la esfinge contiene en su significado un último reducto inexpugnable»),[25] sex («sphynges pour les perversités compliqués, sphynges pour les revenus de tout, sphynges pour le Sphinx lui-même»),[26] cruelty («angélique vampire / Elle rêve sous l'or cruel de ses frisons; [...] Ses yeux sont faux, son coeur est faux, son amour pire...»),[27] transcendental knowledge («Fawn at my feet, fantastic Sphinx! and sing me all your memories!»),[28] art and decoration («ceinte de bijoux»,[29] «your jasper claws» [...] «your agate breasts» [...] «Your eyes are like fantastic moons» [...] «Your tongue is like a scarlet snake» [...] «your black throat»),[30] inaccessibility («Inviolate and immobile»,[31] «a promise of the Ideal»),[32] animality («C'est la Chimère terrestre, vile comme la matière attractive, comme elle représentée par cette tête charmante de la femme avec des ailes, et le corps du carnassier qui déchire»)[33] and exoticism («he read of the Obelisk in the Place de la Concorde that weeps tears

[23] JULLIAN, *Esthètes,* p. 230.
[24] LUCIE-SMITH, pp. 75-6. (From À *soi-même.*)
[25] J. L. CIRLOT, *Diccionario de símbolos* (Barcelona, 1969), p. 199.
[26] VERHAEREN, «Sur la Sphynge de Khnopff», quoted by JULLIAN, *Esthètes,* p. 324.
[27] ALBERT SAMAIN, quoted by JULLIAN, *Esthètes,* p. 325.
[28] OSCAR WILDE, «The Sphinx», in *Complete Works of Oscar Wilde* (London, 1970), p. 834.
[29] VERHAEREN, «Sur la Sphynge...».
[30] OSCAR WILDE, «The Sphinx».
[31] OSCAR WILDE, «The Sphinx».
[32] JULLIAN, *Dreamers of Decadence,* p. 165.
[33] GUSTAVE MOREAU, quoted by JULLIAN, *Esthètes,* p. 324.

of granite in its lonely sunless exile, and longs to be back by the hot lotus-covered Nile, *where there are Sphinxes,* and rose-red ibises, and white vultures with gilded claws, and crocodiles, with small beryl eyes»),[34] and we should bear in mind Mario Praz's statement of what he calls «a more or less obvious truth» that «a love of the exotic is usually an imaginative projection of a sexual desire».[35] Bécquer was quite wrong when he wrote in his mysterious story «Rayo de luna» that it contained «una verdad muy triste, *de la que acaso yo seré uno de los últimos en aprovecharme,* dadas mis condiciones de imaginación»,[36] for the fascination with the mysterious persisted until well into the twentieth century. Bécquer's group of «almas soñadoras»[37] was not extinct when Eugénio de Castro was writing «Interlúnio» more than twenty years later,[38] or Camilo Pessanha the poems which constitute *Clepsidra,*[39] and the Portuguese Modernists could certainly be seen as belonging to it, though they had many additional characteristics. Alfredo Guisado writes:

> Diante de mim essa distância existe,
> Eternamente longe e sempre triste,
> Doida toada que em penumbras fito.
>
> É um descer de bronzes no meu medo,
> É uma curva de Ânsia no arvoredo
> Um gotejar de cinza no infinito.[40]

and:

> Sonho etéreo.
>
> E a Noite receando que lha levem
> Vai guardá-la no estojo da Distância
> Pois tem dentro o retrato do Mistério![41]

and: «Dançava Salomé sôbre mistérios idos»,[42] while Armando Côrtes-Rodrigues has lines like «Colunas de Além-Sonho, arcos de comoção», and «minha Alma / Parte pela noite calma / A caminho do Além».[43] Ronald de Carvalho uses images such as «última glória», «um perfume antigo», «fantasmas de desertas salas», «caçadores ideais», «um perfume

---

[34] OSCAR WILDE, *Dorian Gray,* p. 127.
[35] PRAZ, p. 223.
[36] BÉCQUER, «El rayo de luna», p. 171.
[37] BÉCQUER, «El rayo de luna», p. 184.
[38] EUGÉNIO DE CASTRO, «Interlúnio», in *Obras Poéticas de Eugénio de Castro* (Lisbon, 1968). (First edition, 1894.)
[39] CAMILO PESSANHA, *Clepsidra* (Lisbon, 1969). (First edition, 1920, though this was a compilation —albeit an incomplete one— of work that spanned more than thirty years.)
[40] ALFREDO GUISADO, «Elogio da Distância» (1915), in *Tempo de Orfeu* (1915-1918) (Lisbon, 1969), pp. 5-6.
[41] GUISADO, p. 86 («Sete Orações duma Boca Difunta», III).
[42] In *Orpheu,* ed. Maria Aliete Galhoz, p. 64.
[43] *Orpheu,* pp. 85-6 («Abertura do 'Livro da Vida'»).

de alêm-morte», «um rumor sonâmbulo de asa»,[44] and even Fernando Pessoa/Álvaro de Campos explicitly states the side of the attitude that we find in Sá-Carneiro: «Não, não, isso não! / Tudo menos saber o que é o Mistério!»,[45] though here —writing much later— he takes it to extremes, failing to share Sá-Carneiro's enjoyment of the element. The climate at the time of *Orpheu* was different. As João Pedro de Andrade has written:

> Houve em Portugal uma geração que quis dar forma, através da poesia, aos impulsos interiores, às aspirações indefinidas, a esse conjunto de sensações e percepções tido por inefável. Refiro-me à geração de 1915.[46]

What is important is Sá-Carneiro's personal reaction to mystery. Cleonice Berardinelli is undoubtedly right when she asserts that «tudo que realmente importa é interior», in *contrast* to external circumstances, material objects or other people («o elemento externo sempre *brumoso, nevoento, ténue, irreal*»).[47] He himself is the focal point, and must be seen in interplay with these externals, in his inability to understand, reach or cope with them. If, as Manuel Anselmo maintains, a distinguishing feature of Portuguese poetry in the first thirty years of the century was «uma vontade de autoexplicação»,[48] and of Sá-Carneiro in particular, «uma necessidade psicológica de confidência, de descoberta íntima»,[49] then this emphasis must be seen in relation to outside events and phenomena, and they themselves seen as possible keys to the problem. The mystical journey to the Beyond will often depend on both other people and material objects — aspects of external life, in fact. This may well be a vital facet of Sá-Carneiro's tragic relationship with the world: he despises it in some areas, finds it unexciting in others, and looks on it all as unreal. Yet it *is* real in the sense that he has to cope with it if he is to go on living in it, he had to live *with* it, and adapt his inner reality to it. The unreal nature of the external world is partly wishful thinking, and he comes up against this hard fact when he elects to start his quest for the transcendental, *a Beleza,* in sex and in art, both of which depend to a certain extent on forces beyond his control.

But we shall consider the principal areas in which the manifestations of the ultimate reality can be apprehended after returning to the third of the interchangeable earthly manifestations of the Unknown: *sombra.* Here there is no ambiguity; *sombra* is what it appears to be: it is caused

---

[44] *Orpheu,* pp. 29-34 («A Alma que Passa», «O Elogio dos Repuxos»).
[45] PESSOA/ÁLVARO DE CAMPOS, p. 368 («Demagorgon»).
[46] JOÃO PEDRO DE ANDRADE, *A Poesia da Moderníssima Geração* (Oporto, 1943), p. 10.
[47] CLEONICE BERARDINELLI, p. 52.
[48] MANUEL ANSELMO, *Soluções Críticas* (Coimbra, 1934), p. 115.
[49] MANUEL ANSELMO, *Antologia Moderna* (Lisbon, 1937), p. 231.

by light (the Beyond), it is a reflection of something rather than that something itself and it is an undeniable indication that that something does exist. Even related words such as *auréola* have these connotations. Unlike that of *sonho* and *mistério,* the use of *sombra i*s not a continuation of a literary tradition, nor of any folk customs. A rich source of information about these is Dr Otto Rank,[50] and he reminds us of the many stories of lost shadows, such as those by E. T. A. Hoffmann, Hans Andersen and Goethe, and of the countless traditional superstitions regarding the image, which is thought to be a manifestation of the soul. He refers us to *The Golden Bough,* and to all the primitive beliefs it contains, pointing out, too, peculiarities of language, such as those tongues in which «soul» and «shadow» are the same word. Sá-Carneiro's approach to the image is entirely different. He is largely unconcerned with shadows as reflections of people or material objects; he is much more interested in shadow itself — or rather, Shadow, for it has sufficient of the transcendental about it to warrant a capital letter, in the same way as *o mistério* becomes *Mistério.* (Although personal shadows are not important to Sá-Carneiro, he does, in fact, see the *reflection* as a symbol of survival, as we shall discover when we come to the image of the mirror.)

In «A Estranha Morte do Professor Antena», science is regarded as a means of apprehending truth, but this is a red herring. There are only two apparent paths for Sá-Carneiro — sex and art; in fact, there is really only one, and that is art. Another part of the tragedy of his life may be explained by means of this piece of knowledge. His sexual anguish, immaturity, insufficiency —all the difficulties suggested by his sexual imagery— can be partially accounted for by his insistence on equating sex with art and beauty. His revulsion is caused by the «human» side of sex, the gross nature of the flesh, the lack of pattern, equilibrium, form and style. Excitement and interest are brought about by the adornments and often false veneer of glamour that painting, literature and even dancing have brought to the relationship between the sexes. This attitude has something in common with that which in the late Romantics led them to devote themselves to «fatal sex», «an enhancement rather than a contradiction of a life dedicated to art»,[51] and the traditional association between sex and death acquires an added dimension when ecstasy is seen as a brief moment in which the Beyond may be glimpsed. The logical conclusion is an attempt to extend this moment, *fixar o instante* and if orgasm is a temporary death, death itself must be the desirable next stage. In parallel fashion, sex and death are frightening as well as appealing; both are seen in a melodramatic fashion, sex as the earthly,

[50] Dr. OTTO RANK, *Don Juan. Une Étude sur le double,* trans. Dr. S. Lautman (Paris, 1932).
[51] ALVAREZ, p. 179.

ephemeral solution, death as the key to a permanent, absolute answer. And seeking death is all the more acceptable when we remember the Romantic tradition of suicide; Alvarez points out that:

> in their heyday the Romantics established in the popular mind the idea that suicide was one of the many prices to be paid for genius,[52]

and, as we have already noted, that suicide was a supreme, dramatic gesture of contempt. We have, then, a literary and ideological tradition which demands a journey «N'importe où! n'importe où! pourvu que ce soit hors de ce monde!»[53] even «au fond du gouffre, [...] Au fond de l'Inconnu pour trouver du *nouveau!*»[54] and a real-life tradition of a journey into death which, although not actually advocating suicide, never discards the possibility or rejects it as unacceptable for an artist. Sá-Carneiro obviously feels sympathy towards both these aspects of the Romantic attitude, not only as a philosophy for his fictional characters or his poetic *persona,* but also as an unavoidable standpoint for himself, since «a sua poesia é a sua própria vida a expressar-se», as M. A. Antunes has rightly said.[55] There is, of course, no easy answer; the thought of death is as full of horror as it is of interest. And if the individual is disillusioned with the earthly experiences with he thought could bring him near to the Beyond —sex, for example— then there may arise a worrying doubt as to its very existence. Sá-Carneiro fails, if we accept Walter Pater's definition of success:

> To burn always with this hard, gemlike flame, to maintain his ecstasy, [cf. *fixar o instante*] is success in life.

And he goes on: «In a sense it might even be said that our failure is to form habits»,[56] an interesting comment when we remember Sá-Carneiro's claim that he himself was incapable of any. He has tried, and he has failed, within the boundaries of this world, to make «the highest quality of [his] moments»[57] eternal; there is no alternative but death. As his disillusion with himself, with life, with sex and ultimately even with art, increases, despair sets in and the transition stage between life and death is death in life. But this is not just a comfortable anaesthesia of the emotions, sensations and intellect, but an intolerably painful *dispersão,*

---

[52] ALVAREZ, p. 180.
[53] BAUDELAIRE, «Le Spleen de Paris» XLVIII, in *Le Peintre de la vie moderne. Oeuvres Complètes* (Paris, 1963), pp. 303-4. Quoted in H. H. ABRAMS, *Natural Supernaturalism* (London, 1971), p. 415.
[54] BAUDELAIRE, «Voyage», in *Les Fleurs du mal,* 2nd edition; p. 210 in the Paris, 1924 edition. Author's italics.
[55] ANTUNES, p. 306.
[56] WALTER PATER, *The Renaissance* (London, 1873); p. 222 in the London, 1916 edition.
[57] PATER, p. 224.

a loss of cohesion bordering on madness, a false death without the advantages of real annihilation. Sá-Carneiro's occasional references to the mystery of mankind in general reveal no more than the preoccupation with self and his own survival. He is subjective and egocentric; he may even suffer from real megalomania as well as from what Anselmo has called «megalomania lírica»,[58] and while the road of his despair and disintegration is clearly visible in his poetry and his correspondence, the goal he has failed to achieve is revealed in his prose.

TIME

Sá-Carneiro is, perhaps surprisingly, relatively unconcerned about the passage of time and its metaphysical problems. It is true that one of his short stories, «Loucura», deals with the protagonist's fatal preoccupation with it, but as John Parker rightly points out, the basis of the *Princípio* stories is «the study of various types of obsession, of the psychologies of men in the grip of differing fixed ideas»,[59] and the nature of each obsession is of lesser importance. Nevertheless, Raul Vilar's description of his attitude, «Vivo como todos, à espera da velhice» (P, pp. 78-9), and his anguished cry, «Amanhã... Terrível! Seremos velhos...» (P, p. 79), do bear witness to the Romantic notion echoed throughout Sá-Carneiro's work, that the important things in life do not survive youth. Conversely what is old is necessarily repellent or sinister: the «Rainha, / *Velha* entrevadinha» which is his soul («Não», Po, p. 91), or the «cheiro a madeiras *velhas*» which is part of a list of repulsive images (CF, p. 292). In «O Recreio», we find a possibility of avoiding the progress of the years:

> Se a corda se parte um dia
> (E já vai estando esgarçada),
> Era uma vez a folia:
> Morre a criança afogada... (Po, p. 141),

and there will be no old age.

There is some concern for the passage of time in comparisons of past, present and future, with past and present often linked together to point a contrast. Examples of Sá-Carneiro's despair are those statements in his verse which show up his own awareness of the change in his life and attitudes; some of these changes are indicated only by the vital juxtaposition of verb tenses, some by the use of words such as *hoje* and *ontem,* while others are revealed semantically. An example which involves the first and third techniques is in the poem «O Fantasma»:

[58] ANSELMO, *Caminhos e Ansiedades da Poesia Portuguesa Contemporânea* (Lisbon, 1941), p. 16.
[59] PARKER, p. 126.

A escada é suspeita e perigosa:
Alastra-se uma nódoa duvidosa
Pela alcatifa, os corrimões partidos...

Taparam com rodilhas o meu norte,
As formigas cobriram minha sorte,
Morreram-me meninos nos sentidos... (Po, p. 163)

and here words such as *formigas, tapar, cobrir* and *morrer* convey change. More frequently, we have the explicit use of temporal markers, for example: *«Já* não estremeço em face do segredo; / Nada ma aloira *já,* nada me aterra» («Estátua Falsa», Po, p. 66), or «*Hoje* a luz para mim é sempre meia-luz» («16», Po, p. 96), or «*Outrora* imaginei escalar os céus» («Além-Tédio», Po, p. 73). What is important to Sá-Carneiro is his own *estado de alma* and how it has changed. The obvious extension of this awareness is a sense of nostalgia. Things must have been better in the past, especially in the days of the author's unspoiled wonder and idealism in the face of life. In «Escala», the regrets are obvious: «Oh! regressar a mim profundamente / E ser o que já fui no meu delírio...» (Po, p. 116); in «Elegia», reference is made to «outro tempo mais lilás» (Po, p. 115); in «O Sexto Sentido», we find «*que saudades, que saudades* tenho desse belo tempo já tão distante» (P, p. 137); in «Dispersão» is the revealing statement: «E hoje, quando me sinto, / É con *saudades* de mim» (Po, p. 61), followed by: «Para mim é sempre ontem» (Po, p. 61). The whole concept of *saudades* may eventually cause bitter cynicism:

Cinge tais futilidades
A minha recordação,
E destes vislumbres são
As minhas saudades ...(Po, p. 135)

and the natural outcome is the realisation of lost potential:

(Que história de Oiro tão bela
Na minha vida abortou:
Eu fui herói de novela
Que autor nenhum empregou...) (Po, p. 135)

In addition to a remembered past, we find references both to a fantastic, quasi-mediaeval, chivalric era and to an Edenic home, synonymous with the *Além*. Sometimes the two go together, as in «Partida»: «A minh'alma *nostálgica* de além» determines to find what it needs, «Correr no azul à busca da beleza», and this involves images such as «a espada fulva e medieval», «garra imperial enclavinhada», «clarões e gumes», «licorne e acanto» and a «taça de cristal lançada ao mar, / Diadema e timbre, elmo real e cruz...» (Po, pp. 51, 52 and 53). Transcendental nostalgia is found quite often in the poetry, for example: «Ai que *saudades* da morte...» («Vontade de Dormir», Po, p. 60): the supernatural past was best, and

57

this involves the future too, since paradise is a timeless condition. It is when Sá-Carneiro concerns himself with what might have been, and even what might *still* be, that we find bizarre locutions such as those he comments on to Pessoa in a letter dated February 3, 1913:

> No que lhe escrevo há frases de que gosto deveras: «Os meus lábios de ânsia sofriam já da saudade dos beijos que lhe iam dar.» É a ideia da saudade antes da posse que eu acho qualquer coisa de trágico e grande — *«ter saudade já do futuro»* (C I, p. 69)

«Reminiscências de Aonde / Perturbam-me em nostalgia» («Inter-Sonho», Po, p. 56) also falls into this category, since the «Paulistic» use of *aonde* can hardly have past connotations, only indefinite future ones. In «Dispersão», there is nostalgia for the non-existent: «As minhas grandes saudades / São do que nunca enlacei» (Po, p. 64), and he goes on: «Ai, como eu tenho saudades / Dos sonhos que não sonhei!» (Po, p. 64). In fact, this incongruous paradox, though something of a verbal game, has got a real basis in the emotions of the author, and his eternal consciousness of searching. It is not entirely unconnected either with the episodes in which love is the result of a non-existent relationship or an extremely shortlived encounter; for example, the episode in which Ricardo de Loureiro met the *costureiras,* or in «Ressurreição», when Inácio sends a copy of his book to the dancer, and therefore becomes part of her life (CF, pp. 287-8). Then, in the poem «Elegia» are «cartas nunca escritas» and «orações que não rezei» (Po, p. 114), and all these seem to be stages on the road to despair — part, indeed, of a *declínio*. In this odd context, *saudades* can be regarded as reflecting the existence of hope, and it is only when they disappear and when the key word becomes *nunca* that all appears to be lost; for example:

> Nada me expira já, nada me vive —
> Nem a tristeza nem as horas belas.
> De as não ter *e de nunca vir a tê-las,*
> Fartam-me até as coisas que não tive.
>
> («Além-Tédio», Po, p. 73),

and «Nos cafés espero a vida / Que nunca vem ter comigo» («Cinco Horas», Po, p. 135), and «tudo em mim é fantasia alada, / Um crime ou bem que nunca se comete: / E sempre o Oiro em chumbo se derrete» («Crise Lamentável», Po, p. 161). There is no hope, and the poet states: «A sombra loira, fugidia, / Jamais se abeirará de mim» («Elegia», Po, p. 114).

Último and *derradeiro* are often used to indicate a moment of climax. For example, an «espasmo *derradeiro* da alma» (CL, p. 38), an «*última* perversidade» (CL, p. 42) or an «*último* estertor de cio» (CF, p. 335), while the poetry of Zagoriansky, in «Asas», constitutes «uma nova Arte —

diademada e *última*» (CF, p. 189). In all these cases, the end is, at the same time, a beginning — even the evening of «eu dou-me todo neste fim da tarde / À espira aérea que me eleva aos cumes» («Partida», Po, p. 53), signifies a crossing over from one state to another. The climatic «end» can be linked with the Infinite, which is endless. But yet again, it can have its darker side; like death, there is a chance that it will really sig-nify the end of everything. When all is false («Um cemitério falso sem ossadas, / Noites d'amor sem bocas esmagadas — / *Tudo outro espasmo que princípio ou fim...*», «Escavação», Po, p. 55), when *princípio* and *fim,* as positive elements, have been missed («Quase o princípio e o fim — quase a expansão...» «Quase», Po, p. 68), or when «Em raivas ideais ascendo até ao fim» («A Queda», Po, p. 80), is followed by «Tom-bei...», we are left with «magoados fins de dia» («Vislumbre», Po, p. 105), or discoveries such as «a ponte era falsa — e *derradeira*» («Ângulo», Po, p. 109). In «Não», the narrator wanders through a royal palace; then he says: «Chego ao *fim* dos salões... / *Enfim,* oscilo alguém! / Encontro uma Rainha / Velha, entrevadinha» (Po, p. 91). The quest is over but the result anticlimax. In «Pied-de-Nez», we again have a sense of disillusion which is exacerbated by the glamour of the illusion which it dispels:

> Chora em mim um palhaço às piruetas;
> O meu castelo em Espanha, ei-lo vendido —
> E entretanto, foram de violetas,
>
> Deram-me beijos sem os ter pedido...
> Mas como sempre, *ao fim* — bandeiras pretas,
> Tômbolas falsas, carroussel partido... (Po, p. 146)

In «O Fantasma», a sad end is anticipated: «O que farei [...] Quando este Oiro *por fim* cair por terra, / Que ainda é Oiro, embora esver-dinhado?» (Po, p. 162). One of the poems is actually called «Fim», and it is a bitter, subjective view of death. But even in the negative aspect of *fim,* there can be drama and glamour: for example, the apocalyptic «Há roxos fins de Império em meu renunciar» («Taciturno», Po, p. 102), reminding us of «the dull gold and gory purple» of «the long Byzantine twilight».[60] Horror may sometimes have its compensations.

Sá-Carneiro's treatment of the seasons is conventional. From his early pretentious «o outono, o cavaleiro cinzento da melancolia» (P, p. 234) to the straightforward imagery of the «bruma outonal» («Dispersão», Po, p. 65), there is nothing significant, other than his predilection for autumn. He is even less interested in days of the week, with the exception of Sunday, which he associates with those «que têm família e amor banal-mente, simplesmente» (C I, p. 72):

[60] MARIO PRAZ, quoted by JULLIAN, *Dreamers*, p. 149.

Porque *um domingo* é família,
É bem-estar, é singeleza,
E os que olham a beleza
Não têm bem-estar nem família («Dispersão», Po, p. 62)

The time of day has slightly more importance for Sá-Carneiro, and his interest in crepuscular imagery is a reflection of his use of *outono*. *Manhã* and *noite* are found in conventional locutions (though less obviously *noite* is often seen as a background for Parisian life: a «tablado *nocturno* do grande teatro cosmopolita», CF, p. 264, for example), but *tarde,* with its associated *crepúsculo,* is a much more revealing image. Sá-Carneiro uses *crepúsculo* as the title of a work of art written by one of his characters («o estranho e sombrio poeta do 'Crepúsculo'», P, p. 163), something he often does when images fascinate him — for example, the *concertante* in *A Confissão de Lúcio* is called «Além» (CL, p. 82), «A Chama» is the title of Lúcio's play (CL, p. 142), one of Ricardo's volumes of poetry is «Diadema» (CL, p. 78) and another «Brasas» (CL, p. 23). *Tarde* and *crepúsculo* are found often, and again stand for an intermediary stage between *aquém-* and *além-vida:* they contain elements of darkness and light, of both realities. The difference is that while *sombra, sonho* and *mistério* can be perceived as autonomous elements, *tarde* and *crepúsculo* are used as mere backgrounds, or settings. The unreal qualities given to things by the twilight are emphasised when we read: «Irrealizei-me *a crepúsculo* — emudeci a toda a luz» (CF, p. 87), for example, and this is a positive change, since the cause of it is referred to as a *Maravilha*, a *Triunfo* and a *glória* (CF, p. 86). In «Partida», the *tarde* is seen as an ideal time for departure on a mystical journey, and the visionary element is underlined in «A Estranha Morte do Professor Antena»: «é muito admissível que já fremam em nós *crepúsculos* de sentidos duma vida imediatamente futura» (CF, pp. 243-4), says the Professor. In «A Grande Sombra» the narrator's make-believe as a child involved looking out on his *Império* «ao crepúsculo» (CF, p. 66), while the atmosphere for the «Além» section of «Asas» is created in the first paragraph:

Erravam pelo ar, naquela tarde loira, eflúvios roxos d'Alma e ânsias de não-ser.
Mãos santas de rainha, loucas de esmeraldas, davam aroma e rocio à brisa do *crepúsculo.*
O ar *naquela tarde* era Saudade e Além. (CF, p. 196)

Sometimes the emphasis is on twilight as the remains of something, and then we look backwards rather than forwards. Depending on the mood of the passage, there may be positive or negative connotations: they are obviously negative in «Esta ânsia de me descer é que me *entardece*» (CF, p. 211), in «*Tarde a tarde* na minha dor me afundo» («Como eu não

60

possuo», Po, p. 71), and in «Que foste sempre um adeus em mim / Por uma *tarde* silenciosa...» («Elegia», Po, p. 113).

By far the most important aspect of the imagery of time is the Instant —what M. H. Abrams has called «the experience of eternity in a moment»[61]— and we have already referred to Sá-Carneiro's desire to «fix» this point because of his awareness of the ephemerality of excitement and of the glimpses of the transcendental, the «efémero Ouro» (CF, p. 201). For him, this is often the «momento dourado da posse» (CL, p. 101), and when the hero of «O Fixador de Instantes» kills his mistress after love-making, he achieves his goal: «Glória! Glória! Tenho-a para sempre!» he says, «Vitória! Vitória!» and even: «*Sou o Instante*» (CF, pp. 269-70, author's italics). This is an echo of the theory that beauty must fade with the passage of time (an idea that causes the insanity of the protagonist of «Loucura»), since the *fixador de instantes* adds: «esculpi-a [the *maravilha*] eternamente em saudade [...] Se não a despedaçara, destruíra-a sem remédio — tamanha a sua luz, tamanha a sua altura [...] Infame aquele que, tendo vivido tão admirável sonho, o deixasse esvair» (CF, pp. 269-70). We are left in no doubt as to the nature of his obsession from the very beginning, since the story begins: «O *Instante!* O *Instante!*» (CF, p. 257), and later he explains that «O *momento* dourado, eu posso palpá-lo, revê-lo, tornar a beijá-lo em chama, mas não — ah! mas não! — fazer-lhe brotar outras asas de fogo» (CF, p. 259). An admission of failure is found in the poem «Quase»: «*Momentos* de alma que desbaratei» (Po, p. 69), and in the second «Canção de Declínio»: «O perdulário do *Instante* — / O amante sem amante, / Ora amado ora traído...» (Po, p. 120), whereas there is a certain equivocal success in the conditions of the protagonist's terrible fear in «A Grande Sombra»: «Volvem-se estátuas de ferro *os momentos*» (CF, p. 120), and even the horror of the *A Confissão de Lúcio* climax has the advantage of lifting the hero out of the ordinary rut of life, for: «as horas não podem mais ter acção sobre aqueles que viveram *um instante* que focou toda a sua vida. Atingido o sofrimento máximo, nada já nos faz sofrer. Vibradas as sensações máximas, nada já nos fará oscilar» (CL, p. 16).

A clear pattern is beginning to emerge, and this is based on two overwhelming impressions: that of Sá-Carneiro's insecurity and that of his strong belief in the supremacy of art. We can see a paradox already, for if art is sublime, the artist should be part of the glorious process and impervious to doubts and misgivings. But art is inanimate and artists are not, so that in practice the system fails. We see again the fascination art held for Sá-Carneiro when we consider the glamour of some of the images related to time. The Symbolist preoccupation with twilight, decline and dissolution is echoed in much of the imagery and a lot of it

---

[61] ABRAMS, p. 385.

can be described as Byzantine. The interest of the Decadents in their own *declínio* («la fin de la poésie d'une race», according to the Sâr Péladan),[62] often seen in their representations of the fall of Babylon and of Byzantium, is modified in Sá-Carneiro; like all his circles of interest, decadence is one in which he himself constitutes the central point.

The author's psychological state is clear here too, and it is his ambivalent attitude towards the images and his loss of faith in the salvation that they suggest which reveal his insecurity and, ultimately, his despair. Twilight, for example, lies between two lights; Cirlot says that the image:

> corresponde a la escisión, a la grieta que une y separa a un tiempo los contrarios. [...] El crepúsculo se distingue [...] por esa indeterminación y ambivalencia, que lo emparenta con la situación del ahorcado y de lo suspendido, *entre el cielo y la tierra*. Respecto al crepúsculo vespertino, se identifica con Occidente (el lugar de la muerte).[63]

And autumn can be an end and a beginning. Even *o fim* itself can be a high artistic moment and the source of something new: *fin de siècle* is not, as Dorian Gray's hostess would have it, «fin du globe».[64] A death-agony may be artistic, with the excitement of colour and style, as the thousands of poems, paintings and stories about the fallen empires of the past testify (d'Annunzio, Moreau, Verlaine, Lorrain, Rochegrosse, Kavafy, Couture and Lombard are among those who either represented Byzantium or Babylon in their works or were influenced by the vogue for this kind of splendour).[65] Sometimes Sá-Carneiro shares in the excitement and accepts the existence of an intermediary stage «entre el cielo y la tierra», but hope alternates with despair, positive images are qualified and lose their attraction, while the negative aspects of indeterminate or equivocal images are emphasised. At this stage, even horror and fear, once seen as better than pedestrian reality, are no longer part of his existence: «a minha vida fartou-se» («Serradura», Po, p. 137), he says, «A minha vida não cessa / De ser sempre a mesma porta / Eternamente

---

62 *Vice*, p. 131.
63 Cirlot, p. 159.
64 Oscar Wilde, *Dorian Gray*, p. 137.
65 For example, D'Annunzio's *La Nave* (1908). Philippe Jullian, in *D'Annunzio* (Paris, 1971), p. 176, quotes him as saying of this play: «Je termine une oeuvre extraordinaire forgée avec l'or de Byzance.» See too Gustave Moreau's Byzantine décor in so many of his paintings (though he never actually used Byzantium as a subject); Paul Verlaine's «Langueur» («Je suis l'Empire à la fin de la décadence») from *Jadis et Naguère* (1884); Jean Lorrain, *Le Vice errant* («Coins de Byzance») (1901); Rochegrosse's painting *Les Derniers jours de Babylone*, exhibited in the 1900 *Salon*; Kavafy's «Waiting for the Barbarians», Thomas Coutures painting *Les Romains de la Décadence*, Jean Lombard's *L'Agonie*. There are countless more instances of the taste for this subject: even in music, we find *Götterdämmerung*, Wagner's great example of a twilight.

a abanar» («Torniquete», Po, p. 143), «Que querem fazer de mim com estes enleios e medos? / Não fui feito p'ra festas. Larguem-me! Deixem-me sossegar!» («Caranguejola», Po, p. 157), and «O menino dorme. Tudo o mais acabou» («Caranguejola», Po, p. 159). Bitter resignation comes permanently when the battle is over; even the misgivings about his rôle in life («abria-se às vezes uma inveja salutar, num ante-gozo de felicidade bem outro daquela, quando defrontava os *domingos em família,* na sua peregrinação de boémio impenitente») [66] no longer torment him. He has even abandoned the hope of fixing the moment, an aim which, like so many other elements in his work, he inherited from his artistic antecedents. This is how Arthur Symons defined the birth of art:

> Art begins when a man wishes to immortalize the most vivid moment he has ever lived,[67]

and Symons sees this as true for everyone, for he goes on: «Life has already, to one not an artist, become art in that moment». M. H. Abrams writes about the incidence of what he calls «the unsustainable moment» in the Romantic tradition, «often described», he says, «as an intersection of eternity with time».[68] He refers to St. Augustine as the theological prototype, and mentions the frequent appearances of *der Augenblick* or *der Moment* in the writings of the German Romantics such as Schelling, Hölderlin, Goethe and Novalis, and the related use of the image in Blake, Shelley and Wordsworth. It is a tradition that has survived till the present day and the search for the Instant is still a recurring subject — for example, in Octavio Paz, who combines a visionary attitude inherited from his European predecessors with his Aztec heritage, in which the passage and division of time is of primary importance, and adds a fascination for Oriental religions, such as Tantra, where the Instant reconciles apparent opposites. Timelessness can be achieved in any form of rapture: sexual, religious or aesthetic. For Sá-Carneiro, as for his *homem dos sonhos,* they have all failed. Sá-Carneiro finds that the gulf is too great between life and art and between his present self, a «bobo presunçoso», «o papa-açorda» («Aqueloutro», Po, pp. 166-7), and the idealised figure he once thought he could be. The resultant state, before actual death seems the only possible answer, is one he has labelled *dispersão:* it is surely no coincidence that he should employ this word, which hints at the presence of a modified form of Neoplatonism. Instead of Plotinus's One, equivalent to the Good, the Symbolist Ultimate is Beauty, and Sá-Carneiro, when furthest away from his elevated goal, is in the last of the «hypostases», a living example of division and multiplicity. The word

[66] JOÃO PEDRO DE ANDRADE, pp. 12-13.
[67] ARTHUR SYMONS, «The Choice», in *Studies in Prose and Verse* (London, 1904), p. 291.
[68] ABRAMS, Chapter 7, Part 2, «Moments», pp. 385-90.

«dispersion» is often used in the exposition of Neoplatonic theories. M. H. Abrams gives some examples:

> As early as the third century Origen manifestly Neoplatonized the Christian scheme of history when he described the fall as a lapse into dispersion from the divine One, and, linking the Apocalypse to Genesis, interpreted 'the end or consummation' of all things as a rotation back to their primal unity. 'For the end is always like the beginning', and in the coming world 'that dispersion and separation from the one beginning' will undergo 'a process of restoration to one and the same end and likeness'.[69]

and:

> In his *De divisione naturae* Erigena assimilates the crucial events of sacred history, from creation to apocalypse, to the primary categories of *processio, divisio, reditus,* and *adunatio* [...] and man, as originally created in God's image, was also one and undivided, and hence exhibited no sexual differentiation.[70]

Sá-Carneiro's nadir is complete irrevocable dispersion, and his sexual ambiguity, his inability to love or possess, the Narcissism resulting from his internal division into male and female, all suggest the imagery of his Neoplatonic heritage. There is, however, no gradual decline or fall, and the nadir is reached on several occasions, as Dieter Woll has pointed out:

> A ordem pela qual se sucedem os poemas de Sá-Carneiro é, em grande parte, susceptível de ser alterada. Do primeiro ao último giram sempre à volta da polaridade entre os dois extremos da idealidade e da realidade.[71]

It is a question of sporadic mood, not of a linear descent: when Sá-Carneiro is still capable of hope that «Time present and time past / Are both perhaps present in time future, / And time future contained in time past»,[72] hope that the Christian line of time, Neoplatonized into a circle, will bring him back to the Ideal, to clouds of glory that are non-Christian but not too far removed from Christian imagery or even the idea of redemption, he is alive. He may have *saudades* for himself, he may be living in any time other than the present and he may have lost his sense of unity, but he is alive. All this has a convenient literary and artistic background, as well as fitting in to his psychology: the nostalgia of the Symbolists and the *revalorização* of the past of the Romantics. But in his case, it is an attitude which, like the Instant, cannot be conserved, and he «dies». He becomes old, but without a past, and ultimately, as in *A Confissão de Lúcio,* he is converted into a *morto-vivo.* Ricardo and

---

[69] ABRAMS, pp. 152-3, quoting *De Principiis* I, vi, 1-14, in *The Writings of Origen,* trans. Frederick Crombie (Edinburgh, 1869), pp. 53-59.
[70] ABRAMS, p. 153.
[71] DIETER WOLL, p. 50.
[72] T. S. ELIOT, *Four Quartets* («Burnt Norton»); p. 13 in the London, 1959 edition.

Lúcio represent two sides of one character, the poet and the prose writer; Sá-Carneiro, surely, sees them as the two halves of his own personality, and the irreparable loss of Ricardo is parallel to the loss of his soul (mentioned more than once in the poetry). On Ricardo's death, both «halves» die, though Lúcio is ostensibly still in this world. This total dispersion is not a stage in the journey but ultimate failure. If we accept Woll's division of Sá-Carneiro's ideology into *realidade* and *idealidade*, than *realidade* has won. «Whatever actually occurs is spoiled for art», said Oscar Wilde.[73] And of course, life «actually occurs».

THE «MERVEILLEUX»

The choice of the word *merveilleux* is deliberate, as the structure of virtually all of Sá-Carneiro's prose is descended in a direct line from the vogue for the *conte fantastique* which, though greatly influenced by Edgar Allan Poe and E. T. A. Hoffmann, reached its apogee in France in the nineteenth century. He shows an obvious fascination for all that is bizarre and inexplicable, and, in addition to the narrative mysteries, there is a plethora of adjectives such as *perturbador, estrambótico, inquietador, inexprimível, estranho, raro, assombroso, esquisito, bizarro, extraordinario, singular, milagroso, impossível, incrível, fantástico, maravilhoso, incorpóreo,* and *mágico.* Then there are very many adjectives and nouns referring to human reaction in the face of fantastic phenomena: *aturdido, estonteado, atordoado, assombrado, atónito, perplexo, disperso, abatido, pasmo, perturbação* and *inquietação.* Finally, there are those nouns that refer to the elements that cause *pasmo* and *inquietação: agoiro, encanto, sortilégio, magia, espiritismo, fantasma, monstro, gigante, espectro, feiticero, medium, sabbat, milagre, gnomos, elfos,* and *fadas,* for example.

In *A Confissão de Lúcio,* Lúcio refers to the central events of the story as a «*fantástico* mistério» (CL, p. 153); there is a «*fantástico* teatro» (CL, p. 34), «frases incoerentes, *impossíveis*» (CL, p. 153, author's italics); «duas feras de amor, *singulares, perturbadoras*» (CL, p. 27), an «*estranho* palco» (CL, p. 34), «revelações *estrambóticas*» (CL, p. 51), «uma *estranha* obsessão» (CL, p. 79) and so on. In «A Grande Sombra», there are «animais *estrambóticos, inexprimíveis*» (CF, p. 42), a nocturnal «viagem *maravilhosa*» (CF, p. 43) and «príncipes e rainhas *encantadas*» (CF, p. 43) among other strange elements. In «Abrigo», there is a «*milagroso* carroussel» (Po, p. 131), while in the first of the «Sete Canções de Declínio», is a «*fantástica* bandeira sem suporte» (Po, p. 119); in «O Fantasma», the poet asks: «Que força *mágica* o meu pasmo aguado?» (Po, p. 162); in «Não», we find: «paços reais *encantados*» (Po, p. 89) and in

---

[73] Quoted by ARTHUR SYMONS, «An Artist in Attitudes: Oscar Wilde», in *Writing of the 'Nineties,* ed. Derek Stanford (London, 1971), p. 26.

65

«Ângulo», «transportes *encantados*» (Po, p. 108). There are very many examples.

The reactions of the characters to these phenomena are just as frequently described. «Vou nas ruas, *disperso, atónito*», says the hero of «A Grande Sombra» (CF, p. 110); Lúcio and Ricardo react in a similar way to the «magic» of the «orgy»: «encontrámo-nos na rua, afogueados, *perplexos*» (CL, p. 43) and in the poem «O Resgate», we find: «*Atónito*, parei na grande escadaria» (Po, p. 103). The word *pasmo* is very often found, while the verbs *perturbar, inquietar, pasmar, atordoar* and *assombrar* are also common, usually with supernatural or at least abnormal agents.

Actual manifestations of the fantastic are found too: in «A Grande Sombra» are «*monstros* de bruma verde» (CF, p. 45), for example, while other instances are: «todo se abateu perante o *Milagre!*» (CF, p. 74), «Que *sortilégios* marchetados» (CF, p. 65), «*Milagres, uivos, castelos*» («Rodopio», Po, p. 75), «as suas mãos de *fada,* pálidas e longas» (P, p. 251), «*espectrais* de roxidão» (CF, p. 265), «um êxtase-*fantasma*» (CF, p. 296) and «a gruta dum *feiticeiro*» (CF, p. 226). There are hundreds more phrases involving this imagery.

Sá-Carneiro is not at all concerned with the reproduction or elaboration of folk tales or traditional myths in the manner of Charles Perrault, for example, in his *Histoires ou Contes du temps passé. Avec des Moralitez*,[74] Mme. d'Aulnoy,[75] or any of their many successors responsible for the wide popularity of fairy stories in the eighteenth century. Sometimes there are aspects of his work which do remind us of their conventions, particularly the imagery and atmosphere of the first part of «A Grande Sombra», where a child dreams of penetrating Mystery and creates his own fantastic country, «um mundo bizarro» (CF, p. 42), with forests of multicoloured, sequinned cotton-wool, mountains made of water, rivers which are precious stones, bridges built from stars, and so on. Later, the narrator looks back on his daydreams with pleasure:

> Ah! a imaginação das crianças... onde achar outra mais bela, mais inquietadora, que melhor saiba frisar o impossível? (CF, p. 43).

The imagery is reminiscent of, say, «Hansel and Gretel»:

> ... they followed him till they came to a little house. The bird perched on the roof of it, and when they got up close to it they saw that the little house

---

[74] CHARLES PERRAULT, *Histoires ou Contes du temps passé. Avec des Moralitez* (Paris, 1697). See IONA and PETER OPIE, *The Classic Fairy Tales* (Oxford, 1974).
[75] Marie Catherine Le Jumel de Barnville, Comtesse d'Aulnoy, c. 1650-1705, many of whose stories were translated into English. See the OPIES, p. 24.

was made of bread and the roof was made of cake; the windows, though, were made out of transparent sugar-candy.[76]

or of Hoffmann:

> ... le palais de ma mère [says the *enfant étranger* of the story] est encore plus beau que ceux que tu as vu dans les nuages, car ses colonnes sont de pur cristal et elles s'élèvent jusqu'au bleu du ciel, qui repose sur elles comme un grand dôme. Sous les colonnes sont suspendus de petits nuages brillants bordés d'or; le rouge du soir et celui du matin montent et descendent de chaque côté, et les étoiles étincelantes y forment des figures merveilleuses.[77]

The desire for some kind of supernatural existence, found in the thousands of fairy stories in which the protagonist —often a child— is transported to a setting where all is goodness and light (Tieck's «The Elves», for example) [78] — is not unlike the attitudes of various Sá-Carneiro characters, including the poetic *persona*. The *homem dos sonhos,* for example, is «um homem feliz» (CF, p. 157) since, as he says, he travels «em países longínquos, em nações misteriosas» (CF, p. 160); the joys found in these distant lands are considerably more sophisticated than those in any fairy-tale country — they include a variety of sexes, partialism,[79] «outros sentimentos» (CF, p. 163) and so on — while another difference is that they are explicitly created from within («*Eu tenho o que quero!*», CF, p. 159, author's italics; «Vivo o que quero», CF, p. 160; «eu viajo o que desejo», CF, p. 162) and not conceived of as independent places controlled by others.

The more obvious similarity is between Sá-Carneiro and the later writers of fantastic stories: Nodier, Maupassant, Gautier, Mérimée, Nerval, Balzac, Lautréamont and Villiers de l'Isle-Adam in France, Hoffmann in Germany and Edgar Allan Poe in America. Many of these, as Pierre-Georges Castex has pointed out, follow the age-old tradition of treating «un univers imaginaire» as if it were fact;[80] the difference in the writings of Sá-Carneiro is a subtle one —he is concerned with what he himself calls «a realidade inverosímil» (CL, p. 17)— for him the same thing as «a verdade simples» (CL, p. 15). The problem that faces him

---

[76] *The Juniper Tree and Other Tales from Grimm,* trans. Lore Segal, vol. I (London, 1974), pp. 159-60.

[77] «L'Enfant étranger», in E. T. A. HOFFMANN, *Contes Fantastiques*, trans. Loève-Veimars (Paris, 1964), p. 130.

[78] LUDWIG TIECK, «The Elves», in *The Wishing Ring*, trans. Anthea Bell (London, 1973), pp. 24-25.

[79] «... any special feature of a woman upon which a man's erotic attention is focused may, in a sense, be called a fetish. Where this feature is a part of the body, the breast or the hair, for example, some writers have called the condition 'partialism'». ANTHONY STORR, p. 50. (Storr points out that he dislikes this jargon term, but it is useful in this context.)

[80] PIERRE-GEORGES CASTEX, p. 5.

—and us— is the incredibility of the facts, or what Ione de Andrade has called «o fantástico oculto na própria realidade».[81] With his predecessors in the field, of course, the reverse was often the case. The complaisant reader suspended his disbelief and enjoyed the impossible as if it were real. This is true of Hans Andersen, Grimm, Hoffmann, Tieck, von Brentano[82] and Goethe,[83] for example, as well as of some of the French *conteurs* already referred to. The change between the two approaches came about by means of a gradual but by no means consistent process, full of exceptions to the general tendency, but whose existence is nonetheless undeniable. This is not to suggest that authors no longer invite their readers to believe in the credibility of «un univers imaginaire», nor, conversely, that the nineteenth century produced no advocates of the «realidade inverosímil» approach: Nodier[84] and Edgar Allan Poe[85] were both precursors of Sá-Carneiro in this sense. Nevertheless, there was a growing awareness among the authors of fantastic literature that they could no longer depend on what might be seen as the gullibility of their readers, and explanations of some kind were deemed necessary. Rightly or wrongly, these writers feared that the reader would see himself as the author's dupe, and for this reason, among others, they began to show greater respect for common sense and rationality. One way out was the device of the «rational explanation», making «plausible l'oeuvre tout entière. À l'attrait de l'histoire merveilleuse se juxtapose l'interêt réaliste», and Edgar Allan Poe in particular was greatly admired in France, according to Castex, because his stories were invariably logical.[86] The «rational explanation» itself was presented in one of several ways. Sometimes the author produced a complete set of (often singularly unconvincing) facts at the very last moment to explain away, somewhat after the manner of the detective story, previously puzzling phenomena. In many cases it turns out that there has been some sort of deliberate deception, sometimes for rather shady reasons. An example of this category is Horace Raisson's tale «L'Élixir de jeunesse» (1833),[87] where a magic rejuvenating philtre is presented to the heroine by a strange man

[81] IONE DE ANDRADE, «Realismo Fantástico e Simbolismo dos Trajes na 'Confissão de Lúcio'», in *Bulletin des Études Portugaises*, XXVIII-XXIX (1967-68), 337-54.
[82] See for example «Clever Dick», in *The Wishing Ring*, pp. 46-55.
[83] Another example is «Behind the Evil Wall», in *The Wishing Ring*, pp. 7-20, though part of this story is explained by admitting that it had all been a dream.
[84] CHARLES NODIER classified some of his stories as «histoires fantastiques vraies»; an example is «L'Histoire d'Hélène Gillet» (1832), in *Contes* (Paris, 1961), pp. 330-48.
[85] All Poe's stories expect the reader to accept the outrageous things that happen as part of «everyday life». See EDGAR ALLAN POE, *Tales of Mystery and Imagination* (London, 1971).
[86] PIERRE-GEORGES CASTEX, pp. 70 and 399.
[87] In *L'Artiste*, vol. II.

in gratitude for her hospitality. When the disappearance of her chamber-maid coincides with the sudden appearance of a baby in the house, she assumes that the magic potion has done its work, albeit accidentally and on the wrong person. Any belief the reader may have had in the liquid's supernatural powers is completely dispelled, however, when the *dénoue-ment* reveals, with the arrival ten years later of the chambermaid and the stranger in search of their child, that the whole episode had been contrived in order to get rid of an unwanted baby on a gullible and rich woman. Then Guy de Maupassant is an example of an author who actually *changed* a short story from a version in which no rational explanation was given: his macabre «La Main d'écorché» (1875) [88] tells of the over-night disappearance of the hand of a dead man which has been kept as a morbid souvenir. It has left fingermarks on the protagonist's throat, and is later found by a gravedigger, next to a skeleton. In the second version, now called only «La Main» (1885),[89] we are told that the hand's original owner is not in fact dead: he has merely returned to reclaim it. In many cases, in spite of the author's good intentions, ingenious «so-lutions» add little to the stories' artistic value and even less to their credibility. A second variation of the «rational explanation», aiming to make the incredible credible, was the location of either an episode or the whole tale in the world of dreams. Thirdly, there were authors who revealed that the protagonist's experiences were the outcome of drug-taking or intoxication, and finally, insanity, either temporary or perma-nent, was seen as the cause of the victim's hallucinations. All these techniques presuppose the credulity of the protagonist and often involve a not altogether sympathetic omniscience on the part of the author. The relationship between a story-teller and a protagonist who is apparently normal is surely more appealing to the reader. Even if this «normality» is threatened by extraordinary circumstances, such as the tremendous grief of the Comte d'Athol at the death of his beloved wife in Villiers de L'Isle-Adam's «Véra» (1874),[90] it is more satisfying to have our fears for his emotional stability «allayed» when we are given material proof of the impossible: the key of his dead wife's tomb, left on the nuptial bed, shows that her visit to him was not just a figment of a deranged ima-gination. In any case, there were two ways of treating the supernatural in the nineteenth century: either the incredible was presented as the truth, with no embellishment or apology, or it was seen as only the *appearance* of truth, and a rational explanation was given. Where the reader is concerned, a preference for one technique rather than another may well be no more than a question of subjective taste, but for the

[88] In *L'Almanach de Pont-à-Mousson,* under the pen-name Joseph Prunier.
[89] In *Contes du Jour et de la nuit.*
[90] In *La Semaine Parisienne.*

authors, there were motives other than those based on mere caprice. Charles Nodier shows his disapproval of explanations by heading the final chapter of «La Fée aux miettes» [91]: «Conclusion. Qui n'explique rien et qu'on peut se dispenser de lire.» That he has already given some sort of rational explanation by making the storyteller, Michel, a lunatic is relatively unimportant since his attitude towards the insane is unorthodox: he finds it absurd to assume that they are lacking in sense and lucidity, and is convinced that our concept of normality is an arbitrary one. In the event, the last chapter of this story *adds* incredible new facts. Other writers of the period found no need at all to explain the supernatural, and Mérimée is a good example [92] since, like Hoffmann, he saw no need to give answers to his puzzles. Hoffmann himself eschewed clarification devices and would tie up no loose ends: he would happily use the word «merveilleux», for example, in the literal sense, as in the «merveilleux orfèvre Léonard» of «Le Choix d'une fiancée».[93] This is not to say that he was not aware of the incredible nature of what he was saying — often other characters will point out the unacceptability of the facts as presented by the protagonist, equally often suggesting the excuses used by later writers as explanations: dreaming, insanity, lying, hallucinations or intoxication. In some cases, as in Villiers de L'Isle-Adam's «Claire Lenoir» (1867),[94] a matter-of-fact, pedestrian character is created to point a contrast with the supernatural. This is one way of pandering to the reader. Another is the use of a realistic technique whereby the reader accepts what he is told because of recognition of landscapes, states of mind, conversations, social attitudes and behaviour. This technique is more and more in evidence as time goes by. E. M. de Melo e Castro, in his introduction to the *Antologia do Conto Fantástico Português*, sees this as an important feature of the genre in Portugal: «uma das preocupações dominantes dos contos aqui reunidos é a sua verosimilhança», he asserts. He goes on:

> os factos narrados são autênticos e sobre eles não deve haver dúvidas: que sejam estranhos, anormais, inacreditáveis, raros, isso é da sua própria natureza.[95]

The reproduction of states of mind by European *conteurs* was largely superficial until they came under the influence of Edgar Allan Poe, with his psychological verisimilitude. Psychological verisimilitude and realistic

---

[91] CHARLES NODIER, *Contes*, pp. 167-329.
[92] See for example *Le Guzla* (1827), «La Vision de Charles XI» (1829) and «La Venus d'Ille» (1837).
[93] HOFFMANN, vol. I, p. 157.
[94] In *Revue des Lettres et des Arts*.
[95] *Antologia do Conto Fantástico Português*, ed. E. M. de Melo e Castro, 2nd edition (Lisbon, 1974), p. xvi. (First edition, 1965.)

description are not mutually exclusive however (though one may edge the other out within the limited confines of one short story): **Guy de Maupassant**, for example, achieved an amalgam of both.

So it is that Sá-Carneiro's narrative mysteries and disturbing phenomena have the heritage of two traditions, and he is faced with the problem of whether or not to explain away his enigmas, not «un univers imaginaire», but unacceptable, incredible *facts*. He is on the horns of a dilemma, since to account for the fantastic with one of the standard explanations would defeat his own object: he would be admitting that everything is possible and acceptable if you have the key to the puzzle. On the other hand, to leave a mystery entirely unexplained would be out of keeping with the very structure of his prose which is based on the solution of puzzles, and the value of narrative twists and surprises was something he was obviously aware of. It is clear even from his punctuation, especially the many (often unnecessary) capital letters and the use of italics, that he was concerned to maintain the interest of the reader on the level of superficial suspense. Furthermore, the frequency of such words as *misterioso* suggests that an answer must be forthcoming, as does that of phrases like «Quis [...] fruir o segredo do dominador dos sonhos» (CF, p. 166), «Que vinha a ser aquele homem?» (CF, p. 166), or «Aquela mulher, ah! aquela mulher... Quem seria... Quem seria?... ¿Como sucedera *tudo aquilo?*...» (CL, p. 90, author's italics). The technique that Sá-Carneiro chose was both successful and revealing — revealing because by means of it we have an insight into his personality and traumata. What he does is to give an explanation which is not devoid of internal logic, but which, in fact, is as irrational as the mysteries it purports to clarify. If Edgar Allan Poe was admired in France because his stories were invariably logical, it is clear why Sá-Carneiro was an admirer of Poe.[96] But in both cases logic and credibility are unconnected. Melo e Castro [97] has something interesting to say on the subject of logic when he justifies the exclusion of the Absurd from his anthology:

> O Absurdo só existe em função de uma admitida razão lógica, mas não é uma transgressão. É antes uma categoria (silogística quantas vezes) dessa mesma lógica.

The Absurd, then, is lacking in a logical system but — according to Melo e Castro— is not fantastic. We may add that the fantastic may well be

[96] See for example FRANÇOIS CASTEX, *A Génese*, p. 60: «as suas preferências vão para Stefan Zweig, Oscar Wilde e sobretudo Edgar Poë». (I am indebted to the late Professor Jorge de Sena for pointing out that the reference to Stefan Zweig must be an error, since Sá-Carneiro knew no German and Zweig's works were not translated into French, much less Portuguese, until many years after Sá-Carneiro's death.)
[97] MELO E CASTRO, p. xxiii.

71

entirely logical, but at the same time be completely incredible. Baudelaire was right to see in Poe a taste for «une difficulté vaincue» and «une énigme expliquée»,[98] and we could certainly not fault his judgment of the climate of the short stories — «l'absurde s'installant dans l'intelligence et la gouvernant avec une épouvantable logique»[99] — though his use of the word absurd in the context would be frowned upon by Melo e Castro; nevertheless, it is undeniable that as far as plausibility is concerned, logic is a red herring, however *épouvantable* it may be. Implausibility is, of course, no barrier to the reader's enjoyment: we follow, say, Edgar Allan Poe's «William Wilson»[100] with no less interest because we are unable to accept it as a possible sequence of events. As we have alread noted, «William Wilson», probably one of Poe's best stories and one which has served as an inspiration to many succeeding writers, deals with the materialisation of the protagonist's «other half», which haunts and torments him. Eventually, after years of suffering, in a drunken fury of desperation, he kills his tormentor and condemns himself to a living death, since it is his good half that has died. There is no question of any kind of hallucination: the double actually existed and acted independently. Other people knew him and he had a personality of his own. There is no real explanation and neither is it an allegory; it is truly a tale of mystery and imagination. When we come back to Sá-Carneiro, we see that despite similarities, his method of dealing with the inexplicable is somewhat different: there are explanations and these are not mere technical devices; furthermore, the stories actually pivot on them. Strictly speaking, some of his stories fit into the category described in the *Antología de la literatura fantástica* by Adolfo Bioy Casares as:

> Los que tienen explicación fantástica, pero no sobrenatural («científica» no me parece el epíteto conveniente para estas investigaciones rigurosas, verosímiles, a fuerza de sintaxis).[101]

An example of Sá-Carneiro's technique is «A Estranha Morte do Professor Antena»; the very title suggests the detective story, Science Fiction and the possibility of the fantastic. The narrative is a puzzle which has to be solved, and we know that it actually will be, since the narrator claims that he alone is in possession of the facts which constitute «a alucinadora verdade» (CF, p. 234). The solution —that the eponymous Professor had devised a means of entering other worlds and that in one of them he was accidentally killed— is evidently logical and might even

---

[98] BAUDELAIRE, «Edgar Poe», p. 615.
[99] BAUDELAIRE, «Edgar Poe», p. 616.
[100] Poe, pp. 3-20.
[101] *Antología de la literatura fantástica*, edited by Jorge Luis Borges, Silvina Ocampo and Adolfo Bioy Casares (Buenos Aires, 1971), p. 13.

be classed as scientific, despite Bioy Casares' reluctance to employ the word: the story is set in a scientific ambiance and is embellished by a quasi-scientific formula which is, it seems, evidence of the ineluctable rationality of the answer. So the mystery is solved. But the solution is as meaningless in our material world as the Professor's empty formula. The scientific jargon is part of the explanation, but it is based on groundless theories and it explains nothing. Nevertheless, it is of fundamental importance, both as a pivot for the narrative —since it would be completely pointless if we were told that an eccentric professor's untimely death has no explanation— and for some understanding of Sá-Carneiro. Another example is «O Homem dos Sonhos». Again, mystery is present throughout, from the title and the very first sentence («Nunca soube o seu nome», CF, p. 157) to the flash of inspiration, like a «relâmpago de claridade» (CF, p. 167) by which the answer is revealed to the narrator. This story of a mysterious happy man who has learned to control his dreams, manages to find the Ideal, is disappointed in it and then disappears for ever out of the narrator's life was described by Sá-Carneiro as «uma história de *além*-vida, de além-terra; desenvolve-se», he claimed, «noutros mundos, noutros sentimentos» (C I, p. 57, letter to Fernando Pessoa dated January 21, 1913, author's italics). There are two explanations in this particular story: the strange man explains the reason for his happiness (he has escaped from everyday life), and the narrator works out for himself just who this man is (a creature out of a dream, living dreams and dreaming life: «o homem estranho sonhava a vida, vivia o sonho [...] Ele derrubara a realidade, condenando-o ao sonho. E vivia o irreal», CF, p. 168). Once again, this eminently logical solution is meaningless. In *A Confissão de Lúcio*, the identity of Marta is the principal mystery. And the mystery is solved: Ricardo had created her in order that his homosexual love for Lúcio might be consummated. Thus, when he kills her, he kills himself (an idea repeated in «Eu-próprio o Outro»: «Mata-*lo*-ei esta noite... quando *Ele* dormir...», CF, p. 222, and found in many other stories including the Hans Heinz Ewers film already referred to and which Sá-Carneiro may conceivably have seen, since the French version, *L'Étudiant de Prague*, was shown in Paris in 1912). Attendant psychological mysteries, such as the reasons for Ricardo's *tédio* and for Lúcio's revulsion when he makes love to Marta, are cleared up at the same time... and yet, nothing is cleared up. Although *A Confissão de Lúcio* has suffered from critical neglect, there are, as Dieter Woll points out,[102] several interpretations of it: this shows that although superficial puzzles may be superficially solved, the real mystery is open to various readings. It is the great Mystery that we have already dealt with —the

---

[102] DIETER WOLL, «Decifrando 'A Confissão de Lúcio'», in *Miscelânea de Estudos em Honra do Prof. Vitorino Nemésio* (Lisbon, 1971), pp. 425-38.

Unknown, the Beyond, the only thing worth knowing— with an element of terror: «o medo é Mistério» («Não», Po, p. 89). The narrative puzzles constitute a surface under which lies the idea of the Unknown presiding over everything, and in the few stories where there is no narrative puzzle, the emphasis falls directly on Mystery itself, often manifested in psychological problems. In all these stories, there is an ironic reversal of the concept of the omniscient author: the hero's new experience after death in «Página dum Suicida», for example, is not shared with the reader, but neither is it shared with the author. This is not the first time that authors have explained mysteries with mysteries, or just left them unsolved. But it is unlikely that there have been many who suffered as much bewilderment as Sá-Carneiro reveals in the use of this technique. And the bewilderment is made more intense, though perhaps arouses slightly less sympathy, by the fact that it is based on complete egocentricity. He does not write about Man but about a man — himself. He is not so much concerned about Death as about his own death. He deals not with universals, but with one personality and its problems, and this causes little surprise since he is prey to a sense of isolation from other people. For a moment, as he ties up the loose ends of his stories, he may appear to have found an answer, but this means nothing, for his loose ends make an irrational tangle; he is not omniscient but ignorant, not powerful but weak, and the mysteries are no less oppressive and haunting for having been put in another key. This is a very different attitude from that of many of the nineteenth-century *conteurs* in France who did so much to make the genre of the fantastic popular: Villiers de L'Isle-Adam, for example, headed his stories «Claire Lenoir» and «L'Intersigne»: «faire penser» when they were first published in the *Revue des Lettres et des Arts*,[103] and he had something to say about life, literature and philosophy. Other French writers, particularly the so-called 1830 Generation, used the *conte fantastique* as a therapeutic exercise, as Miriam Hamenachem points out, because of their disillusionment with religion, science, politics and society in general: «Le thème de l'effet maléfique des sciences a fait couler beaucoup d'encre de la plume de Nodier tout au long de sa carrière littéraire», for example.[104] Needless to say, their stimuli came partly from within too, but with Sá-Carneiro,

---

[103] VILLIERS DE L'ISLE-ADAM, «Claire Lenoir», in *Revue des Lettres et des Arts*, October 13, 20, 27, November 3, 10, 17, 24 and December 1, 1867. «L'Intersigne», December 8, 1867 and January 12, 1868.

[104] MIRIAM HAMENACHEM, *Charles Nodier. Essai sur l'Imagination mythique* (Paris, 1972), p. 32. She also maintains that Nodier was impelled to create the «côté noir de son univers» by witnessing the horrors of the French Revolution (p. 10). PIERRE-GEORGES CASTEX, *op. cit.*, points out that «la plupart des écrivains fantastiques [were] des contempteurs du monde moderne», and shows how similar are the ideologies of Nodier and Villiers de L'Isle-Adam despite the fifty years between them (p. 400).

it would appear to come almost *exclusively* from inside himself. Even those who see the absence of any religious faith as a main source of his problems do not suggest that he was intellectually disenchanted with the worldly manifestations of organised religion, or with the social system, or with human injustice. What he does have in common with some of his French predecessors is a consciousness of what Guy de Maupassant called a «mal [...] inconnu»,[105] and Sainte-Beuve's aphorism about Mérimée applies equally well to Sá-Carneiro: «Mérimée», he wrote, «ne croit pas que Dieu existe, mais il n'est pas bien sûr que le diable n'existe pas».[106] The French *conteurs* did, in very many cases, suffer from personal *Angst,* but its ratio to social disenchantment was different. (Gérard de Nerval is an obvious exception. Even in life there are similarities: the loss of his mother at an early age, his irregular life in Paris, the desire to shock the *bourgeoisie,* financial disaster when founding a literary journal, the love of travel, the ultimate suicide — all these link him to Sá-Carneiro. And in his writings, as we have already noted, there is the common aim of capturing the ineffable — «fixer mon idéal», he says in *Sylvie,* like the *fixador de instantes* — and some imagery in common: mysterious cities, the concept of the double and so on.) Urbano Tavares Rodrigues' assertion that Sá-Carneiro wrote «contos [...] sem parentesco, a não ser estilístico, na nossa prosa de ficção»,[107] may well be true, but they are certainly not without *parentesco* in the realms of French, German, English and American literature. M.-J. Durry has described Nerval's writings as a revelation of his soul, and this is true for Sá-Carneiro too: if Nerval's use of myth is «l'explication poétique du monde»,[108] Sá-Carneiro's use of the fantastic is an *explication poétique* of himself. But he does not understand the *explication,* and he feels isolated and alienated. The mystery explained by a mystery is a kind of irrational explanation

---

[105] GUY DE MAUPASSANT, «Le Horla», in *Gil Blas,* October 26, 1886. Reprinted in *Le Horla* (Paris, 1909); p. 6: «ce pressentiment qui est sans doute l'atteinte d'un mal encore inconnu, germant dans le sang et dans la chair». «Le Horla» has many features in common with stories of Sá-Carneiro. For example, at one point the protagonist's musings regarding the limitations of this world (cf. the *homem dos sonhos*): «Pourquoi pas un de plus?» he asks, referring to an «être nouveau»; «Pourquoi pas aussi d'autres arbres aux fleurs immenses, éclatantes et parfumant des régions entières? Pourquoi pas d'autres éléments que le feu, l'air, la terre et l'eau? [...] Comme tout est pauvre, mesquin, misérable!» (p. 41). In «O Homem dos Sonhos», the stranger says, «A vida, no fundo, contém tão poucas coisas, é tão pouco variada... [...] Por toda a banda o mesmo cénario, os mesmos acessórios: montanhas ou planícies, mares ou pradarias e florestas — as mesmas cores...» (CF, pp. 158-9).
[106] *Portraits Contemporains* (Paris, 1855). Quoted by PIERRE-GEORGES CASTEX, p. 248.
[107] URBANO TAVARES RODRIGUES, Introduction to *Mário de Sá-Carneiro, Cartas a Fernando Pessoa,* vol. I, p. 19.
[108] M.-J. DURRY, *Gérard de Nerval et le mythe* (Paris, 1956), p. 80.

of himself. He deals with the possible, not the impossible, and this is what is terrifying. As Villiers de L'Isle-Adam said of the «facts» of «Claire Lenoir», «la seule idée de *leur simple possibilité* est tout aussi terrible que le pourrait être leur authenticité démontrée et reconnue».[109] For Sá-Carneiro, the «incredibility of the facts» was intolerable.

---

[109] VILLIERS DE L'ISLE-ADAM, p. 12 (author's italics).

CHAPTER 3

«ESTADOS DE ALMA»

In spite of Sá-Carneiro's debt to the Symbolist movement, the *estados de alma* which are most frequently found in his works do not coincide exactly with those cited by his Symbolist predecessors (Cirlot gives the list as «severo, extático, doloroso, entusiástico, activo, erótico, melancólico» in his *Diccionario de símbolos*),[1] and we have already dealt with the erotic *estado*. For the Portuguese writer, there seem to be four dominating moods: fear, alienation, pain and ecstasy.

FEAR

In addition to fear in connection with sex, we sometimes find it related to art. At one point it is literature: «estrebuchando a louca do poema *medonho*» (CF, p. 265). Then there is architecture: «Nossa Senhora de Paris! — a Catedral Tragédia elançando-se ao ar, *temível*, pálida de exorcismos» (CF, p. 280); although there are connotations of the supernatural in this particular instance, again it must be pointed out that Sá-Carneiro's fascination with the manifestations of religion was largely aesthetic. He goes on: «Lá dentro abóbadas, naves de pasmo — milagre e *medo* na luz de imagens que os vitrais coam...» (CF, p. 280). Even colour can be frightening: «uma cor repugnante *que metia medo*» (CF, p. 232, author's italics). Then, there is the effect of settings and décor that are theatrical in their descriptions: «sigo nas salas douradas. Os pares volteiam em mil cores. Lembram rosas as valsas. E, no entanto, mais do que nunca se me acentua *um calafrio de receio*» (CF, p. 102). Architecture provides the background for Ricardo de Loureiro's «*horror* dos arcos» (CL, p. 52) and his «sensação misteriosa de *pavor*» on discovering a small archway at the end of a lonely street (CL, p. 52), and he adds «*apavoravam-me as ogivas*» (CL, p. 52). Not surprisingly, mystery is another source of fear: the protagonist's childhood memories in «A Grande Sombra» are evidence of this: «numa febre de *medo*, a ranger de mistério, voguei pela

---

[1] CIRLOT, p. 208, under the heading «Estado de ánimo».

sombra» (CF, p. 44), and he adds: «dava-me asas o próprio *terror*» (CF, p. 45). In the poem «Não», we find the lines: «Mistério é riqueza — / E o *medo* é Mistério!...» (Po, p. 89), while the converse is evident in «Estátua Falsa» — all is false, worthless and invalid, «nem sequer um arrepio de *medo!*» (Po, p. 66) since there is no longer a *segredo*. But there are still «lembranças de *pavor*» in the storyteller's soul in «A Grande Sombra» as long as the enigma has *not* been clarified (CF, p. 120). The strange man of «O Homem dos Sonhos» reacts to the mysteries of the city to which he has escaped from everyday life in the same way: «Ah! que estranho calafrio de *medo* me varou, delicioso e novo» (CF, p. 161), while the mystery of the poem «Álcool» is represented by the image of *bruma*: «Fecho os meus olhos com *pavor* da bruma...» (Po, p. 59).

Two things are obvious: that any form of excitement can cause fear, and that, yet again, the author has an ambivalent attitude towards the reaction. It was Arthur Symons who wrote:

> In his escape from the world, one man chooses religion, and seems to find himself; another, choosing love, may seem also to find himself; and may not another, coming to art as to a religion and as to a woman, seem to find himself not less effectually? [2]

Some years earlier, he had said the same thing:

> Allowing ourselves, for the most part, to be but vaguely conscious of that great suspense in which we live, we find our escape from its sterile, annihilating reality in many dreams, in religion, passion, art; each a forgetfulness, each a symbol of creation; religion being the creation of a new heaven, passion the creation of a new earth, and art, in its mingling of heaven and earth, the creation of heaven out of earth. [3]

If we see the destination of an «escape from the world» as represented by the obsessive *Mistério* found in the writings of Sá-Carneiro, it is clear that the interchangeable areas of excitement that we have considered —sex, art and any mysterious element in life— constitute the means by which this destination may be reached. All of them may be tried even if there is no guarantee of success, but Sá-Carneiro chooses to ignore Symons' first suggestion, religion, leaving only its beauty and the vague mystery that non-believers see in it as possible ways of gaining the goal. All Sá-Carneiro's efforts are strivings in an act of creation; he *is* trying to create «a new heaven out of earth», and it *is* a kind of forgetfulness, since a religious heaven is not even considered, and the «new earth» brought about by passion is seen to be incomplete, though not entirely worthless. Sexual relationships have their brief moments

---

[2] ARTHUR SYMONS, «The Choice».
[3] ARTHUR SYMONS, *The Symbolist Movement in Literature* (London, 1899); pp. 171-2 in the 1911 edition.

of ecstasy, and these afford glimpses of the great Mystery. All of this is inevitably accompanied by feelings of fear. This is not unusual in religious experiences: St. Augustine refers to «ictu *trepidantis* aspectus» when his understanding recognised «the sight of the God who IS»; [4] St. Paul when granted a vision of God on the road to Damascus, was *trembling and astonished*»; [5] when the shepherds saw the angel of the Lord, «they were sore *afraid*». [6] As M. H. Abrams has pointed out, «such experiences [...] were of common report among the philosophers and poets of the Romantic generation», [7] and he quotes, among other examples, Coleridge's «To William Wordsworth»:

> of moments awful
> Now in thy inner life, and now abroad,
> When power streamed from thee, and thy soul received
> The light reflected as a light bestowed. [8]

In Sá-Carneiro, these moments of revelation invariably have something of the «moments awful», with the exciting phenomena, whatever they happen to be, giving rise to *arrepios* at the very least.

But in addition to this terror which may be seen as reasonable and justifiable as well as being part of Sá-Carneiro's literary and religious heritage, there are irrational fears. There are some aspects of painting, architecture, sculpture, décor and the performing arts that give rise to phobias apparently unconnected with the perception of the transcendental. For example, in the short story «A Grande Sombra», the narrator confesses that as a child «*receava* os campanários das igrejas, sombriamente [...] e *temia* sobre as tapeçarias espessas... vinham-me *calafrios* defronte dos reposteiros pesados, de veludos quentes...» (CF, p. 48), while Ricardo, in *A Confissão de Lúcio*, tells Lúcio about his «*medos* inexplicáveis» (CL, p. 51) which include dancing-girls, who seem to be impassively identical: «Não as posso destrinçar do seu conjunto: daí o meu *pavor*» (CL, p. 52), archways, especially «arcos triunfais» (CL, p. 52), and ogives, or pointed arches, but he adds that the arches themselves are less terrifying than the «espácio aéreo que eles enquadram» (CL, p. 52). As a child, he had feared «as abóbadas, as sombras de altas colunas, os obeliscos, as grandes escadarias de mármore...» (CL, pp. 52-3); his psychological make-up, he says, is no more than an extension of his childhood phobias, and part of this is his adult terror of «o céu das ruas, estreitas e de prédios altos, que de súbito se partem em curvas apertadas» (CL, p. 53). Now

---

[4] ST. AUGUSTINE, *Confessions*, VII, xvii: p. 151 in the Harmondsworth, 1961, edition, trans. R. S. Pine-Coffin.
[5] ACTS 9, v. 6.
[6] LUKE 2, v. 9.
[7] ABRAMS, p. 386.
[8] ABRAMS, p. 389.

79

it is clear that these fears have nothing to do with what Sá-Carneiro once called the «calafrio supremo» (C II, p. 140) and which he explained in «O Fixador de Instantes»: «Em face da maravilha todos têm medo» (CF, p. 269). There is no *maravilha* here, no equivocal reaction, and the protagonists suffer without relief. The author's Unconscious would appear to have chosen images with obvious sexual significance — tall columns, obelisks and bell-towers on the one hand, archways, domes, staircases, the thick pile of carpets and upholstery, space which apparently leads to the infinite («uma porta aberta sobre o infinito», CL, p. 52) on the other. In addition to the phallic connotation of towers and obelisks, there are hints of the supernatural. Once again, in fact, sex and the Unknown are linked. Cirlot tells us that the tower is:

> en el sistema jeroglífico egipcio, signo determinante que expresa la eleva-ción de algo, o la acción de elevarse por encima de la norma vital o social. [...] En la Edad Media, torres y campanarios [...] tenían un significado de escala entre la tierra y el cielo

and there is also the «analogía: torre, hombre».[9] The images connected with feminine sexuality show a similar duality: Cirlot says that «según Leo Frobenius, toda bóveda constituye una representación de la unión del dios del cielo y la diosa de la tierra», and he adds, «la separación de ambos creó el vacío».[10] Ascension is, of course, implicit in the staircase image, while that of the archway has also been regarded as half the circle which is totality.[11] At the same time it leads to the infinite and its insecurity: «un arco al espacio ilimitado», as Luis Cernuda said many years later.[12] The pattern is clear: the images are both transcendental and sexual. They are representations of the first stage on a journey to the Unknown with sex seen as its reflection in the finite world, and therefore they incorporate fear on that count. The sexual aspect of the author's attitude stems from his sexual ambivalence, with fear of the male co-existing with fear of the female. (The fear of the female as a general concept is emphasised by Ricardo's inability to make individuals of the chorus girls.) In the two stories where these images are most densely concentrated, *A Confissão de Lúcio* and «A Grande Sombra», there is bisexuality even on a narrative level, with, in the first case, a character whose *anima* materialises and, in the second, a man who is the carnal manifestation of a woman's death.

The second area of irrational fears is indicated by the frequent refe-

9 CIRLOT, pp. 457-8.
10 CIRLOT, p. 111.
11 CIRLOT, p. 89.
12 LUIS CERNUDA, «El acorde», in *Ocnos* (Xalapa, 1963), p. 192. (First edition, 1942.)

rences to disintegration; in «Eu-próprio o Outro», the protagonist is losing his identity:

> Venho para casa cheio de medo.
> Olho-me a um espelho...
> Horror!
> Descubro no meu rosto, caricaturizado, o rictus de desdém do *seu* rosto. (Cf, pp. 216-17, author's italics)

In *A Confissão de Lúcio,* Ricardo's «tenho medo — medo de soçobrar, de me extinguir no meu mundo interior, de desaparecer da vida, perdido nele...» (CL, p. 63) is not unconnected with Lúcio's fear of madness («chegando mesmo a recear enlouquecer» (CL, p. 82) nor with that of the protagonist of «A Grande Sombra»: «receio então que a minha alma seja apenas um líquido verde, oleoso e turvo, enjoativo, fechado nesse depósito» (CF, p. 61). And the image of «molduras... sem retratos» (CF, p. 100) and «telas [...] sem retratos» (CF, p. 112) with, eventually, «os retratos desconhecidos» becoming «o *seu* retrato» (CF, p. 116, author's italics), when the dominant element is victorious, have the same significance. The Unknown is present here too in the incomprehensible nature of the workings and make-up of the individual. These fears may be irrational but they are not uncommon. Jung said that:

> one of the most common mental derangements that occur among primitive people is what they call «the loss of a soul» — which means [...] a noticeable disruption (or, more technically, a dissociation) of consciousness.
> Among such people, whose consciousness is at a different level of development from ours, the «soul» (or psyche) is not felt to be a unit.[13]

And he goes on:

> Beyond doubt, even in what we call a high level of civilization, human consciousness has not yet achieved a reasonable degree of continuity. It is still vulnerable and *liable to fragmentation.*[14]

This fragmentation, like the dispersion we have already considered, is a possibility, if not a fact, in Sá-Carneiro, and this is frightening since it reflects chaos. Ultimately there are two kinds of fear: that which is acceptable and even desirable, for it serves as proof that there is indeed something ineffable with which the artist is sporadically in touch, and that which is the result of the awareness that this may not, after all, be the case. And the second variety is found in the absence of the first, when all is lost and hope is non-existent:

---

[13] CARL G. JUNG, *Man and his Symbols* (London, 1964), p. 24.
[14] JUNG, p. 25.

81

Já não estremeço em face do segredo;
Nada me aloira já, nada me aterra:
A vida corre sobre mim em guerra,
E nem sequer um arrepio de medo!

(«Estátua Falsa», Po, p. 66)

There is no sense of direction and this is terrifying. «Man positively needs general ideas and convictions that will give a meaning to his life and enable him to find a place for himself in the universe», said Jung.[15] Even more significantly, he added that «the individual is the only reality».[16] The abstract idea of what is necessary for mankind in general must be adapted to the case of one man in particular: not only are «general ideas and convictions» lacking, but the individual for whom these are essential is disintegrating and is on the point of disappearing entirely.

ALIENATION

Sá-Carneiro was sporadically tormented by the distance that lay between him and everyday life, and this awareness led to the fear of madness, if not to madness itself. He was, in the sense that Colin Wilson gave to the word, an Outsider,[17] but essentially a passive one, a victim. Wilson says: «the basic point of my 'outsiders' is their feeling of rejection of the everyday world»;[18] for the Portuguese author, life was to a certain extent made up of rejection *by* the everyday world, or at least, his certainty that it was, which comes to the same thing. As he sees things, there is first of all action, represented by verbs such as *derrotar, vencer, amarfanhar,* then the process gets under way in the individual with images such as *despedaçar-se, soçobrar* and *tropeçar;* this bring a reaction which is made up of *vertigem* and struggling (*estrebuchar, lutar,* etc.); the result is madness, alienation and incomprehension, sometimes indicated by the word *ilusão* as well as by the usual explicit adjectives *doido, possesso* and *louco.*

In «A Grande Sombra», the protagonist refers to «esse mesmo peso do meu sono que me *aflige* e *amarfanha*» (CF, p. 101); in the poem «Apoteose», the poet says: «Levanto-me... / —*Derrota!*» (Po, p. 182); even in a letter to Pessoa (dated May 3, 1913) Sá-Carneiro refers to «o ritmo *amarfanhado* da minha alma» (C I, p. 111). In «O Incesto» there is fear of a «círculo férreo, *estrangulador*» (P, p. 319); in the poem «Álcool» is the line: «*Ferem*-me os olhos turbilhões de gumes» (Po, p. 58);

---

15 JUNG, p. 89.
16 JUNG, p. 58.
17 COLIN WILSON, *The Outsider* (London, 1970). (First edition, 1956.) The original Outsider was, of course, the *étranger* of Albert Camus.
18 WILSON, p. 313.

in *A Confissão de Lúcio,* the light «*invadia* o sangue» (CL, p. 38), while most explicitly, the protagonist of «Eu-próprio o Outro» claims: «[O Outro] Foi-me *sugando* pouco a pouco. O seu corpo era poroso. *Absorveu-me*» (CF, p. 221). There are innumerable examples of these verbs of conflict and conquest, and sex is a battle too: its setting is described on one occasion as a «grande alcova da *vitória*» (CF, p. 197). Mystery is another enemy, but Professor Antena «*venceu* o Mistério» (CF, p. 253). The self, or at least part of it, is a source of hostility: «Não me pude *vencer*» («A Queda», Po, p. 80). Victories are few; *conquistar* and *vencer* are frequently in the negative or the passive — «era sempre *vencido*» (P, p. 332), «Ei-los *vencidos, vencidos*» (P, p. 301) and «nem um espasmo *venço!*» («A Queda», Po, p. 79) —or speculative (especially using the word *triunfo)*— «ah, se conseguisse semelhante *triunfo*» (CF, p. 143), or «Ah! se eu fosse quem sou... Que *triunfo!*» (CF, p. 211). There are often barriers in this warfare: «Fora esta a *barreira* em que sempre tropeçara» (CF, p. 136), or «foi essa a extraordinária empresa a que o Prof. Antena se decidiu meter ombros, *embora todas as barreiras!*» (CF, p. 249). Then, things and people may be obstructive and cruel, and we find adjectives such as *feroz, cruel, agressivo, brutal* and *assustador.*

Despite the frequently-stated desire to conquer or, at the very least, to fight back, the process is almost always one in which the victim suffers and loses. To conquer, in Sá-Carneiro's terms, involves either death, deviation from normality or both. The alternative is a process of defeat and disintegration. The victim stumbles «por becos e saguões» (CF, p. 149) and is afraid and confused: «numa agonia *estonteada*» (CL, p. 54), «cheio de cansaço, *aturdido*» (CL, p. 147). Then disintegration and destruction begin: «esse *quebranto* infernal» (CF, p. 145), and in real life, «a zoina silva sobre mim *despedaçadoramente*» (C II, p. 161). «O próprio corpo [...] *se desmorona*» (CF, p. 176), and so does everything else. We end up with «*devastação* completa» (CF, p. 61). The resulting state of incoherence —«Não posso descrever melhor esta *incoerência*» (CL, p. 74)— is accompanied by incomprehension and dizziness: «O Universo é *incompreensível* para os homens» (P, p. 116), «uma *vertigem* nos rodopia» (CF, p. 58). Many of these images have dual connotations: we need look no further than the line «Sombra, vertigem, ascensão — Altura!» from the exuberant poem «Partida» (Po, p. 53), and the juxtaposition of *vertigens* with *erros* and *falhas* in «Rodopio» to see this. Similarly, *quebranto* is not necessarily a negative image. What they all have in common is their connection with the same stage of the process of disintegration, with its accompanying abnormality. The victim's reaction is to curse, struggle or flounder. But the result is often madness. The peripheral symptoms are illusions: «Pobre alma humana, criança louca, sempre em busca de *ilusões!*» (P, p. 308), and then comes insanity: a «*loucura* furiosa» (CF, p. 131), «Sou um *louco*... um *louco*... Que me importa?» (P, p. 176). «Enlouqueço. Compreendo. Isto é a *loucura*» (P, p. 169) — there are countless examples. Then, «*Doido! Doido! Doido!* Tenha muita pena de mim» (C II, p. 183) writes Sá-Carneiro in a letter dated April 18, 1916, just over a week before his suicide.

As he himself asked in one of his *Princípio* stories, «Mas afinal o que vem a ser a loucura?» (P, p. 60), and the answer will be a key one as far as he is concerned, since it obsessed him. Here is another example of the tragic incompatibility between two attitudes towards the same thing: on the one hand, the desire for it, the enjoyment of it and even pride in the awareness of its existence, and on the other, horror and fear of its implications. This time it is a question of the distance between the artist and his fellow man. There is a vast gulf between the real-life cry of «Doido; Tenha muita pena de mim» and the exaltation and exultation of «Loucura... loucura... A Perfeição» (CF, p. 193); the stages that lead up to insanity can be both thrilling and horrifying, at times simultaneously: the verb *dilacerar* is sometimes used with *ternura, amor* and *triunfo* as its subject, and with *fustigar,* we may find *ternura* and *orgulho.* Yet even in these cases, the protagonist/*persona* is a *victim,* there is oppression and repression and he is not in control; he is conscious of persecution and unreality. Colin Wilson has said that «what can be said to characterize the Outsider is a sense of strangeness, or unreality»,[19] and he qualifies this:

> ... what he sees is essentially *chaos.* For the bourgeois, the world is fundamentally an orderly place, with a disturbing element of the irrational, the terrifying, which his preoccupation with the present usually permits him to ignore. For the Outsider, the world is not rational, not orderly.[20]

Later he points out that «the Outsider's sense of unreality *cuts off his freedom at the root*».[21] Life is a constant battle, with traps, pitfalls and barriers, and it is all the more intolerable for those who are aware that it is not the real thing: «The Outsider», says Wilson, «has glimpsed a higher form of reality than he has so far known. Subsequently he loses that glimpse and has to accept a second-best».[22] But those who cannot have no option but to accept something which may well be a great deal worse: the torture of madness. Before recognising the real nature of insanity because of the intensity of their suffering, it can seem attractive, a *vitória,* as Sá-Carneiro called it, a withdrawal from reality into the euphoria of the moments when they feel «curiously immortal, god-like,

[19] WILSON, p. 13.
[20] WILSON, p. 13.
[21] WILSON, p. 40.
[22] WILSON, p. 43.

as if hovering above the world, untouched by its dullness.[23] Even struggling and floundering can be exciting, and in Sá-Carneiro, both verbs are used in areas that contain promise for those who are characterised by a «non-acceptance of life».[24] But as was the case with fear, it is the conventional, terrible side of madness which dominates: «the old, familiar aesthetic experience; art giving order and logic to chaos» [25] has not worked. This final stage is certainly a question of degree: it is the *extent* of the victim's alienation which decides when he could be declared insane. Many artists are aware of a gulf between themselves and their more prosaic neighbours without becoming insane; many people withdraw from life to a greater or lesser degree; many are aware of and concerned about supernatural forces and alternative realities. As in the question of Sá-Carneiro's homosexuality, all that one can do is to list the evidence: it proves, at the very least, that the author was preoccupied by insanity, if not that he himself was (as he thought) a victim of it. And there is a great deal of evidence.

i) *Loucura* and its associated terms are used with a frequency that the few examples we have given do not reveal. Many Sá-Carneiro characters are thought mad, look forward to madness, fear madness or, of course, are explicitly said to *be* mad.

ii) The emphasis on disintegration highlights a symptom often found in schizoids tending towards psychosis. R. D. Laing, in *The Divided Self*, refers to this both in its undeveloped and its advanced stages.[26] Gaspar Simões sums up this aspect of Sá-Carneiro: «dispersão total, fraccionamento das sensações, rodopio das imagens que de si mesmo retém, vertigem ao encarar-se interiormente. Sá-Carneiro é apenas — um caos».[27] (Wilson's Outsider *saw* chaos; Gaspar Simões sees this Outsider as chaos itself.)

iii) Frequent references to the violence with which the protagonist/*persona*/author himself is surrounded (wardrobes that strangle, whirlwinds that wound, breezes that thrash, light that invades, etc.) remind us of what Laing calls implosion: «the full terror of the experience of the world as liable at any moment to crash in and obliterate all identity»,[28] a «persecutory, impinging aspect» [29] of it.

iv) The sense of unreality, both within the narratives and poems and also in real life, is significant. The very creation of a world of the imagination may itself be regarded as the result of what Gaspar Simões called

---

[23] WILSON, pp. 313-14.
[24] WILSON, p. 16.
[25] WILSON, p. 23.
[26] R. D. LAING, *The Divided Self* (Harmondsworth, 1972), pp. 89 and 162. (First edition: 1960.)
[27] GASPAR SIMÕES, «A Ilusão», p. 128.
[28] LAING, p. 45.
[29] LAING, p. 46.

x) There are, too, references in Sá-Carneiro to turning into things which are not human: «Serei uma nação? Ter-me-ia volvido um país? O certo é que sinto praças dentro de mim. É isso! Volvi-me nação... ... Grandes estradas desertas... arvoredo... rios... torres... pontes... muitas pontes...» (CF, pp. 211-12), for example, or «Sou hierarquias em Bizâncio...» (CF, p. 88), or «sou naufrágios embandeirados a negro» (CF, p. 107), or «Sou funerais em Memphis...» (CF, p. 123), or «A sua alma de hoje era toda vidros partidos e sucata leprosa» (CF, p. 127), etc., etc. Psychiatrists call this depersonalization, and it would appear to be closely linked to the tendency described by William Blake to become what one perceives.[42]

xi) The frequency of being turned into stone in Sá-Carneiro is also significant. In addition to the conventional use of phrases such as «fiquei *petrificado*» (CF, p. 104, for example), there are frequent references to statues: «regressar, íntimo, ao meu cioso alheamento-*Estátua*» (CF, p. 98), «*esculpe-me* em desconhecido» (CF, p. 110), «*Estátua* Falsa» (Po, p. 66), «A chuva, o vento, o sol — e eu, a *Estátua*» («Escala», Po, p. 117), etc. It is obvious that this image will have many other connotations and we shall discuss it later. Nevertheless, turning other people into stone and being turned into stone are common symptoms of schizoid depersonalization.[43]

xii) The extension of this, as Tillich has pointed out, is non-being: «neurosis is the way of avoiding non-being by avoiding being».[44] Laing calls it «the denial of being, as a means of preserving being».[45] One of his patients once said: «I had to die to keep from dying».[46] This apparent paradox is clear in much of Sá-Carneiro's work: the common death-in-life symptoms and the resignation and inertia of the poem «Caranguejola», for example:

> Noite sempre p'lo meu quarto. As cortinas corridas,
> E eu aninhado a dormir, bem quentinho — que amor!...
> Sim: ficar sempre na cama, nunca mexer, criar bolor —
> P'lo menos era o sossego completo... História! era
> a melhor das vidas...

The poem finishes:

> Nada a fazer, minha rica. O menino dorme. Tudo o
> mais acabou. (Po, pp. 158-9)

This is the first stage of «non-being». The final move is suicide.

[42] Referred to by LAING, p. 198.
[43] LAING, pp. 112-13.
[44] P. TILLICH, *The Courage to Be* (London, 1952), p. 62.
[45] LAING, p. 150.
[46] LAING, p. 176.

Any attempt to judge the extent of Sá-Carneiro's mental abnormality must be doomed to failure and, furthermore, seen as presumptuous if made by a layman many years after his death. Insanity is a relative term, and there is no agreement even among psychiatrists as to its levels or frontiers. Thomas S. Szasz, in *The Myth of Mental Illness,* queries the whole of what he calls «the traditional definition of psychiatry»,[47] and claims that «psychiatric interventions are directed at moral, not medical, problems».[48] This imprecision in definition is the first inhibiting factor in our search for some sort of helpful conclusion. The second is that we are using information taken from literature rather than from life, and the accusation of mixing the two indiscriminately and thereby arriving at the wrong answer has already been levelled at one critic of Sá-Carneiro.[49] Yet an answer springs to mind in the face of these objections: the vast majority of critics have seen the writings of Sá-Carneiro as virtually autobiographical, and his own correspondence and his ultimate suicide confirm that the symptoms and attitudes, neuroses, prejudices and inhibitions of his fictional characters were all felt by him at one time or another. It is therefore admissible to say that Sá-Carneiro was certainly neurotic, probably schizoid and «depersonalized», possibly psychotic and even, conceivably, in the early stages of schizophrenia. To make this kind of deduction from the images and *mots obsédants* of the poetry and prose alone would be foolhardy. But his correspondence and death make all these images acquire a new depth and a new significance.

It should be pointed out that, as Erwin Stengel has stated, «it is reasonable not to accept the suicidal act alone as a criterion of mental disorder, but to assume the presence of such a disorder only if symptoms other than suicidal behaviour can be established».[50] This, surely, is the case with Sá-Carneiro. In addition to the evidence gleaned from the images and metaphors, *mots obsédants* and themes of his writings, we should, perhaps, add that many of the criteria listed by Stengel [51] as indicative of an impending suicidal act can be found in Sá-Carneiro's life and literature. They are:

(1) Depression with guilt feelings, *self-depreciation,* and self-accusations, associated with tension and agitation [«O mago sem condão, o Esfinge Gorda...» («Aqueloutro», Po, p. 167), «Gostava tanto de mexer

---

[47] THOMAS S. SZASZ, *The Myth of Mental Illness* (St. Albans, 1975), p. 17. (First edition: 1961.)

[48] SZASZ, p. 11.

[49] Joel Serrão's assertion that onanism was a key to Sá-Carneiro's real-life character (in «*Perfil de Mário de Sá-Carneiro*», in *Temas de Cultura Portuguesa,* Lisbon, 1960) was not well received by other critics.

[50] ERWIN STENGEL, *Suicide and Attempted Suicide* (Harmondsworth, 1971), pp. 58-9. (First edition: 1964.)

[51] STENGEL, pp. 61-2.

na vida» («Crise Lamentável», Po, p. 160), «Eu não sou eu nem o outro» («7», Po, p. 94), «Cansei dentro de mim, cansei a vida» («Além-Tédio», Po, p. 73), etc., etc.].

(2) Severe hypochondriasis, i.e. a tendency to *continuous complaining*, usually about physical symptoms [«a zoina silva sobre mim despedaçadoramente» (C II, p. 161), «Vivo há semanas num inferno sem nome» (C II, p. 161), «Tudo isto e as minhas desolações conhecidas me torturam, me despedaçam» (C II, p. 165), «a Zoina silva cada vez mais forte» (C II, p. 172), «É como se estivesse bêbado» (C II, p. 173), etc., etc.].

(5) Previous suicidal attempt.

(6) Suicidal preoccupation and talk.

(7) Unsympathetic attitude of the relatives *or life in social isolation*.

(8) Suicides in the family [in the case of Sá-Carneiro, the influence was, rather, that of Tomás Cabreira Júnior, who killed himself at school.

(9) History of a broken home [52] before the age of 15 [Sá-Carneiro's mother died when he was two years old, as we have seen. According to Pessoa, the very character of Sá-Carneiro's work is dictated by this fact. In a letter to João Gaspar Simões he says:

«A obra de Sá-Carneiro é toda ela atravessada por uma íntima desumanidade, ou, melhor, inumanidade: não tem calor humano nem ternura humana, excepto a introvertida. Sabe porquê? Porque ele perdeu a mãe quando tinha dois anos e não conheceu nunca o carinho materno. Verifiquei sempre que os amadrastados da vida são faltos de ternura, sejam artistas, sejam simples homens; seja porque a mãe lhes faltasse por frieza ou afastamento. Há uma diferença: os a quem a mãe faltou por morte (a não ser que sejam secos de índole, como o não era Sá-Carneiro) viram sobre si mesmos a ternura própria, numa substituição de si mesmos à mãe incógnita».[53]

Stengel claims that «the lack of a secure relationship to a parent figure in childhood may have lasting consequences for a person's ability to establish relationships with other people. Such individuals are likely to find themselves socially isolated in adult life, and social isolation is one of the most important factors in the causation of suicidal acts».[54]]

(13) Dreams of catastrophes, *falls,* and self-destruction [...].

(14) Unemployment and *financial difficulties*».[35]

---

[52] According to STENGEL, p. 54, BRUHN has defined a broken home as «one characterized by absence or loss of one or both parents, by death or separation due to marital disharmony for periods of six months or more before the patient reached the age of fifteen years».

[53] FERNANDO PESSOA, *Cartas de Fernando Pessoa a João Gaspar Simões* (Lisbon, 1957), pp. 98-9.

[54] STENGEL, p. 55.

[55] Although of the fourteen characteristics given, only nine can be proved to be relevant to Sá-Carneiro, some, at least, of the other five may well have been. The

Out of fourteen conditions, nine apply to Sá-Carneiro. With hindsight, we can see that he was highly likely to commit suicide as the climax of any crisis; what we can also see is the importance of his preoccupation with mental derangement. *Any* of his problems —sexual, financial, social, artistic— may have been enough, in theory, to inspire him to commit suicide. And yet thousands of people suffer from terrible problems of all kinds without resorting to this solution. As Stengel has pointed out:

> Normally, people do not ask themselves whether their life has a meaning and purpose and then decide to end it if they cannot think of a positive answer. If this was the case of suicide the human species would long be extinct. *Life has its own dynamics which are independent of social and other values.* However, mental states which are associated with suicidal tendencies often lead to questioning and depreciation of values held dear by individuals and society, and consequently to the feeling that life is empty.[56]

His death proved that Sá-Carneiro was in this sort of «mental state»; his writings prove that it was a state of disorder.

PAIN

Dor, tortura, martírio, calvário, suplício, sofrimento and, by extension, *tristeza, amargura, tédio, aborrecimento* and *modorra* crop up all the time, and not entirely unrelated to these key words is the concept of *doença,* with its related terms *náusea, febre* and *delírio.* It would be tedious indeed to give all the examples, but there are literally hundreds of expressions of unrelieved suffering in Sá-Carneiro's work. On the other hand, pain is yet another image that is used, albeit not very frequently, to suggest the moment of contact with the Unknown: «A minha *dor* enclavinhou-se em Mistério» (CF, p. 110), for example, or «Como é que em *dor* genial eu me eternizo?» («Álcool», Po, p. 52). It is certainly worth noting that Sá-Carneiro, who once wrote to Pessoa that «o título muitas vezes pode ter importância» (C I, p. 100), calls his hero Lúcio's best short story *João Tortura* (CL, p. 33).

Those who avoid actual pain are nevertheless often victims of boredom, sadness and *tédio.* There are expressions such as «*tristeza e tédio desolador*» (CF, p. 61), «*desilusão amarga*» (P, p. 287), «tudo me *aborrece*» (CL, p. 47), «profunda *modorra*» (CL, p. 90) and «endureci de *tédio*» («Além-Tédio», Po, p. 74).

others are: (3) Sleeplessness with great concern about it; (4) Fear of losing control, or of hurting others or oneself; (10) Serious physical illness; (11) Alcohol or drug addiction; (12) Being at the end of a depressive illness, when the depressed mood still persists but when initiative is returning.
[56] STENGEL, p. 132.

Sadness and boredom have no connection with exaltation, and the images are of unrelieved gloom. On the other hand, illness, fever, delirium and their related words may be stimulating and interesting, or indicative of areas which are. For example, we find that one of the dancers in *A Confissão de Lúcio* is «uma rapariga frígida, muito branca e macerada, esguia, evocando misticismos, *doença,* nas suas pernas de morte — devastadas» (CL, pp. 39-40), and there are countless references to delirium as the result of sex, literature and modern city life. Fever and delirium can be caused by the excitement of the search for the Ideal too: the sexual ideal, for example, with its «mágicos *delírios*» (CF, p. 330), the ideal of happiness, «em *febre* ideal» (CF, p. 150) and the ideal of personal perfection: «ser o que já fui *no meu delírio*...» («Escala», Po, p. 116). Perhaps the most interesting emphasis on illness as a partially positive image is that which reflects the preoccupations of Decadentism: Lúcio describes the group of friends who meet at the beginning of *A Confissão de Lúcio*: «Que belo grupo! [...] duas feras de amor [...] evocando mordoradamente perfumes esfíngicos, luas amarelas, crepúsculos de roxidão. Beleza, perversidade, vício e *doença*...» (CL, pp. 27-8). Then we have an «ouro pálido, *doentio*» (CL, p. 42), «um além-gosto a *doença*» CL, p. 101), «crepúsculos amarelos, / Mordidos, *doentios* de roxidão» («Álcool», Po, p. 58) and, referring to António Nobre, who was tubercular, «Caprichos de lilás, *febres* esguias» («Anto», Po, p. 110). Sometimes, though, even these images indicate unrelieved suffering. For example: «uma grande *náusea*» (CL, p. 147), a «*doença* terrível» (P(p. 301), «incompreensíveis *náuseas*» (CL, p. 101) and «asco de um *vómito*...» («Aqueloutro», Po, p. 166).

If the artist feels more than his fellows, then he will also suffer more. In theory, it would appear to be churlish to complain, and in practice, *real* complaints are found only when the suffering becomes intolerable. There is even a certain satisfaction in being numbered among the *doentes de beleza,* as the Visconde de Vila-Moura called those with an aesthetic temperament,[57] and Sá-Carneiro is not the first to be conscious of this. Henri de Groux was entirely convinced of the need for suffering as an ingredient of the artistic life:

> Que pourrait-on penser d'un artiste qui n'aimerait pas la douleur, qui serait même incapable de l'aimer pour elle-même? Serait-il autre chose qu'une boussole sans aiguille, une aiguille sans aimant?...
> Le travail d'art est un engagement terrible, une sorte de duel grave et silencieux où l'espirit doit se concentrer dans une discipline impavide.[58]

By extension, illness is considered a special state; as Hubert Juin has said, writing about Georges Rodenbach: «C'est enfin éprouver l'extrême

---

[57] VISCONDE DE VILA-MOURA, *Doentes de Beleza* (1913).
[58] HENRI DE GROUX, *Notes sur l'Art*; quoted by JULLIAN, *Esthètes*, p. 338.

pointe de l'être, dans cet endroit fragile où l'être va céder et disparaître au fil d'une onde noire».[59] And he adds: «Georges Rodenbach vante les vertus de la maladie. [...] La maladie rapproche de la vie véritable, qui est une vie secrète, feutrée, tissée d'incertaines métamorphoses», etc.[60] This attitude sees suffering as inevitable, possibly necessary and perhaps even desirable. It is not a far cry to seeing suffering, pain and illness as actually thrilling, and this, of course, was one of the more bizarre and perverse features of the Decadents. Verlaine wrote *Mes Hôpitaux* in 1891; the hero of Jean Lorrain's *M. de Phocas. Astarté* (1901) is fascinated by tuberculosis, by cemeteries and by hospitals, Octave Mirbeau's *Le Jardin des supplices* (1898-99) has been called «the breviary of morbid exoticism»,[61] there are innumerable descriptions of death agony, especially that of young girls (see, for example, Barrès, *Le Jardin de Bérénice*, 1891) — in fact, «the whole universe is suffering and in pain», as Mario Praz put it, quoting a poem by Ivan Gilkin called «Amour d'Hôpital», which begins: «Ô Reine des Douleurs, qui rayonnes de sang...» [62] Sá-Carneiro shares these attitudes: suffering exists, and indeed it must, if the artist is not to join the ranks of the *lepidópteros;* having accepted and even desired it, there are two possible extensions — a glimpse of the Beyond, with suffering as the means to this end, and new excitement in life. Pain and illness can serve the same purpose as death, insanity and mystery: they can be good elements, they can act as a key to another reality and, too, they reflect a literary and aesthetic legacy from a group of artists in the recent past. But like some of the other images we have already discussed, they can also represent states so frightful as to be intolerable, and this side of the coin is that which ultimately triumphed in Sá-Carneiro's life and, it may be added, in his work, since all victories are won by means of eschewing accepted normality.

Unlike other forms of suffering, tedium and boredom are invariably without advantages. Boredom combines the distaste for the common herd with self-deprecation and impatience and despair with life: the only defence is to withdraw from life entirely. The grounds for the withdrawal are varied, but overlapping: they are made up of the nihilism of the self-confessed Outsider, the sense of aristocratic alienation felt by the artist, the emotional alienation felt by the schizoid, the exasperation of the man disillusioned with himself (largely for sexual reasons) and, perhaps, the emptiness of the *menino bem* with nothing to do. We have already considered the first three attitudes as motives for Sá-Carneiro's *taedium vitae,* for in spite of Andrée Crabbé Rocha's certainty that his introspec-

[59] HUBERT JUIN, *Écrivains de l'Avant-siècle* (Paris, 1972), p. 44.
[60] JUIN, p. 44.
[61] JULLIAN, *Dreamers of Decadence*, p. 134.
[62] PRAZ, pp. 159 and 197-299.

93

«ÊXTASES»

Life may not be made up of ecstatic moments, but the desire for them does seem to be ever present in Sá-Carneiro's characters. These longings are both the bane of their lives and the spice which makes them worth living. The key word, *ânsias,* may be used in the context of almost any circumstances or emotions that heighten the sensibilities, or that arise as the result of heightened sensibilities, It is all a question of excitement of one sort or another. Generally, *ânsias* indicate the first stage of the journey towards ecstasy, and there are few reservations. It is often used sexually: «espasmos de aurora, em êxtases de chama, ruivos de *ânsia*» (CL, p. 26) or «beijos de *ânsia*» (CF, p. 164). At other times, longings are explicitly transcendental: «*Ânsia* revolta de mistério e olor, / Sombra, vertigem, ascensão —. Altura!» («Partida», Po, p. 53) or «Nunca em meus versos poderei cantar, / Como *ansiara,* até ao espasmo e ao Oiro, / Toda essa Beleza inatingível, / Essa beleza pura!» («Apoteose», Po, p. 182). Conversely, the gradual advance of the death-in-life state that we have already referred to is signalled by the disappearance of these longings; first there is an awareness that they are being stifled, then that they are absent, and all is lost: we find «*ânsias* lassas» («Taciturno», Po, p. 102), «Desistamos. A nenhuma parte a minha *ânsia* me levará» («Caranguejola», Po, p. 158), «uma *ânsia* irrisória» (CF, p. 62), «a minha *Ânsia* é um trapézio escangalhado» («16», Po, p. 96), «Rendas da minha *ânsia* todas rotas...» («Pied-de-nez», Po, p. 145), «a *ânsia* abatida» (CF, p. 145) and then, ultimately, in «Aqueloutro»: «O sem nervos nem *ânsia*» (Po, p. 167). The line separating the various *ânsias* is artificial: although the means may vary (sex or art or mystery, for example), the end is the same.

Longings may occasionally be fulfilled, and the climax is seen as a *triunfo,* a *vitória* and the condition, however transitory, comprises *êxtases* and *espasmos;* key verbs are *arfar, fremir, crispar, vibrar* and *oscilar,* with *convulsivo* a frequent adjective. Sex is again an area that provides its victories, but there are other areas of potential triumph: in the story «Mistério», the hero «*triunfara.* Deixara de ser um isolado» (CF, p. 149) when he found a friend. In the poem «Não», we find: «*Vitória! Vitória! /* Mistério é riqueza» (Po, p. 89), while the narrator of «O Fixador de Instantes» refers to his experience as «voos de *triunfo!*» adding, «eis no que reside o meu segredo; é essa a minha arte, a arte perdida que admiràvelmente *venci!*» (CF, pp. 258-9). The goal has not yet been reached in «Partida», but we are aware of it: «Ao *triunfo* maior, avante pois!» (Po, p. 54), while in the «Bailado» section of «Asas», we read: «Olha o carro do *Triunfo,* ascendendo o Capitólio» (CF, p. 202). Triumph is the goal, as the author states explicitly in Princípio: «O *triunfo...* Oh! a quimera de ouro, astro radiante» (P, p. 202), and some actually do achieve it: «*vitó-ria* sem resgate» (CF, p. 86).

Whatever the field of triumph or victory, the imagery used to convey the thrill tends towards the sexual, if only implicitly. *Êxtases,* of course, are not confined to sex, but other terms used by Sá-Carneiro are exclusively physical and largely sexual: *espasmos, vibrar* and *fremir* for example. The moment of ecstasy, then, may actually *be* sexual orgasm or may be represented by its terminology. There are frequent examples of actual sexual climax, sometimes in speculative conversation, such as that of the American woman at the beginning of *A Confissão de Lúcio*:

> a voluptuosidade é uma arte ... *fremir* em *espasmos* de aurora, em *êxtases* de chama, ruivos de ânsia — não será um prazer bem mais arrepiado, bem mais intenso do que o vago calafrio de beleza que nos pode proporcionar uma tela genial, um poema de bronze? (CL, p. 26)

At other times, it is a question of fact not speculation: «*êxtases arfados*» (Cl, p. 101), «*êxtases* e lírios» (CF, p. 147), «um *êxtase* fantástico, de *vibrações* infinitas, sumptuosas» (CF, p. 292), an «*êxtase* dos sentidos» (P, p. 56) and «violentos *êxtases*» (P, p. 319). But this terminology is, in fact, more frequently found in speculative locutions or is used metaphorically. The *homem dos sonhos,* for example, discusses heterosexual lovemaking: «Ah! o mistério fulvo dos seios esmagados, a escorrer em beijos, e as suas pontas loiras que nos roçam a carne em *êxtases* de mármore...» (CF, p. 163). Inácio, in «Ressurreição», «tinha ideado [...] *êxtases* de íris» (CF, p. 285), like the character who «Puro ainda, sabia fantasiar [...] todos os *êxtases*» (P, p. 287). The tense of the verb *fremir* is important in the line from «Como eu não possuo»; «São *êxtases* da cor que eu *fremiria*» (Po, p. 70), and the speculation goes on: «Eu *vibraria* só agonizante / Sobre o seu corpo de *êxtases* doirados» (Po, p. 71). Then the future is mentioned in «O Fixador de Instantes»: «quando a tiver possuído em *êxtases* de cor e ânsias de harmonia» (CF, p. 266), and the narrator imagines an «*espasmo* sem fim» (CF, p. 266); Inácio is sure that one must know how to «*vibrar,* rugir, arder» (CF, p. 280) and later, he suffers from the occasional «saudade de não saber *oscilar* os seus *espasmos*» (CF, p. 296). When ecstasy is brought about by means other than sex, the same terminology is used: «Sou chuva de oiro e sou *espasmo* de luz» says the poet in «Partida» (Po, p. 53); the hero of «Mistério» finds ecstasy in the excitement of a great city: «Subira-lhe ao cérebro, como um álcool de *êxtase,* toda a agitação urbana» (CF, p. 138); a strange light may have the same effect: «sorvíamos essa luz que, num *êxtase* iriado [...] se nos engolfava pelos pulmões» (CL, pp. 37-8). Works of art are another means to the same end; Inácio de Gouveia is, or should be, consoled by his own works, «ah! as suas obras esquivas, roçagando

97

miragens, *extáticas* de ouro, ungidas de Incerto» (CF, p. 277). The Music Hall surroundings in another part of «Ressurreição» are sources of excitement too: Inácio is «*extático* no ambiente que os cercava» (CF, p. 282). Décor, in *A Confissão de Lúcio,* adds to the ecstasy created by perfumes, lights and music, and dancing does so with impressive frequency.

Whereas Sá-Carneiro reveals an ambivalent reaction to *ânsias,* his reaction to ecstasy is clear and consistent. As far as *ânsias* are concerned, there are many pathetic complaints —lives are «torturadas de ânsias»— but like artistic hypersensibility, this «torture» is justified and even welcomed. It is Ricardo, in *A Confissão de Lúcio,* who sums this up, and Sá-Carneiro takes advantage of the opportunity to express his sentiments on the subject of popular art:

> olhe que é lamentável a banalidade dos *outros*... Como a «maioria» se contenta com poucas ânsias, poucos desejos espirituais, pouca alma... Oh! é desolador!... Um drama de Jorge Ohnet, um romance de Bourget, uma ópera de Verdi, unas versos de João de Deus ou um poema de Tomás Ribeiro — chegam bem para encher o seu ideal. Que digo? Isto mesmo são já requintes de almas superiores. As outras —as verdadeiramente normais— ora... ora... deixemo-nos de devaneios, contentam-se com as obscenidades lanteojuladas de qualquer baixo-revisteiro sem gramática... (CL, pp. 60-1, author's italics)

The opposition is explicitly stated: «almas superiores» and «as verdadeiramente normais». To be incapable of feeling is to exist, but to feel is to live. Sá-Carneiro, in a letter to Pessoa dated January 21, 1913, considers the possibility of dedicating a projected book «à gente tranquila» since it comprises «páginas de alucinação e de ânsia» (C I, p. 61); in a later letter (May 14, 1913), he again emphasises the gulf between the artist and the common herd who are indifferent to beauty: «Há que lamentá-los, só», he concludes, «São os anquilosados da chama; incapazes de fremirem em frente do que não está catalogado dentro deles» (C I, p. 131). *Ânsias* are both desirable and, ultimately, intolerable. The difficulty with longing for something is that, by definition, the state is an indication of an end. The *ânsias* themselves will continue to be welcomed only if there is a possibility of reaching the goal, and if the goal, once reached, is found to be worthwhile. Now it is obvious that there *is* always the possibility of reaching the longed-for condition, and the means of success are apparently found in a number of fields, though in the end they are all facets of art. Thus, the presence of desire, however nebulous, is healthy and stimulating, and the author's attitude, though ostensibly ambivalent, at least tends towards the welcoming. But there are problems: disappointment after sexual ecstasy reflects the fact that any search for the Ideal is fated. The strange *homem dos sonhos* «era um homem inteiramente feliz» we are told (CF, p. 157), he will never exhaust the store of desirable things (CF, p. 165). But he *does*: «Já conheço o ideal», he confesses one day, «No fim de contas é menos belo do que imaginava...» (CF, p. 165). The triumph at the end of the story belongs to the narrator: «eu pude entrever o infinito» (CF, p. 168), for the *homem dos sonhos* has gone beyond it. Sá-Carneiro is ever-conscious of this: in a letter to Pessoa (January 21, 1913), he talks about his «projectos literários» (C I, p. 55). He is working out the basic framework for «Asas»: «o título de ASAS, querendo simbolizar a perfeição que se não pode atingir porque, ao atingi-la, evola-se, bate asas» (C I, p. 59), and he considers the possibility of changing the title to «A Perfeição» to make his point clearer. He has already mentioned this idea in an earlier letter (January 7, 1913):

> Acerca das ideias novas, esta nascida ontem à noite: Um artista busca a perfeição — é esta a sua tortura máxima e desfaz e refaz a sua obra. Vence: atinge a perfeição e continua a querer fazer maior: porém, a tela em que trabalha evola-se por fin, dilui-se torna-se espírito — desaparece. *Esse artista ultrapassou a perfeição.* (C I, p. 49, author's italics)

The Ideal, too, may cause revulsion, and the artist may strike so hard that he goes beyond his goal and loses it. The third possibility is that ecstasy is found to be incomplete. The protagonist of «Mistério» finds true love, and his life, which had been «um canal estreito, viscoso e mefítico» becomes «uma torre branca erguida a meio de mar» (CF, p. 149). The images are exclusively positive — «vitória azul», «Auréola! Auréola!» (CF, p. 146), «conquistador iriado da sombra», «dedos ansiosos», «lábios dourados», «a carne velada em rubor, ondeante de rosas», «êxtases e lírios» (CF, p. 147), and so on. But it is not enough: «alguma coisa faltava ainda — uma pequena luz para chegar ao fim: ao além» (CF, p. 147); complete triumph is achieved only with death. Incompleteness may, as in «Mistério», be a question of a missing final stage, or of some doubt, worry or difficulty: in both cases there is something wrong. The fourth and final possibility is that perfection *is* achieved, that it *is* complete and unblemished, but that it is of so transitory a nature as to be almost a form of torment: the hero of «O Fixador de Instantes» hesitates before launching himself into a sexual adventure because he is aware of the inevitability of decline and disillusion.

The solution lies in death, or abnormality, or both. In the same way that his explanations do not really explain anything, we now find that Sá-Carneiro's solutions solve nothing. The only moment of unblemished sexual triumph in his writings is the homosexual experience in «Ressurreição», which is a variation from normality. Victories through art are unsatisfying and the continued striving of the artist brings its own disaster. The final step of the journey must be taken, and, as for the heroes of «A Grande Sombra», «Mistério» and «O Homem dos Sonhos», the «solution» involves death, and only a madman will understand. Finally, the solution to the problem of the ephemeral nature of the perfect instant is to «fix» it by terminating life at the moment of triumph.

The desire for paradise, the thirst for infinity, the need to extend and preserve moments of ecstasy are part of our human and literary heritage, and as M. H. Abrams has pointed out, this attitude is still with us.[72] He quotes Allen Ginsberg: «burning for the ancient heavenly connection»,[73] and sees the Beat Generation as «heirs [...] of the *fin de siècle* writers». Sá-Carneiro is another of their heirs, and at the same time an heir of the Romantics. But these people were not strange creatures, merely sensitive human beings in whom universal desires and needs were, for various reasons, exaggerated and exacerbated. In other words, the question is one of degree, not principle, and the inevitable failure of a transcendental aim is bound to have more tragic effects in some cases than in others: given a certain nervous instability, the prospects are not encouraging if a constant and obsessive desire is continually thwarted and if the only hope of success is thought to lie outside the confines of normal life. Again, the obvious parallel to Sá-Carneiro is Gérard de Nerval,[74] and the characteristic most relevant to Sá-Carneiro's attitude towards ecstasy, perfection, paradise or the Ideal, is Nerval's desire to «fixer le rêve»,[75] «pénétrer encore le mystère dont j'avais levé quelques voiles»[76] (cf. Sá-Carneiro's «são véus rasgados sobre o além», CL, p. 83) and «conquérir et fixer mon idéal».[77] Both writers suffered from a «frustrated desire for transcendence»,[78] and neither could cope with it, since, unlike their more prosaic fellow human beings, their desire was obsessive, and their experiences of earthly ecstasy linked in their minds with their ultimate goal. Nerval «knew that the love that he imagined was not capable of consummation in this world»;[79] Sá-Carneiro discovered that the ecstasy that he had both experienced and imagined could not be maintained. Albert Béguin's judgment of Nerval[80] could equally well be applied to the Portuguese author: «Chaque parole de Nerval oriente l'esprit vers quelque chose qui autrement reste insaisaissable».

[72] ABRAMS, p. 424.
[73] ALLEN GINSBERG, *Howl and Other Poems* (San Francisco, 1956); (p. 182 in *The New American Poetry 1945-1960*, ed. Donald M. Allen, New York, 1960).
[74] See NORMA RINSLER, *Gérard de Nerval* (London, 1973), p. 8: «That he was afraid of love is clear enough in many of his writings.»
[75] *Aurélia*, p. 281.
[76] *Aurélia*, p. 246.
[77] «Sylvie», in *Les Filles du feu*, p. 154.
[78] NORMA RINSLER, introduction to Gérard de Nerval, *Les Chimères* (London, 1973), p. 23.
[79] RINSLER, p. 24.
[80] ALBERT BÉGUIN, *Gérard de Nerval* (Paris, 1945), p. 93.

CHAPTER 4

NATURE

Sá-Carneiro was very much the urban artist and his interest in Nature was minimal: «A vida, a natureza, / Que são para o artista? Coisa alguma» («Partida», Po, p. 52), he claims. Yet he does use natural imagery.

ELEMENTS

It is, perhaps, unsurprising that of the four elements earth should be the least popular with Sá-Carneiro, or that when it is used it is almost invariably a negative image, especially within the heaven/earth opposition with its associated words *lama* and *lodo*. But sometimes it is positive, and it is in these cases that we realise the significant fact that for a natural image like *terra* to be acceptable, it has to be reshaped —made artificial— either by becoming part of a fantastic or an urban landscape. The marvellous panorama imagined by the child in «A Grande Sombra» is one example: «pássaros sem cabeça, coelhos com asas, peixes de juba, borboletas que fossem flores, nascessem da *terra*» (CF, p. 42). Another is the «grande capital» described by the *fixador de instantes,* with its «*solo* ultra-civilizado!» (CF, p. 260), and the «*terra* dos boulevards» (CF, p. 262).

Air is far more frequently found, and it takes several forms: it is, of course, used in opposition to *terra* to convey heaven, the *azul,* the ether, the unreal and the Unknown, and in this context we find words such as *etéreo, aéreo, vaporizar-se, neblina* and *bruma* in addition to *ar* itself. Then it, too, may be artificial. Thirdly, it represents space, the environment. Lastly, it is a refreshing element, like water, and it is welcomed to soothe feverish excitement and heat. In the first category, there is no dearth of examples: «eu dou-me neste fim de tarde / À espira *aérea* que me eleva aos cumes» and «Sei a distância, compreendo o *Ar*» (both in «Partida», Po, p. 53); in *A Confissão de Lúcio* we find «*etéreos* sonhadores de beleza» (CL, p. 62), «pobres catedrais de *neblina*» (CL, p. 113), and that «listas úmidas de sons *se vaporizavam*» (CL, p. 38). In «Rodopio» are the lines: «Há vislumbres de não-ser, / Rangem, de vago, *neblinas*» (Po, p. 77); in the second of the «Sete Canções de Declínio» we find:

101

citação do *fogo*» (CF, p. 330), «carne a *arder* — virgens supliciadas» («Bárbaro», Po, p. 106) and «requintes de *brasa*» (CL, p. 95). But fire frequently reflects other forms of passion, even at times representing life itself. Ricardo's comparison of the «gente média» and the «sonhadores de beleza» in *A Confissão de Lúcio* shows that the latter are the victims of passion: *«lume que nos arde!»* (CL, p. 62, author's italics). Later, Lúcio cannot resist the excitement of Ricardo's explanation or of Ricardo himself: «eu acompanhava-o como que arrastrado por fios de ouro e *lume*» (CL, p. 149). Inácio, in «Ressurreição», is described as «cheio de ânsias maravilhosas na imaginação, bem certo de as poder eternizar a oure e *lume*» (CF, p. 273). In «Distante Melodia», the poet looks back at the «Domínio inexprimível de Ópio e *lume*» (Po, p. 99). After an unforgettable musical experience, Lúcio goes home through a shower of rain: «sentia-me silvado por um turbilhão de garras de ouro e *chama*» (CL, p. 83); later he talks about the mystery of Marta: «esse mistério ia ser [...] a *chama* e o rastro de ouro da minha vida» (CL, p. 91). The attraction of the dance, half sexual, half aesthetic, is emphasised in the «Bailado» section of «Asas» (CF, p. 203): «A *chama* subtiliza-me», while it is literature that provides the thrill in «Ressurreição»: «livro de *brasa* onde lograra enfim estilizar todos os seus estrebuchamentos, os seus requintes» (CF, p. 317). Passion is both mystical and sexual in the projected tale of the sculptor in the same short story: «para iludir a sua *chama,* esse Artista —um escultor— ergueria uma estátua de Cristo» (CF, p. 335), while Inácio is convinced that he will now write one of his greatest works, «uma das suas maiores novelas — das mais convulsas, fustigando *brasas*» (CF, p. 336). He hears that Paulette has died after a period of debauchery and this excites him: «[she] tinha a coragem de *arder*... de se entregar à chama audaciosamente» (CF, p. 348). In «Loucura», fire is equated with life itself: «Sim! fui eu que formei, que dei *fogo*... vida a este corpo!» (P, p. 55), while the simile used by Lúcio when Marta disappears at the death of Ricardo is not as conventional as it seems: «Marta, essa desaparecera», he says, «evolara-se em silêncio, como se extingue uma *chama*...» (CL, p. 154). When the lovers disappear from this world in «Mistério», we have the same image: «[the madman] vira sair por essa janela uma *chama,* uma grande e estranha *chama*» (CF, p. 152). In «O Incesto», Sá-Carneiro refers to a tubercular patient's life as a *«chama* bruxuleante prestes a extinguir-se» (P, p. 300). And it is not just a question of life but of *real* life, the only sort of life worth having; one has to «saber sofrer, saber vibrar, rugir, *arder*» (CF, p. 280), to emulate Paulette in «Ressurreição» who «tivera [...] o génio de *arder* até ao fim» (CF, p. 349). It is the same as being an «arco de oiro e *chama* distendido» («Partida», Po, p. 52) and the poet says: «sou luz harmoniosa / E *chama* genial que tudo ousa» («Escavação», Po, p. 55). It is clear to see that the reason is that fire is an earthly manifestation of the Beyond, «Dormindo *fogo*, incerto, longemente» («Apoteose», Po, p. 97), and therefore, very special people are described in these terms. Gervásio Vila-Nova in *A Confissão de Lúcio* is one of them: «Ao falar-nos, brilhava ainda mais a sua *chama*» (CL, p. 21), while he himself praises another artist by saying: «era todo *chama*» (CL, p. 29). The image may be qualified, perverted or, indeed, absent: for example, Ricardo's sensibility, in *A Confissão de Lúcio,* is manifested in a strange way: *«uma ânsia sexual* de possuir vozes, gestos, sorrisos, aromas e cores!...» «... *Lume* doido! *Lume* doido!» (CL, p. 63). In the poem «Escavação», there are «cinzas, cinzas só, em vez de *fogo*» (Po, p. 55). In «A Grande Sombra», the narrator says: «sonho grandes *incêndios* em ruínas» (CF, p. 113), while in the poem «16», the poet claims that his dreams are «leões de *fogo* e pasmo domados» (Po, p, 95). But it is in «Quase» that we find the most pathetic lines: «Um pouco mais de sol — eu era *brasa* [...] Quase o amor, quase o triunfo e a *chama* [...] Um pouco mais de sol — e fora *brasa*» (Po, pp. 68-9).

The elements are important features of Sá-Carneiro's work since they both represent life and are themselves life-giving. When Prometheus brought fire to the earth, he brought life itself; when the phoenix rises from the ashes it is a manifestation of the renewal of life, with fire the transforming element as it was in alchemy and as it is in modern metallurgy and chemistry; the Egyptians associated it with life and health;[1] by means of its purging powers, Christians believe they can reach eternal life. Water is equally significant: for the Chinese «todo lo viviente procede de las aguas»;[2] the Indians consider it the element on which life itself depends; baptism is a rebirth, a re-creation of life; water is both fertility and birth. As for the air, man was made by God when He «breathed into his nostrils the breath of life»:[3] it is creative factor as well as a vital one. Finally, earth is the symbol of fecundity, the setting for seedtime and harvest, for continuing life. Nevertheless, it appears relatively little in Sá-Carneiro. The reasons are twofold. First, the element is too indissolubly associated with an area with which the author has no *rapport* and in which he shows no interest; the essential and primordial character of the soil is something natural that can hardly be transposed into an artificial setting, and on the odd occasions when it is, the imagery is singularly ineffective and clumsy («A terra dos boulevards», for example). Second, it is a heavy, solid image, by definition terrestrial and physical, and in direct opposition to the spiritual connections of air and the so-called fifth element, the ether. Indeed, it is to point this opposition that it is most frequently used.

[1] CIRLOT, p. 219.
[2] CIRLOT, p. 62.
[3] Genesis, 2, vii.

It was Ortega y Gasset who said that «la verosimilitud estética es la congruencia interna del microcosmos creado por el autor, no la coincidencia del libro con el detalle del mundo que hay fuera»,[4] and in Sá-Carneiro's prose (and even the poetry) this internal verisimilitude based on consistency does exist in spite of exaggeration, excesses and eccentricities. However diverse the images we may investigate, our conclusions fit together and overlap in a convincing manner: the «microcosmos creado por el autor» is one in which everything points in the same direction. With the four elements, we find that there *is* a «coincidencia [...] con el mundo que hay fuera», but the internal consistency is also fascinating. Sá-Carneiro is creating «heaven out of earth», but his heaven is what Arthur Symons, after Baudelaire, has called an «artificial paradise», adding that «every 'artificial paradise' is within one's own soul, somewhere among one's own dreams».[5] Sá-Carneiro has to control natural images, to reshape them as his own dreams would have them. They also become spiritualised, ordered, beautiful and aesthetically pleasing, which is to say they are now art, not nature, *and only in this way are they physically exciting*. We have already seen how this process takes place with sex: it is a re-creation of sex that we find in Sá-Carneiro, not an acceptance of the facts. Nature in general suffers the same manipulation and the elements are a particular aspect of this. The «new heaven» is urban, sexual and artificial, but the images which evoke it are those of life itself, of its creation and renewal.

«A city is no part of nature», wrote Arthur Symons, but it is certainly the «natural» habitat that most pleased Sá-Carneiro: everything is controlled by man, technical progress makes life colourful and comfortable, artistic awareness and talent make it entertaining. At the same time, everything is sexual, even though this sexuality is an artificial substitute for the real thing, since this natural, physical area is, in many ways, revolting. In addition to the many examples of this already referred to, we now discover the image of humidity. All the examples we have already given were explicitly repellent; those we have not mentioned are explicitly sexual — the «espasmos *húmidos*» which is all love amounts to (CF, p. 137), the «carne palpitante e *húmida*» of the dancers (P, pp. 340-1) and the thought of the woman «oferecendo-lhe o sexo, colando-lhe à sua boca, ansioso e *húmido*» (P, p. 333) — and it is impossible not to see this combination as significant. Artificiality has, as we have said, the consoling feature of being under man's control, while nature is free and menacing. The coloured waters of an indoor fountain, for example, are safe and

---

[4] JOSÉ ORTEGA Y GASSET, «*El obispo leproso, novela de Gabriel Miró*», in *Caracteres y circunstancias* (Madrid, 1957), p. 217.
[5] ARTHUR SYMONS, «London: A Book of Aspects», in *Cities and Sea-Coasts and Islands* (1918); first published in a private printing: 1908. See ARTHUR SYMONS, *Selected Writings*, ed. Roger Holdsworth (Cheadle, 1974), p. 90.

beautiful and their movement is within our power to regulate. Most marvellous of all, the excitement is the same as that evinced by great works of art or moments of sexual ecstasy: it constitutes a brief glimpse of the inexplicable. In its essential state, fire is often seen as having dual qualities —the erotic, with physical energy, and solar heat on the one hand, and the mystic, with spiritual, purifying heat on the other,[6]— and it can be an intermediary, joining the world of the flesh to that of the spirit; in the Christian tradition, as Mircea Eliade points out, «Paradise has been rendered inaccessible by the fire that surrounds it»,[7] so that mystical union is possible for those who penetrate and conquer the flames. And for Sá-Carneiro, all this is possible when fire is part of art. Similar observations could be made about air and about water: countless primitive rituals bear witness to the intermediary qualities of these elements, and many myths are based on man's deep-rooted desire to use any feature of his habitat as a symbol in a transcendental search, a symbol which, as Jung has put it, «always stands for something more than its obvious and immediate meaning».[8] Water and air join together the physical and the metaphysical in rituals and myths. It is with the air that the so-called fifth element, the ether, is most closely connected. The elements have often been placed in a hierarchy of their own, and this clearly demonstrates the link they constitute between matter and spirit: Cirlot says:

> La ordenación de los elementos según una jerarquía de importancia o de prioridad ha variado según autores o épocas, influyendo en ello también la inclusión o no inclusión del «quinto elemento», a veces llamado éter, a veces designado abiertamente como espíritu y quintaesencia, en el sentido de alma de las cosas. Se comprende que la ordenación gradual ha de verificarse *desde lo más espiritual a lo más material* (creación es involución o materialización).[9]

In theory, then, the use of the elements, once reshaped to fit an urban, artificial context, should be a happy one: like sex, music, painting, literature, sculpture, architecture, mystery and many other areas of life, they act as a link with the unknowable. But of course, the moments of insight they afford must be ephemeral. More important, they may well be invalidated by the very conditions of their generation. If sexual desire, for example, is brought about by unreal conditions, it may be difficult, if not impossible, to assuage it satisfactorily in a real, physical relation-

---

[6] CIRLOT, p. 220, refers to MARIUS SCHNEIDER, *El origen musical de los animales-símbolos en la mitología y la escultura antiguas* (Barcelona, 1946), who points out this divison.

[7] MIRCEA ELIADE, *Myths, Dreams and Mysteries* (London, 1972), p. 67. (First edition: Paris, 1957.)

[8] JUNG, p. 55.

[9] CIRLOT, p. 191.

ship. If life is envisaged as art, there is little hope of avoiding grave disappointment: the «À tout chercheur d'impossible, la déception est due», that we have already quoted [10] bears repeating here.

In spite of the relevance of all this to Sá-Carneiro in particular, his preoccupation with the area was by no means original and may even be seen as part of fashion. This time it is less to his literary background than to his social and artistic ambiance that we must turn to find his inspiration. His love for Paris and his obvious cosmopolitanism are inextricably tied up with his attitude towards Nature and towards the elements in particular. He was devoted to Paris in an uncritical and child-like way, so much so that Pessoa once wrote:

> Recordo-me de que uma vez, nos tempos de *Orpheu,* disse a Mário de Sá-Carneiro: «V. é europeu e civilizado, salvo em uma coisa, e nessa V. é a primeira vítima da educação portuguesa. V. admira Paris, admira as grandes cidades. Se V. tivesse sido educado no estrangeiro, e sob o influxo de uma grande cultura europeia, como eu, nao daria pelas grandes cicades. Estavam todas dentro de si».[11]

For Sá-Carneiro, salvation lay in the colour and life of great cities and in particular of Paris, an attitude he shares with the French Decadents — Jullian tells us, for example, how Jean Lorrain spent his adolescent years «rêvant de Paris».[12] The artificiality and sophistication was not wishful thinking but fact. Rudorff calls the Paris of the nineties (which was very similar to the Paris that Sá-Carneiro knew, in spite of the War) «the pleasure capital»,[13] and many of its real-life entertainments involved the appropriation of natural elements and their conversion into *décor* and stage effects. We have already referred to the dancer Loie Fuller who used changing colours in lighting so that she became «a flower of flame»[14] as Rudorff put it, or so that she floated «dans une mer de ténèbres» becoming «la flamme elle-même» as Jean Lorrain once said.[15] In 1891, Paul Fort described his forthcoming theatrical productions in the *Écho de Paris*:

> as from the month of March the performance of his Théâtre d'Art would end with the display of the stage of a «painting unknown to the public or in progress by a painter of the new school». The curtains would be raised for three minutes and the display of the work would be accompanied by specially written music and *the release of perfumes* corresponding to the subject of the painting.[16]

---

[10] See above p. 12.
[11] *Páginas da Doutrina Estética* (Lisbon, 1946), p. 138.
[12] *Jean Lorrain,* p. 27.
[13] RUDORFF, title of Chapter II.
[14] RUDORFF, p. 315.
[15] Quoted in JULLIAN, *Jean Lorrain,* pp. 140-1.
[16] See RUDORFF, p. 141.

What Sá-Carneiro does with the elements is no more nor less than what Paris did to Nature in general with the zinc palm-trees of the Élysée-Montmartre garden,[17] the plaster elephant of the Moulin Rouge,[18] the artificial garden in the hall of Montesquiou's apartment,[19] the smart designs based on flora and fauna that were found in fabric, furniture and wall-coverings and the use of pools and fountains in Music Halls, cabarets, hotels and restaurants. By the time Sá-Carneiro arrived there, though much evidence of the so-called *belle époque* remained, there were also many new trends which led away from the natural and simple towards the sophisticated and artificial, towards the elegance of the Art Deco movement which was to flourish later. It is not just the influence of the *fin de siècle* that we find in Sá-Carneiro, however strong that influence may be: his images and metaphors spring from the ambiance in which he lived during the short creative period of his life, an ambiance that was entirely to his taste but which, according to Arthur Symons, takes mankind «further from nature and further from our needs», creating about us «unnatural conditions which are really what develop in us these new, extravagant, really needless needs».[20] Sá-Carneiro deliberately created artificial needs and substituted «unnatural conditions» for the «natural» ones he associated with the majority of other people. It is yet another example of his rôle as Outsider, and Symons understands this attitude:

> The artist, it cannot be too clearly understood, has no more part in society than a monk in domestic life: he cannot be judged by its rules, he can neither be praised nor blamed for his acceptance or rejection of its conventions. Social rules are made by normal people for normal people, and the man of genius is fundamentally abnormal.[21]

The obvious objection to this assessment of his position is to say that he was by no means alone in his love for the sophistication of Paris and his contempt for the natural and earthy, for the provincial or rural. How can his sense of estrangement from his fellow man be compatible with his participation in a general movement of taste which involved many thousands of people? It is Pessoa's judgment of Sá-Carneiro's attitude towards Paris that gives us the clue to the answer: Sá-Carneiro never ceases to be Portuguese, never ceases to see Paris as exotic, and for that reason is able to classify himself as different. He *is* different — from his fellow-countrymen: unlike them, but like his character Inácio, in «Ressurreição», «vangloriava-se de [...] ser duma capital europeia» (CF, p. 298).

---

17 RUDORFF, p. 46.
18 RUDORFF, p. 51.
19 RUDORFF, p. 218.
20 SYMONS, *Selected Writings*, p. 90.
21 ARTHUR SYMONS, *Wanderings* (London-Toronto, 1931), p. 77.

image is used: *abismo*. In «Mistério», though, the gulf is between people (who see each other «de cada margem *do abismo*», CF, p. 136), but since the bridging of this gap is tantamount to achieving a glimpse of the Unknown, the image can be said to be serving the same purpose here as in those examples where it explicitly represents the no-man's land between this and the other world: «Lançara pontes sobre *o abismo* insuperável» says the author when the hero finds love (CF, pp. 146-7). In «O Homem dos Sonhos», *o abismo* is clearly linked with mystery: «não sei o que teria sido do meu pobre cérebro que a asa do mistério roçara, se por fim não conseguisse mergulhar mais fundo o abismo azul» (CF, p. 167). In «Ressurreição», the protagonist feels admiration for *os doidos,* who «tiveram o génio de arder, de dar o grande salto, de mergulhar *o abismo*» (CF, pp. 283-4), while the décor, with colours, lights, perfumes and breezes, in the *Confissão de Lúcio* «orgy», penetrates the souls of the spectators «em febre de longe, em vibração *de abismos*» (CL, p. 41). The fact that Pessoa wrote a poem called «Abismo» reveals that it was a metaphor that interested both Sá-Carneiro and his friend: the key line of the Pessoa poem is: «E súbito encontro Deus» (quoted in C I, pp. 190-191, Appendix). A related image is *precipício*: «eu decidi não fugir mais do *precipício*» says Lúcio, adding, rather clumsily, «entregarme à corrente — deixar-me até onde ela me levasse» (CL, p. 93). In «Mistério», *precipício* is used as *abismo* was — to indicate the gulf between people: «nenhuma destas almas diligenciava sequer aproximar-se da outra que existia além do *precipício*» (CF, p. 136), but in the poem «Manucure», part of the *beleza* in the air is made up of «inflexões de *precipício*» (Po, p. 171), while the frustration of «Quase» is revealed by incomplete or spoiled images, and the poet complains that:

> ... mãos de herói, sem fé, acobardadas,
> Puseram grades sobre os precipícios... (Po, p. 69)

Moments of perception and vision are indicated by *sol, lua, noite, luz, astro* and *nuvem,* together with associated words such as *claridade, estrela, sideral* and *luminoso.* The least complicated of these is, of course, *sol.* The simple, the cheerful, the good and pure may be suggested by this image. It may also be connected with uncomplicated sex, as in «a sua carne esplêndida de *sol*» (CL, p. 39). But both of these areas of allusion are somewhat ordinary, and the beginning of real excitement is when the sun sets, often accompanied by mysterious *nuvens*: for example, the «*Sol*-poente a arder em horizontes de *bruma*» (CF, p. 281) or «Asas perdidas no *Solposto*...» (CF, p. 203). *Noite, penumbra* and *trevas* constitute the next stage: «corpo de esfinge, talvez, em *noites* de *luar*» (CL, p. 20), for example, where the added element of moonlight is seen. Equally significant and frequent is the use of *astro, estrela* and their associated

words: these are links connecting earth and heaven and touching terrestrial objects with the transcendental. They are also very fashionable
words, given the current vogue for the Occult, theosophy and astrology.
For example, there is a «recordação *astral* de certa aventura amorosa»
(CL, p. 68), there are «insinuações *astrais*» (CF, p. 83), «certas manhãs
astrais» (CF, p. 89), an «Emigrado/*Astral*» («O Fantasma», Po, p. 162),
«um desconhecido *astral*» (CF, p. 146), and «meu desdém *Astral*» («Taciturno», Po, p. 102). An apparent paradox is the importance of light to
Sá-Carneiro; there are many examples of the attraction of mysterious
darkness, and yet *luz* and associated words have equal, if not more significance. The answer is that *luz* represents the goal which may be reached
via darkness; it is not the «simple» light of the sun, but a supernatural
light which man should be striving for. In this world, its reflection is
artificial light. We have countless examples of the transcendental source
of light and its influence on our lives: «esse momento *luminoso*» (CL,
p. 17), «Um relâmpago de *luz* ruiva me cegou a alma» (CL, p. 150), «um
país *luminoso*» (CF, p. 146), «alguma coisa faltava ainda — uma pequena
luz» (CF, p. 147), and so on. An ambivalent attitude is evident, and
there is also the possibility of failure. Other examples reveal that the
image can be wholly bad, or that the author's relationship with it is unsatisfactory or painful: Lúcio's suffering, in *A Confissão de Lúcio,* is
represented by a series of images which includes «manchas de *luz* podre»
(CL, p. 92); while praising mystery, the protagonist of «A Grande Sombra» actually complains of «a *luz* sempre sobre mim» (CF, p. 41); later,
his cry is more desperate: «Como hei-de suportar esta *luz* sem fim —
inevitável e obcecante...» (CF, p. 72); in «Além-Tédio», the poet says:
«Cansei dentro de mim, cansei a vida / De tanto a divagar em *luz* irreal»
(Po, p. 73); again, in «A Queda» are «Agonias de *luz* eu vibro ainda
entanto» (Po, p. 79); in the *Confissão* «orgy» there is «essa *luz* de além-
Inferno» (CL, p. 38) and Ricardo, in the same work, complains that «a *luz*
cega os olhos» (CL, p. 62). But electric light represents the absolute
Light. The American woman in *A Confissão de Lúcio* talks about *a luz*
as one of the potentially voluptuous elements of life (CL, p. 26), and
demonstrates her theory later on, but with artificial lights — she refers to
«os arrepios misteriosos *das luzes*» (CL, p. 26), for example — and when
her *soirée* actually takes place, she asks the guests for their opinions,
adding: «*sobretudo o que pensam das luzes*» (CL, p. 35, author's italics).
The *espectáculo* is a combination of «*Luzes,* corpos, aromas, o fogo e a
água» (CL, p. 36), and the narrator asserts that «o mais grandioso, o mais
alucinador, era *a iluminação*» (CL, p. 37), with its «*torrentes luminosas*»
(CL, p. 37). He says that «a maravilha que nos *iluminava* nos não parecia
luz» (CL, p. 37), and «sorvíamos essa *luz*» (CL, p. 37), «essa *luz* mágica» (CL,
p. 38). Light is magic on other occasions too: there are «Guinchos de

luz» (CF, p. 203) in the dance in «Asas» and it is *«Luz* maquilhada»; then we find *«luz* negra» (CF, p. 235), «uma nuvem de *luz»* (CL, p. 94), «vértices de *luz* e sombra» (CF, p. 61) and «uma cintilação *luminosa, relampejante»* (CF, p. 81), which may or may not be artificial, but which are certainly seen in an artificial way. And this artificiality is only one step away from sheer fantasy, the only context in which we find the landscape images of *paisagem, montanhas* and words of that kind.

Sá-Carneiro's principal preoccupation as an artist is the apprehension of the existence of «glory» and, ultimately, its acquisition; therefore he is a kind of *náufrago* —a «náufrago do irreal», like the madman in his story «Mistério»— but for him, to a large extent, it is *this* world that is *o irreal.* He is like o *homem dos sonhos* who «sonhava a vida» and «vivia o sonho» (CF, p. 168).

Moments of awareness have to be expressed by imagery belonging to this world, in the same way that mystics are obliged to use worldly allegory or analogy to communicate their experiences. What is revealing is which areas of conventional imagery he chooses. The dearth of maritime imagery would appear surprising for a Portuguese writer, and the few images he does use are commonplace in the extreme. The explanation is found in the extent to which he «discards» his Portuguese nationality: he sees himself as «European», he adores Paris, and Lisbon has few charms for him; he is a Parisian by adoption and a city-dweller by option; he despises the provincial and feels no *rapport* with Nature. Those who write explicitly about the sea and the problems of those who work and live with it very often have a sociological as well as a literary purpose, and this is the last thing that could be attributed to Sá-Carneiro. Furthermore, his contact with the sea as a child was minimal, so that maritime images would be less likely to come naturally to him.[22] Nevertheless, the image of the aimless, drifting boat, together with that of the safe harbour, however conventional, are important. In the awareness of a lack of destination and the wish to anchor somewhere we see again his alienation. But the rootless, independent existence may well be an attractive one and we can also see that it is a form of escapism. The difficulty is that you cannot have it both ways. At the same time the negative qualities of the sea underline the sense of revulsion with both Nature and man that have already emerged in Sá-Carneiro, and the fate of the «barco de vela que parou / Em súbita baía adormecida» (Po, p. 127) is a warning to the artist who thinks he can compromise: the images in the rest of that passage of the sixth «Canção de Declínio» indicate the end of life as it *should* be («dormente», «miragem», «duvidosa», «tremulante» for example), and the boat «não mais aparelhou». The only appealing possibili-

[22] Cf. RAFAEL ALBERTI, *Marinero en tierra,* for example, in which all his childhood love of the sea emerges.

ty is to sail away on a voyage of discovery, to search for the world as it should be, not as it is — the real world, the artist would say. It is the goal of the fairy story, the magic country, the lost island, the other side of the rainbow; Rupert C. Allen, in *The Symbolic World of Federico García Lorca* [23] has this to say on the subject:

> This is perhaps the single great issue of the fairy-tale quest: how to acquire a treasure which will successfully resolve the problem of life,

and this is certainly a judgment that could be applied to Sá-Carneiro. But when Allen goes on:

> and this treasure may be described as the development of inner potential which allows the hero to establish himself as a sound adult, safely beyond the threat of regressive tendencies,

it is brought home to us that the quest is doomed to be a hopeless one. For Sá-Carneiro, the goal is a paradise in which he would be a passive, hedonistic inhabitant; there is little question of «inner potential» and his life reveals that he in fact never became «a sound adult». Immaturity is evident in his writings, and Joel Serrão sees his major problem as the determination to «regressar a um passado próximo», rather than accept the passage of time; [24] the same critic points out that:

> os personagens de Mário de Sá-Carneiro são, neste primeiro livro [*Princípio*] (e o mesmo ocorrerá nos subsequentes!) *artistas* e *adolescentes*.[25]

The successful quest ends with the hero living happily ever after, but:

> The passage through adolescence is successful only if the youngster's own inner forces are mobilized and integrated into a viable adult personality. If this can be accomplished, then his chances are very good for meeting and dealing with the accidents and crises of everyday living which await him as an adult — and it is in this sense that we can speak of living «happily ever after».[26]

As a psychiatric patient of R. D. Laing's said when he felt himself to be normal once again, «You have to live in this world *with* other people. If you don't something dies inside»; [27] for Sá-Carneiro, all the «accidents and crises of everyday living» centre around his inability to accept this world and to accept other people, to establish with it and with them a working relationship. In the end, something *has* died inside him and it may well be that the solution of suicide was, as we are told that it so

[23] RUPERT C. ALLEN, *The Symbolic World of Federico García Lorca* (Albuquerque, 1972), p. 62.
[24] SERRÃO, p. 129.
[25] SERRÃO, p. 128, author's italics.
[26] ALLEN, p. 62.
[27] LAING, p. 133.

often is,[28] that of dying in order not to die. The hero of «Mistério» considers the possibility: his soul is a large dusty house in winter, and it belongs to the past (CF, p. 12), he is the victim of «um torpor constante, um sono invencível» (CF, p. 129), he wants to rest (CF, p. 130), he is stagnant (CF, p. 131) and he is aimless (CF, p. 132). He considers suicide to escape from this death in life. In fact, in this case he restrains himself for he is not yet entirely devoid of hope: «Ainda se, ao menos, o não suicidar-se lhe evitasse a morte...» (CF, p. 133). In real life there was, it seems, none; at least there was none in this world and the voyage of discovery could only be what Cirlot has referred to as «volver al mar», that is «retornar a la madre» — death.[29]

The landscape imagery that underlines the gulf between heaven and earth is that which links the two areas — again by no means an original choice: either we are concerned with stars and moonlight and light in general, for example, or, where more prosaic features of the landscape are concerned such as fields, hills and mountains, with a fantasy world. The truth is twofold: the artist cannot stay here, but the journey will involve fearful dangers. There has to be an abyss, a precipice: the search must be a struggle, and will involve suffering. The key conditions are darkness, night, clouds and mist. In the same way as «a única coisa interessante que existe actualmente na vida, é a morte» (P, p. 174) and the only thing worth knowing is the unknowable, the only thing worth seeing is darkness. «Eu via as trevas», boasts the *homem dos sonhos,* «Que triunfo! Que triunfo!» (CF, p. 161). Only moonlight is acceptable until the real light is reached: it belongs to the mystical night, is unreal, misleading, variable and maleficent but, for the artist, influential and real. Like the stars, it is touched by the supernatural — apprehensible but inaccessible, associated with death and reincarnation, with woman and with deception.

The awareness of glory must be followed by its acquisition, and again we find that the means are thought to be the conversion of life into art. The most striking example is artificial light. But this is no more successful than the structured, ordered sex which has so little to do with the real thing.

Sá-Carneiro's choice of imagery here is very largely a sign that he is part of literary and social fashion. Many of his images are part of the

---

[28] LAING, p. 150, refers to this attitude as «the denial of being, as a means of preserving being» and later (p. 176) quotes a patient who says: «I had to die to keep from dying.» STENGEL writes about the school of thought which maintains that suicide is a «paradoxical self-assertion through which man achieves a phantasy immortality» (p. 53). This, of course, is going a little further and regarding the act as partly positive rather than as entirely evasive, but it does seem to have some bearing on the attitude in question.

[29] CIRLOT, p. 310.

116

legacy of the Symbolists, while many are more specifically those of Decadentism. In the poetry of his Portuguese predecessors such as Nobre,
Guerra Junqueiro, Cesário Verde, José Duro, Camilo Pessanha, Teixeira
de Pascoaes, Eugénio de Castro and Gomes Leal, and in *Nefelibatismo*,
we find a very large number of them. Even titles confirm this: *As Clari-
dades do Sul* of Gomes Leal (1875), *Interlúnio* and *Saudades do Céu* of
Eugénio de Castro (1894 and 1897), *Vida Etérea* and *Senhora da Noite*
of Teixeira de Pascoaes (1906 and 1909) are instances of the images from
this particular chapter. A cursory glance at the poetry itself will produce
«Este anseio que tens das *Ilhas Impossíveis*» (Leal, «O Anticristo»), «*A
onda do luar...*» (Pessanha, «Roteiro da Vida»), «Sou fraga da montanha,
névoa astral» (Pascoaes, «Sempre»), «de cada *estrelinha* um raio de ouro
desce» (Castro, «Saudades do Céu»), «Sobre o verde jardim caem *penum-
bras* lentas» (Castro, «Oaristos»), «Quero subir em *fumo* e, à *luz do sol,* pai-
rar...» (Pascoaes, «Elegias»), «Lendária *ilha* afastada» (Leal, «Misticismo»),
and it goes without saying that there are countless more examples. It
is through these poets that the new French poetry reached Portugal, but
in addition to these direct links, this kind of imagery was in the air,
influential and unavoidable, especially in Paris. The abyss, for example,
constituted an image frequently found amongst artists of all kinds, and
Towards the Abyss, by Henri Martin, was one of the paintings exhibited
in the Grand Palais in the 1900 Paris Exhibition (another —significantly—
was Beauversi's *Evening penetrating the Mist*).[30] Other paintings of the
period were *The Clouds* by Pinky Marcius-Simmons, an American painter
who exhibited at the *Salon des Rose + Croix*,[31] Giacometti's *Night,* Clai-
rin's *The Great Wave,* Kandinsky's *Night,* Rimmer's *Evening: Fall of
Day,* Hughes' *Night with her Train of Stars,* Payne's *The Enchanted Sea,*[32]
Bower Davies's *Full-orbed Moon,* Böcklin's *Calm Sea,* Mikalojus Čiurlio-
nis's *Sonata of the Stars,* Hodler's *The Night,*[33] and there were many
more paintings that contain the motifs in question even though they may
not appear in the titles. For example, the current preoccupation with the
Chimera led to a great deal of emphasis on the sky, flying, clouds and so
forth,[34] while the interest in mysticism, the Beyond and ascension led
to a plethora of paintings with a similar background to those of the

[30] See PHILIPPE JULLIAN, *The Triumph of Art Nouveau. Paris Exhibition 1900,*
trans. Stephen Hardman (London, 1974), pp. 122-3.
[31] Reproduced in JULLIAN, *Dreamers of Decadence,* p. 240.
[32] JULLIAN, *Dreamers of Decadence,* pp. 178, 176, 125, 180, 90 and 58, respectively.
[33] Reproduced in LUCIE-SMITH, *Symbolist Art,* pp. 145, 152, 158 and 160
respectively.
[34] See ROCHEGROSSE, *Déesse et Chimère;* SÉON, *Le Désespoir de la Chimère;*
POINT, *La Chimère* (in this painting the Chimera, or «siren» as Lucie-Smith
translates it, is riding over the waves of the sea on a horse); MOREAU, *La Chimère,* etc., etc.

Chimera paintings.[35] From the point of view of what might be termed social fashion, Sá-Carneiro's delight in the modern and artificial reveals his awareness of the style and trends which had been part of Paris for several decades. His concern with electric light and the effects that can be achieved with it shows that he shared the excitement of those about him when confronted with this new phenomenon, though it was as far back as 1889 that Paris first acquired the name of «Ville Lumière».[36] The 1889 Exhibition was the first one to be, as Jullian has put it, «transformed into a kind of fairyland magic» [37] because of electricity; he quotes Charles Simond, writing in *Paris sous la IIIème République*: «If the organizers had succeeded in spreading the magic of life over its vast surface [that of the Exhibition ground], this was because a new force, electricity, had given them the assistance of a mysterious power»,[38] and in his book *The Triumph of Art Nouveau. Paris Exhibition 1900,* he entitles one chapter «The Fairy Electricity». There was, of course, a *Palais de l'Électricité* in the 1900 Exhibition in which «the apotheosis of the new source of power was given a theatrical fairyland setting».[39] The Hachette Guide, quoted by Jullian, describes the coloured lights at the *Palais de l'Électricité:*

> At night the whole façade is illuminated with the changing lights of its 5,000 multicoloured incandescent lamps, its eight monumental lamps of coloured glass, the lanterns of its sparkling pinnacles and its phosphorescent ramps. At the top the Spirit of Electricity, driving a chariot drawn by hippogryphs, projects showers of multicoloured flames. At night the openwork frieze forms a luminous embroidery of changing colours.[40]

Jean Lorrain is more lyrical, and is obviously thrilled by the combination of water and coloured lights:

> ... in a sparkling of stained glass, under its multicoloured pediment [that of the Water Tower], can be seen the jets and cascades of liquid sapphires and rubies, then topazes and sards. [...] Oh, the magic of the night, the many-sided and changing night! [41]

It is interesting that Jullian comments on the attitude of the people, who thought that «humanity was finally entering upon the age of light; everything seemed possible and happiness was within reach of all».[42]

---

[35] For example, RODON's *L'Oeil comme un Ballon bizarre se dirige vers l'Infini*; DELVILLE's *L'Amour des âmes*; WAGNER's *Le Rêve*; PUVIS DE CHAVANNES' *Le Rêve* and *Le Bois sacré*; GAUGUIN's *Figure de Spectre*; SCHWABE's *L'Idéal.*
[36] See JULLIAN, *The Triumph of Art Nouveau,* p. 10.
[37] JULLIAN, *The Triumph of Art Nouveau,* p. 16.
[38] JULLIAN, *The Triumph of Art Nouveau,* p. 16.
[39] JULLIAN, p. 73.
[40] JULLIAN, p. 82.
[41] Quoted by JULLIAN, *The Triumph of Art Nouveau,* p. 87.
[42] JULLIAN, *The Triumph of Art Nouveau,* p. 94.

Electric power, as Jullian has said, was known in Paris as the *fée électri-cité*;[43] it was magic, and the whole of life was, it seemed, undergoing some kind of metamorphosis. It was Péguy who, in 1913, said «the world has changed less since Jesus Christ than it has in the last thirty years»,[44] and in the pre-First World War years of this century, life in the French capital has been described by one critic as a «paroxysm of activity».[45] This critic —Roger Shattuck— maintains that these «Banquet Years», as he calls them, lived life to the full, and he talks about sumptuous parties and exotic homes such as the famous «Pink Palace» of Boni de Castellane and his wife, the American heiress, Anna Gould.[46] There was a mixture of what remained of the *belle époque* with the *avant-garde*, and all of this was new and thrilling for a young Portuguese for whom Paris evoked «um grande salão *iluminado a jorros* — perfumes esguios, luas zebradas, cores intensas, rodopiantes...», while Lisbon was no more than «*luz de petróleo,* tons secos, cheiro de alfazema...» (CF, p. 281). And if the stimula-tion he felt in Paris should, because it was felt by so many others, seem incompatible with his sense of being different, it must again be borne in mind that Sá-Carneiro was Portuguese, not French. The degree to which he discards his original nationality is one of the keys to understanding him. As far as the imagery of landscape and seascape are concerned, in their natural state they mean nothing to him. Nature is life but Paris is art. As Gustave Moreau said:

> What does Nature matter in itself? For the artist it is only an oppor-tunity to express himself... Art is the strenuous attempt to express inner feeling in plastic form.[47]

FLOWERS, ANIMALS

With his lack of interest in Nature *qua* Nature, Sá-Carneiro's flower and plant images are almost entirely conventional: they are either clichés such as *folhas secas, folhas mortas* and the verb *embrenhar-se,* or con-ventional motifs of *fin de siècle* art, such as *lírios, orquídeas, amaranto, girassóis* and *violetas,* with the adjective *marchetado,* or they are conven-tional Romantic images, such as *rosas, camélias* and *acanto.* The only examples of a slightly more individual approach are found in artificial or sexual contexts.

[43] RUDORFF, p. 35.
[44] Used by ROGER SHATTUCK as an epigraph to Part One of *The Banquet Years. The Origins of the Avant-Garde in France: 1885 to World War I,* revised edition (London, 1969). (First edition: 1955.)
[45] SHATTUCK, p. 353.
[46] SHATTUCK, Chapter 12, pp. 353-60.
[47] Quoted by JULLIAN, *Dreamers of Decadence,* p. 257. (From Moreau's unpub-lished notes.)

Revealing further the extent of the author's affinity with the aesthetic world of the turn of the century are the floral elements of painting and literature that find their way into his writings. The most common of these was the lily, so beloved of the Aesthetic movement — the *lírio (branco)*. Other flowers that were popular with the Aesthetes and the Decadents are found too, but it must be added that there is not a great deal of evidence of floral imagery of any sort.

Sá-Carneiro's Romantic heritage is visible in the two girls who are said to have «pele de *rosas* e leite» (CL, p. 22), in the «ternura de *camélias*» (CF, p. 89), flesh that is «ondeante de *rosas*» (CF, p. 147), and a «companheira das *rosas*» (CF, p. 150). «Lembram *rosas* as valsas», we are told in «A Grande Sombra» (CF, p. 102), and in the same story, «as *rosas* eram encantamentos» (CF, p. 45). In «Loucura», Raul says: «Morreríamos românticamente [...] rodeados de *flores* [...] de *rosas*... de muitas *rosas*» (P, p. 81). An interest in mediaeval imagery is revealed in the choice of the heraldic or decorative flower emblems acanthus and lily: «Sou laberinto, sou licorne e *acanto*» says the poet in «Partida» (Po, p. 53), «incerta de *lis*» is found in «A Grande Sombra» (CF, p. 92) and there are «*flores de lis*» in «Nossa Senhora de Paris» (Po, p. 85).

Animal imagery is partly sexual, partly decorative, and very often both at the same time. *Leonino* and *tigrado/trigrino* are favourite adjectives, and these also combine the decorative and sexual; for example: «as suas tranças *leoninas*» (P, p. 292), «*possuíra* enfim exclusivamente [...] sideralmente, a *leonino*...» (CF, p. 352, author's italics), «que ânsia *leonina*» (CF, p. 48); «*Leonina,* ela arremessa a carne arroxeada» («Certa Voz na Noite Ruivante...», Po, p. 92), and «essa noite tigrada» (CF, p. 87). When the use of these images is not specifically sexual, they deal with the excitement brought about by those experiences interchangeable with sex. More specifically decorative are: «Mordiam-se-lhe nos braços *serpentes* de esmeraldas» (CL, p. 35), «Enroscam-se-lhe ao tronco as *serpentes* doiradas» («Bárbaro», Po, p. 107) and the «*cisnes* de brasa» of «Bailado» (CF, p. 201). Even the fantasy animals found from time to time have a certain decorative quality, suggesting the illustrations for children's stories, with bold colours and glittering surfaces: there are good examples in the marvellous *mundo bizarro* in «A Grande Sombra», «*borboletas* que fossem flores», «uma grande *formiga* multicolor», «*coelhos* com asas», «*pássaros* sem cabeça», «*ratos* dourados com asas de prata», «*peixes* de juba», «toda uma *fauna de animais* estrambóticos» (CF, p. 42). They are all interesting and admirable, and only man is ridiculous.

Flowers and animals in Sá-Carneiro reveal both his interest in fashion (and this includes decoration as well as literature, painting and music) and something of his psychology. Even the clichés, so fossilized as to have become divorced from their original semantic field, are significant. Sá-

Carneiro was interested in two things: art and himself, and this is visible in his choice of natural imagery. In his use of conventional natural images, we are made aware of the trends of the previous forty or fifty years or so, particularly in France, trends that formed part of the artistic atmosphere. No artist could help being aware of them, even if he had not actually read, or even heard of all the writers, and even if he had seen none of the paintings in question. Who could fail to be influenced by the eternal but currently popular image of dead leaves, for example?

> Et je m'en vais
> Au vent mauvais
> Qui m'emporte
> Deçà, delà,
> Pareil à la
> *Feuille morte.*

said Paul Verlaine in a famous poem; [48] Maurice Maeterlinck wrote about «Les *feuilles mortes* de leurs fièvres»; [49] in another poem, he said: «J'attends pour voir leurs *feuilles mortes* / Reverdir un peu dans mes yeux», [50] and it was the same poet who wrote about «*les feuilles effeuillées*». [51] It is no accident that so much art of all kinds centred on the autumn (the Verlaine poem is, of course, called «Chanson d'Automne»), and from Baudelaire onwards we find a plethora of poems with titles such as «Chant d'Automne» (Baudelaire), or «L'Hiver qui vient» (Jules Laforgue), or simply «L'Automne» (Vielé-Griffin), or whose neutral titles disguise the fact that the poetry treats of autumn (e.g. Baudelaire's «Causerie», which begins: «Vous êtes un beau ciel d'automne, clair et rose!»). By the time the century reached its end, the preference had almost become a cult: Jullian [52] tells us about «that autumnal atmosphere» in which «summer was bound to seem vulgar and spring ingenuous. The Decadents' favourite season», he adds, «was the season of faded glory», and it is clear that this taste for nostalgia and pleasure in decline is closely connected to the taste for suffering. In Chinese symbology, the falling leaf denotes lost happiness, [53] and the Symbolists and the Decadents had no interest in, and indeed no possibility of happiness. Splendour may be far away or it may belong to the past; Sá-Carneiro's *marchetações* are reflections of the preoccupation with decline and decomposition found right through the poetry and the art in general of the Symbolist period — the «lèvres *fa-*

---

[48] PAUL VERLAINE, «Chanson d'Automne», in *Poèmes Saturniens* (1866).
[49] MAURICE MAETERLINCK, «Tentations», in *Serres Chaudes* (1889). (In *Poésies Complètes*, Brussels, 1965, pp. 91-126.)
[50] «Âme de Serre», *ibid.*
[51] «Fauves Las», *ibid.*
[52] *Dreamers of Decadence*, p. 116.
[53] See CIRLOT, p. 252.

121

nées», «lys *jaunis*» and «lys *fanés*» of Maeterlinck, for example,[54] the «Don Juan *se fanait*» of Remy de Gourmont,[55] and the prevailing sadness, pessimism and morbidity of «Quand la vie est passée» of Maurice Magre,[56] and in Portugal, «meu *cair-das-folhas, em Abril!*» and «*Murchou* na jarra de oiro o púdico jasmim», both from António Nobre.[57] It would be difficult, too, to avoid the «contamination» of the lily motif, surely one of the most popular artistic emblems of all time. It was Oscar Wilde who made it fashionable in England, though it had already been used as a symbol of purity in the work of Dante Gabriel Rossetti, and it is interesting that to justify his choice of the lily and the sunflower as symbols of the Aesthetic Movement, Wilde claimed that they were «the two most perfect models of design, the most naturally adapted for decorative art — the gaudy *leonine* beauty of the one and the precious loveliness of the other, giving to the artist the most entire and perfect joy».[58] Referring to Ellen Terry, he wrote on another occasion:

> She stands with eyes marred by the mists of pain
> Like some wan *lily* overdrenched with rain,[59]

and, too, the flower «found contemporary appropriateness as a mark of homage to the beautiful Mrs Langtry, the Jersey Lily, who was then the admiration of London».[60] Lionel Johnson was responsible for a poem with a refrain which ran: «Lily, O Lily of the valley! / Lily, o Lily of the Calvary Hill»,[61] in which the symbol obviously retains its properties of purity and virginity, and the goddess of the Symbolist «mystics» was Isis, holding a lily in her hand.[62] The lily was a popular Christian symbol with French artists even before becoming entangled in the world of «Nature peopled with shadows»[63] which was the world of the Decadents. For example, lilies are plentiful in the paintings of Puvis de Chavannes and the Rosicrucians. (That is not, of course, to deny that these artists were Symbolists and —in the case of the Rosicrucians— Decadents too, but the flower was used first as a *Christian* symbol.) Once the image took hold with the writers of the *fin de siècle,* it was used with a frequency that is almost ludicrous: in the poetry of Maeterlinck (one of the worst offenders),

---

[54] «Désirs d'Hiver», in *Serres Chaudes*; «Oraison», *ibid*; «Visions», *ibid.*
[55] REMY DE GOURMONT, «Le Secret de Don Juan», in *Histoires Magiques* (Paris, n. d.), p. 47.
[56] In *La Chanson des hommes* (1898).
[57] ANTÓNIO NOBRE, «Ao Canto do Lume» (1890-1891) and «Menino e Moço» (1885), in *Só* (Oporto, 1944), pp. 99 and 121.
[58] Quoted by SPENCER, p. 98.
[59] Quoted by JULLIAN, *Oscar Wilde*, p. 68.
[60] WILLIAM GAUNT, *The Aesthetic Adventure* (Harmondsworth, 1957), p. 129. (First edition: 1945.)
[61] Quoted by JULLIAN, *Dreamers of Decadence*, p. 242.
[62] JULLIAN, *Dreamers of Decadence*, p. 19.
[63] JULLIAN, *Dreamers of Decadence*, p. 119.

even a cursory glance produces: «Des oiseaux de nuit sur des *lys*», «Les *lys* jaunis des lendemains», «Des *lys* au fond des eaux lointains», «Au milieu des *lys* que j'attouche», «Semez des *lys* le long des fièvres», «des *lys* dans un vestibule de marbre!», «Ses *lys* de glace», «ses *lys* à jamais épars», «dont les *lys* n'éclosent pas», «Les *lys* contre les verres clos» and, of course, the «*lys* fanés» already referred to.[64] Not surprisingly, artists themselves began to make fun of the excessive use of the image — Rimbaud in a letter to Banville, for example, and Octave Mirbeau in his critique of the Rosicrucians, entitled «Lilies! Lilies!»[65] Both of these, in fact, were scornful in their attitude *before* the lily reached its peak of popularity, but their contempt did nothing to impede its use in painting, literature and décor. The fact that Sá-Carneiro, almost twenty years later, can still use the image seriously is proof of this. Other Portuguese poets went on using it well into the twentieth century — «Entre as rosas, os *lírios* e os perfumes» and «Alto, divino *lírio*» (Teixeira de Pascoaes, «Regresso ao Paraíso», 1912), for example — and so indeed did the French, despite the superior attitude of many of their fellow countrymen: Vielé-Griffin's «D'un baiser de *lys* sur la bouche» from *La Partenza* dates from 1906, and there are many more examples. And despite the indisputable fact that, as S. Tschudi Madsen has pointed out, «the decline of Art Nouveau was swift. The popularity enjoyed by the style in Paris in 1900 evaporated within two years»,[66] there was still a great deal of evidence of it for many years later, especially in fabrics and —obviously— in the lasting architecture and décor that had been created when the style was at the peak of its popularity. (In any case, those who discarded it and looked to new areas of inspiration during the first decade of the century were leading designers in France, Belgium, Austria, England and Germany, not young artists from Portugal who were discovering it for the first time.) For Sá-Carneiro, its floral forms, together with the motifs of an earlier generation of poets —Rostand's «Les Nénuphars» (1890), «Les Violettes» by Jacques Normand (1878), «Le Miracle des roses» by Vielé-Griffin (1906); the «nénuphars blêmes» of Verlaine's «Promenade sentimentale» (1866), Stuart Merrill's «lassitude des lilas», from «Fête au Parc» (1887-1897), his «crépuscule de roses», from «Fastes» (1891), Maeterlinck's «Nénuphars mornes des plaisirs», from «Feuillage du coeur», his «bulles des songes lilas», from «Oraison», his «roses des attentes mortes», from «Âme chaude», his «roses de joie écloses sous leurs pas», from «Lassitude» (all dating from 1889), among many others— are still the height of

---

[64] «Serre Chaude», «Oraison», «Offrande Obscure», «Âme Chaude», «Oraison» («Mon âme a peur»), «Hôpital», «Aquarium», *ibid*, «Attente», «Âme de Serre», «Visions», all from *Serres Chaudes*.

[65] See JULLIAN, *Dreamers of Decadence*, pp. 173 and 83.

[66] S. TSCHUDI MADSEN, *Art Nouveau*, trans. R. I. Christopherson (London, 1967), p. 232.

fashion, though he does add his personal touch to them as well as revealing the influence of fellow countrymen such as Eugénio de Castro, Camilo Pessanha and Teixeira de Pascoaes. In addition to this area of influence is that of the mediaeval aspect of Art Nouveau. Sá-Carneiro's fascination for the motifs of the Middle Ages is something that will be dealt with in more detail later: in this context, the heraldic lily motif is an image that is both fantastic and connected to a distant Golden Age. This escapism into what is both past and marvellous is also revealed in his choice of animal images, which recalls the frequent use of lions, serpents, swans and dragonflies in poets such as Maeterlinck and Rameau, as well as reflecting the fascination shown by the painters and writers of the *fin de siècle* for Celtic folklore, fairy stories and the Nordic sagas.

Sá-Carneiro's flower and animal imagery is also significant as a guide to his psychology. In spite of his lack of originality, the fact that he chooses to prolong a style —or even a principle, for this is what it was according to Oscar Wilde— which is already moribund, if not dead, for so many of his contemporaries shows us how relevant it was for him personally. The quest for beauty was one with which he felt himself in sympathy; escapism was necessary, sadness and suffering (for even the most hardened clichés indicate these states) are unavoidable and even enjoyable; impotence (also clearly revealed by means of fossilized terms such as *embrenhar-se* and by the desire to change Nature and control the world) is part of his condition; sex and other stimuli are desired and feared simultaneously; decoration and order and style are all-important, but Nature *qua* Nature is not; art is sublime. All this applies to Symbolism and all of it applies to Sá-Carneiro too, though this is by no means all there is to him. In the end, whatever area of his work we investigate, Sá-Carneiro's tragedy is the result of the combination of incompatible attitudes, incompatible desires and incompatible styles. In spite of all the evidence, he is *not* a Decadent and he is *not* a Symbolist: indeed, life might have been marginally easier for him had he fitted neatly into one of these categories.

PART TWO

"ARTIFICIAL" IMAGES

Fuller; in this context the typical adornments are quite different, they are the gauzy veils and translucent, floating panels more commonly associated with the image of a sweet young virgin. In the first category —that of the *femme fatale*— we find the American woman in *A Confissão de Lúcio*: at her party, she greets the guests in «uma túnica de um tecido muito singular [...] Era como que uma estreita malha de fios metálicos — mas dos metais mais diversos [...] *Todas as cores enlouqueciam na sua túnica*» (CL, p. 35, author's italics). Furthermore, «por entre as malhas do tecido [...] divisava-se a pele nua: e o bico de um seio despontava nume agudeza áurea» (CL, p. 35). The combination of brilliant colours and a glittering surface with nakedness is echoed later in the same party: in the description of the three dancers, we are told that «blusas *vermelhas* lhes encerravam os troncos, *deixando-lhes os seios livres,* oscilantes» (CL, p. 39). In «A Grande Sombra», the fantasy princess falls into the same category, with *«o brilho roçagante* do seu traje» (CF, p. 47), and Vitorino, in «Ressurreição», is prey to a form of fantastic desire where the «raparigas dos teatros» are concerned: he wants to possess «os seus vestidos multicolores» (CF, p. 330). The American woman's second costume in the *Confissão* «orgy» is strikingly coloured too: «Envolvia-a uma túnica *branca,* listada de *amarelo*» (CL, p. 41), while later in the story, Lúcio describes the «linha escultural das pernas que uns sapatos muito abertos mostravam *quási nuas,* revestidas por *meias de fios metálicos,* entrecruzados em largos lozangos *por onde a carne surgia...*» (CL, p. 93). Then even the tension and excitement on his first sexual experience with Marta do not prevent him from mentioning the «*tecido ruivo* do quimono de seda» (CL, p. 95). The «estranho disfarce» worn by the *princesa velada* of «A Grande Sombra» is described in detail: it is «o costume, por certo, dos pagens dalgum país distante e azul de conto de fadas». The author goes on:

> Encerrava-lhe o tronco um corpete de brocado de ouro, por onde assomava em perniciosa audácia o bico petulante dum seio moreno.
> Cingia-lhe as pernas quase nuas, um «maillot» violeta, imponderável.
> Um gorro de setim escarlate sobre os cabelos torrenciais, com uma pluma desconhecida, de ave mágica — ofuscante e multicolor.
> À cintura, um cinto negro de coiro lavrado, misterioso, donde, na sua bainha, pendia um estreito punhal.
> Um «loup» de seda verde a ocultar-lhe o rosto... (CF, p. 76),

and it is not long before «ao ageitar o corpete áureo, fizera surgir mais livremente a ponta maquilhada do outro seio» (CF, p. 77). These costumes are nothing if not strange: in *A Confissão de Lúcio,* the American woman «Calçava umas estranhas sandálias, nos pés nus... *nos pés nus de unhas douradas...*» (CL, p. 28, author's italics) and her guests were «estranhas mulheres quási nuas nos seus trajos audaciosos de baile» (CL,

p. 36). Part of the colour and exoticism is created by make-up: the dancer's fingers in «Ressurreição» are «esguios, *maquilhados, perturbantes*» (CF, p. 288); the imaginary victims of Vitorino's sadistic fantasies in the same story have «carnes *maquilhadas*» (CF, p. 330); Marta, in *A Confissão*, «dava a trincar o seu sexo *maquilado*, o seu ventre obsceno de *tatuagens roxas*...» (CL, p. 95); the American woman's dance reaches its climax when she covers herself with her veils, «deixando apenas nu o sexo *áureo*» (CL, p. 42), while the other dancers reveal at the waist «um cinto de carne nua *onde se desenhavam flores simbólicas*» (CL, p. 39). Make-up is so exciting, in fact, that we even find expressions such as «um ambiente propício, *maquilhado*» (CF, p. 298), «Luz *maquilhada*...» (CF, p. 203) and «Meus sentidos *maquilados*» («Sete Canções de Declínio», II, Po, p. 121). The world of the dance serves as a link between the traditionally innocent dress of the Romantic heroine and that of the «prostituta de carne à mostra, de seios pintados» (P, p. 327). And the link is shown clearly by the juxtaposition of *véus* and *lantejoulas* (CF, p. 291) or *laços* and *lantejoulas* (CF, p. 330), since both veils and bows are conventionally romantic, even if veils have also been associated with erotic dancing since the time of Salome. The dancing of the period made the most of the mysterious and provocative nature of translucent materials, and we find that «Ténues *gases* rasgadas lhes pendiam das cinturas» (CL, p. 39) in the case of the three dancers in *A Confissão de Lúcio*, that the *mulher fulva* «de novo tomou *os véus* e se ocultou» (CL, p. 42) after having danced naked and that the seductive woman in «O Fixador de Instantes» had gyrated and «Espasmo a espasmo, em insídia, os *véus* tinham soçobrado» (CF, p. 265). Further evidence of theatricality in dress is the frequency with which Sá-Carneiro uses the mask image: «Ah! os bailes de *máscaras* maravilhosas... Um baile de *máscaras* do Império, na grande Ópera...» says the narrator of «A Grande Sombra» (CF, p. 75). And he adds, significantly, «se eu estivesse lá — seriam minhas amantes todas as mulheres que me rodeassem: *porque todas viriam de máscara!*» (last phrase italicised in text). Later, the mysterious woman he has met at the masked ball takes him to her house, undresses and «Ficou toda nua. No rosto sempre a *máscara* verde...» (CF, p. 81); when he kills her, after making love to her, he lacerates her face with her own jewelled dagger «para ninguém mais a poder ver» (CF, p. 84). In the poetry, we find the image again, but this time it would appear to suggest that the thrill of mystery has become a false façade: «Eu fui alguém que se enganou / E achou mais belo ter errado. / Mantenho a trono *mascarado* / Aonde me sagrei Pierrot» («Elegia», Po, p. 114) for example, or «O dúbio *mascarado*, o mentiroso / Afinal, que passou na vida incógnito; / O Rei-lua postiço, o falso atónito; / Bem no fundo o covarde rigoroso...» («Aqueloutro», Po, p. 166). One other area of fascination in Paris was the sheer luxury of the appearance of some of the women about him, and we find references to «princesas de unhas lustrosas, vermelhas — oiro, véus, rendas, plumas, zibelinas» in the Place Vendôme and the Rue de la Paix (CF, p. 280), and «uma mulher sumptuosa de zibelinas e rendas...» (CF, p. 57), while Inácio, in «Ressurreição», feels scorn for Lisbon because «na Lisboa medíocre não circulavan mulheres luxuosas na audácia semi-nua dos últimos figurinos» (CF, p. 283). Nearly all Sá-Carneiro's detailed sartorial descriptions are of women; certainly all the colour and sheen and brilliance are found in feminine clothing. But he does refer to men too, and in this field we find the paradox that Ione de Andrade has pointed out, that of the sombre nature of the attire of men who are nevertheless dandies.[2] Gervásio Vila-Nova, in *A Confissão de Lúcio,* is a good example: he has long hair, is ascetic looking and «trajava sempre de preto, fatos largos, onde havia o seu quê de sacerdotal — nota mais frientemente dado pelo colarinho direito, baixo, fechado». His headgear consists of «um *bonet* de fazenda — esquisito, era certo», and on seeing him in the street, it was impossible not to say: «ali deve ir *alguém*» (all CL, p. 20, author's italics). This debonair and interesting kind of appearance is what Ricardo de Loureiro longs for; he knows he has a «corpo dobrado, [um] rosto contorcido», but wants to be «belo, esplêndidamente belo» with a «chapéu petulante» and «na testa, uma madeixa juvenil» (CF, p. 65). Professor Antena, too, must be conscious of the effect he makes with his unusual dress: «o sobretudo negro, eterno de verão e de inverno, na incoerência do feltro enorme de artista; e os cabelos longos e a lavallière de seda, num laço exagerado» (CF, p. 225), but despite its eccentricity, it is again sombre. On the other hand, the «inquietante viscondezinho» of *A Confissão de Lúcio* is slightly more colourful, «louro, diáfano, maquilado» (CL, p. 24), and the narrator's strange friend in «A Grande Sombra» is more noticeable too with his «mãos esguias, maquilhadas», his «longa cabeleira» and the «grande rosa vermelha» in his buttonhole, though there is no mention of his attire as being anything other than dark in colour (CF, p. 69).

Jewels provide additional colour and glamour, as does everything that glitters and shines. A few examples are: «gomos de *cristal*» (CL, p. 38), «aquela garganta *adiamantina*» (CL, p. 76), «beijos de *esmeraldas*» (CL, p. 38), «obscenidades *lantejouladas*» (CL, p. 61), «compassos de pontas de *ágata*» (CL, p. 67), a «minuto a *safiras*» (CF, p. 87), an «obra a *Diamantes*-mármore» (CF, p. 85), «sensações de *filigranas*» (CF, p. 89), «*incrustações* exóticas» (CF, p. 64), «*madrepérolas e jades*» (CF, p. 64), «ondas de neblina e *jaspe*» (CF, p. 82), «*pedrarias* e estrelas» (CF, p. 74), «as *gemas* esquecidas» (CF, p. 81), «um colar de *safiras*» (CF, p. 263), «cetins e *esmeraldas*» (CF, p. 280), «seios de *jaspe*» (CF, p. 330), «as mulheres

[2] ANDRADE, p. 342.

esplêndidas [...] cobertas de *jóias*» (P, p. 287), «*anéis de jade*» (Apoteose», Po, p. 176), and «Há Oiro marchetado em mim, *a pedras raras*» («Taciturno», Po, p. 101). At times there is a sparkling and gleaming in somewhat unexpected places: «palácios *rutilantes*» (P, p. 225), and «Pontes de *brilho*» («Distante Melodia», Po, p. 99). Lustre is used as a characteristic feature of anything that is beyond our immediate understanding, of the things and experiences that suggest the Unknown, and of those people who are touched by its charisma: «A vida não se pode tactear: é *brilho* só» (CF, p. 258), «Uma linda mulher *brilha*» («Cinco Horas», Po, p. 134), «auréola de *cintilações* fantásticas» (P, p. 292), «ecos circulares, *rútilos*, farfalhantes» («Apoteose», Po, p. 176), «versos *coruscantes*» (P, p. 215), «o aroma *rutilante* da hora que fugia» (CF, p. 263) and so on. Most frequent of all are the references to those special people who have in them —particularly in their eyes— some undefinable brilliance: for example, «Os olhos [...] *fulguram-lhe em brilhos*» (CF, p. 94), «os seus passos divergem noutros *brilhos*» (CF, p. 103) and «foi-me impossível sustentar o *brilho* dos seus olhos» (P, p. 159). Sá-Carneiro takes great pleasure in actual materials too — sometimes lustrous, almost always beautiful and expensive: «um corpete de *brocado de ouro*» (CF, p. 76), «rua da Paz *dos cetins*» (CF, p. 280), «uma blusa negra *de crepe da China*» (CL, p. 93), «um gorro *de setim* escarlate» (CF, p. 76), the «*crepe da China* verde da blusa de Leonor» (P, p. 326), «a minha voz ressoa coada por *damascos* e *pelúcias*» (CF, p. 87), «estiraçada sobre um leito *de rendas*» (CL, p. 66), «sob cortinas *de damasco* púrpura» (CF, p. 120), «*as sedas, as peles, as rendas*» (CF, p. 268), «oiro, véus, *rendas, plumas, zibelinas*» (CF, p. 280). «Harém *de gaze*, e as odaliscas *seda*» («Escala», Po, p. 118), «*veludos* quentes» (CF, p. 48), «Ó êxtases *de Arminho!*» (CF, p. 122), «um manto *de peles* riquíssimas» (CF, p. 78) and many more. Ivory and marble are two other favourite materials: we find «ameias *a marfim*» (CF, p. 40), «tronos de *marfim*» (CF, p. 84), «ecos de *marfim*» (CF, p. 89), «êxtases de *mármore*» (CF, p. 163), «*mármores* arraiados» (CF, p. 87), «degraus de *mármore* rosa» (CL, p. 34) and «corpos de *mármore*» (CL, p. 66) among other things. Closely connected to these materials are their qualities: if Sá-Carneiro's favourite characteristic is lustre, his interest in the transparent comes a close second, and the adjectives *transparente, diáfano, hialino* and even *translúcido* are used in many different contexts.

All this confirms the impressions already gained from the study of natural imagery: it reveals a need for fantasy, an obsessive interest in mystery and an awareness of fashion.

The element of fantasy is evident in the costumes of the *femmes fatales*. However permissive Paris had been, or was, there is an obvious discrepancy between Sá-Carneiro's bare-breasted Salomes and real life.

His figures are made up from paintings (especially those of Moreau and his imitators), the Music Halls, the theatres, and from his own sexual fantasies, and constitute a mild form of pornography. At times this is not only fantastic, but incongruous. Ione de Andrade points out one example:[3] Marta's stockings («meias de fios metálicos, entrecruzados em largos lozangos por onde a carne surgia») which are infinitely more suitable for a Music Hall dancer than a respectable married woman. What all the *femmes fatales* have in common is that they are unreal. It is probably true to say that the most characteristic quality of pornography is exaggeration; exaggerated make-up and dress represent drama, and the more excessive they are, the further away we move from the ordinary world. Make-up is a «form of illusion», according to Arthur Symons, who admired the new kind of exciting savour it gives to a charming face. It has, too, he maintains, «a certain sense of dangerous wickedness, the delight of forbidden fruit. The very phrase, painted women, has come to have an association of sin, and to have put paint on her cheeks [...] gives to a woman a kind of symbolic corruption». How apt this is for Sá-Carneiro's women, who paint a great deal more than their cheeks. Arthur Symons is talking about theatrical performances, in fact, and he goes on to say that the painted woman «seems to typify the sorceries, and the entanglements of what is most deliberately enticing in her sex: Femina dulce malum, pariter favus atque venenum — with all that is most subtle, *least like nature,* in her power to charm».[4] Sá-Carneiro's women are characters in theatrical performances too, whether this is stated explicitly or not: they are what he would like them to be. And his fantasy life in aristocratic and opulent society means that their clothes, jewels and settings must be sumptuous in the extreme: if there is no limit to voluptuosity, there need be none to glamour and luxury either. Since the author is creating figures whose connections with real life are tenuous, then they might just as well be blessed with what he considers to be all the virtues. With women of this sort he does not share life but escape from it. Another area of escape is the fantasy world of the mediaeval setting, the fairy story, the Roman palace — any exotic ambiance, in fact, where a prince may live and be attended by seductive dancers.

The need for fantasy and an interest in mystery often overlap. In this particular context, the fascination with veils and transparency —which on their own may serve to conjure up the transcendental— is linked to the interest in shadow, clouds and mist: there is something visible, and something hidden. With provocative dancers, the glimpses are exciting, and the existence of beauty is not open to doubt, even if it may prove inaccessible. The mysterious qualities of what can be only partly seen are

[3] ANDRADE, p. 348.
[4] SYMONS, *Selected Writings,* p. 92.

found, too, when beautiful women wear masks: the element of the unknown is not only present but stimulating and obvious. And lustre is a
conventional image of the transcendental, found in the shining angel, the
glittering star, the flash of inspiration or revelation. Cirlot says that «en
sí, el brillo tiene siempre algo de sobrenatural, es como un mensaje des-
tacado nítidamente sobre un fondo negativo o neutro. El brillo se rela-
ciona naturalmente con el fuego y la luz en su aspecto benéfico o des-
tructor»,[5] so that it causes us no surprise to discover that it is one of
Sá-Carneiro's favourite images. Even the painting of the female body is
connected to some higher beauty, since it invariably involves «os bicos
dos seios e o sexo [...] *dourados*» (CL, p. 42), a «boca [...] *dourada*»
(CF, p. 261; «Dispersão», Po, p. 63), «seios *doirados*» (CF, p. 203), «o
sexo *áureo*» (CL, p. 42) or «unhas *douradas*» (CL, p. 28).

The images of costume, jewellery and materials in general paint a clear
literary and social picture. The use of veils in dancing was particularly
fashionable because of Loie Fuller's almost unbelievable popularity, and
there were countless reproductions of the rhythm of her dancing and the
swirling of her celebrated veil. Martin Battersby says:

> Painters and poets alike fell under the spell of the dancer Loie Fuller after
> her début in 1893, and endeavoured to portray the movement and colour
> of her performances on canvas and in verse; sculptors, too, were fascinated
> by the shapes made by her fluttering draperies in which the figure of the
> dancer was half seen or completely disappeared.

He goes on to mention in particular the sculptors Raoul Larche and
Pierre Roche.[6] In the 1900 Exhibition, she even had her own theatre, and
above the entrance stood a statue of her «with its mass of floating draperies».[7] There was a great sale of Louie Fuller statuettes which could be
used as lamps, and «her fluttering veils inspired the glass tulips enclosing
the electric bulbs [of the Exhibition] and also the precious ornaments of
Lalique».[8] But of course, her dancing inspired other dancers, not just
artists and craftsmen, and free expression with floating draperies and
veils became common, with interpreters as famous as Isadora Duncan.
Sá-Carneiro's interest in masks reflects his artistic background as well
as his psychological make-up. Philippe Jullian has pointed out the frequency with which we find masks in the writings of the Decadents,[9]
citing Vielé-Griffin, Henri de Régnier, Marcel Schwob, Jean Lorrain and
Aubrey Beardsley. Many painters used this motif too, including Félicien
Rops, Carrière, Klinger, Odilon Redon and, of course, Ensor. Jullian

---

[5] CIRLOT, p. 111.
[6] MARTIN BATTERSBY, *Art Nouveau* (Feltham, 1969), p. 15.
[7] JULLIAN, *The Triumph of Art Nouveau*, p. 88.
[8] JULLIAN, *The Triumph of Art Nouveau*, p. 90.
[9] *Dreamers of Decadence*, pp. 126-8.

ficative. Mais de quoi? [...] Le dandysme est la face visible d'une condition humaine revendiquée et vécue comme condition esthétique.» And this condition is that of the artist-hero, one inherited from the Romantics: «Les romantiques», says Juin, «se voulaient *héros*». He quotes Albert-Marie Schmidt [18] who has affirmed that «Le Symbolisme est avant tout 'littérature'», and who explained the behaviour of its adherents by saying that «les Symbolistes mettent leur orgueil à respecter les règles d'une éthique du parfait littérateur, qu'ils précisent continuellement», deducing that dressing with an affected elegance was one of the rules for those who wanted to write. This would appear to be the case for so many of the literary and real-life dandies of the period, though it is not just a question of «comment on devient écrivain», as Juin has said in a paraphrase of Péladan himself,[19] but «comment on devient artiste». This theory may, then, be incompatible with Balzac's assumption that

> en se faisant dandy, un homme devient un meuble de boudoir, un mannequin extrêmement ingénieux qui peut se poser sur un cheval ou sur un canapé, qui mord ou tète habilement le bout de sa canne, mais un être pensant... jamais! [20]

(which any case we may take with a pinch of salt, since Balzac was something of a dandy himself), for the Symbolist artists certainly considered themselves *êtres pensants*. If we accept, then, that someone wishes to be an artist, and that the very condition of the artist is something quite different from that of ordinary men, it becomes reasonable and obvious that he will want to dress differently. Émilien Carassus, in his *Le Mythe du dandy*,[21] says that «Le dandy, lui, pense que la différence se prouve, se montre et se crée en se montrant», and he adds, «Le dandy [...] veut arriver».[22] Despite this latter assertion, he is sure that snobbery is not the automatic ingredient of dandies: «le dandy», he says, «cherche à paraître *autre*, le snob à paraître *parmi*».[23] Yet there *is* a kind of snobbery involved, even though it may not be that of wishing to be a member of the highest social stratum. And in a way, the snobbery of the would-be artist of the Symbolist period is even more egocentric and reprehensible, since he is bent on becoming a member of what he considers to be an élite on a cosmic rather than a social scale. Another reflection of fashion in the context is Sá-Carneiro's emphasis on make-up. If men were dandies, women were obliged to go to even greater lengths to be colourful and

---

[18] ALBERT-MARIE SCHMIDT, *La Littérature symboliste* (Paris, 1942).
[19] JUIN, pp. 17-18. The Sâr Péladan called volume one of his *Amphithéâtre des Sciences mortes* (1891), *Comment on devient mage*.
[20] HONORÉ DE BALZAC, «Traité de la vie élegante», in *La Mode,* Paris, October-November, 1830.
[21] ÉMILIEN CARASSUS, *Le Mythe du dandy* (Paris, 1971), p. 46.
[22] CARASSUS, p. 47.
[23] CARASSUS, p. 53, author's italics.

striking, and the use of make-up was less and less confined to theatres and Music Halls. Nevertheless, it was to be a long time before «respectable» women used obvious make-up freely and without self-consciousness, and the interest in paint and powder among the *fin de siècle* writers is yet again to do with unreality. Aubrey Beardsley, in *Under the Hill* (1904),[24] describes how Venus's «three favourite girls [...] waited immediately upon her with perfume and powder in delicate flacons and frail cassolettes, and held in porcelain jars the ravishing paints [...] for those cheeks and lips», setting his unreality in mythology. John Henry Gray's poem «The Barber» (1896), seems to have Byzantine paintings as its source:

> It was my task
> To gild their hair, carefully, strand by strand;
> To paint their eyebrows with a timid hand;
> To draw a bodkin, from a vase of kohl,
> Through the closed lashes; pencils from a bowl
> Of sepia to paint them underneath;
>
> [...]
>
> and the waist
> I touched; and pigments reverently placed
> Upon their thighs in sapient spots and stains,[25]

and the excitement of make-up is such that the poet, who has dreamed that he is a barber, «laughed and wept», so maddened was he. With make-up we find the glorification of sexuality. Women become more feminine, more animal and, paradoxically, less real in this way. They become works of art.

The mask motif is important. Jean Lorrain is said to have loved masks because his appearance disgusted him,[26] and there is certainly evidence of this attitude in Sá-Carneiro too. But there is more to it than that. To preserve the anonymity of a mistress by never seeing her face, going to the extent of actually killing her without removing the mask, and lacerating her features, suggests the need for relationships with anonymous women. If the woman is a prostitute, it is as though she were nobody; if she is masked, the same purpose is served and there is no danger of humiliation, while at the same time, the woman becomes more seductive in a theatrical way. She reflects the sophistication of modern life and the beauty of art. Furthermore, masks —like veils— reveal only part of what exists, and create an aura of mystery. If the mask is removed, the mystery —which is one of the few things worth having in this world— is destroyed.

---

[24] AUBREY BEARDSLEY, *Under the Hill* (privately printed by Leonard Smithers, 1904). Reproduced in *Writing of the 'Nineties*, pp. 59-66. Quotation: p. 63.
[25] Quoted in *Writing of the 'Nineties*, p. 156.
[26] JULLIAN, *Jean Lorrain*, p. 190.

Sá-Carneiro's delight in clean, shiny, brightly-coloured things, and his accompanying squeamishness and fastidiousness (the insistence on taking great care of his hands in real life, for example)[27] again mark the distance he regards as necessary between nature and art, between the flesh and beauty. Finally, his interest in dandies is of great significance too, and for several reasons. First, as we have already mentioned, the admiration with which they are described is indicative of a certain sexual ambivalence, which is echoed by the fact that they are relatively sombre in appearance, despite their eccentricity. This allows the feminine element to attract more attention. Furthermore, the rejection of too much flamboyance may suggest the acceptance of some sort of compromise — the basic compromise between one extreme and the other which his life was forced to reflect. And it is yet another area in which we see that Sá-Carneiro and his friends were very much the country cousins. For them, fashions which had long since lost favour with those who were really what Sá-Carneiro called «European» were *le dernier cri*. Even Jean Lorrain has an air of superiority, and of amusement, when describing Paris society, its dress and its habits, «toute la comédie coutumière de cette ménagerie de luxe»,[28] for example, and he was writing in the heyday of the Decadent movement and has himself been called «the young colossus of the decadence».[29] Raymond Rudorff sums up attitudes in Paris:

> The fashions of the *fin de siècle* did not survive the decade in which they reached their climax. Ridicule and reactions against influences from abroad helped to kill them. The public's image of the *avant-garde* crusader as an effete young man with a craze for lilies and mauve colours, who swooned before esoteric paintings, who was homosexual if not impotent, and who could appreciate nothing unless it was abnormal and *outré*, was hard to destroy and often seemed confirmed by reality. Cultural dandyism and snobbery was fiercely satirised in humorous magazines and in novels, as well as in jingoistic newspapers, which urged their readers, in a time of acute nationalism, to sweep away such unhealthy, foreign-inspired pseudo-art and return to what was French and sane.[30]

But for those who had only recently arrived in the French capital from Lisbon, this was not pseudo-art but Art, and even as late as the second decade of this century they took it all as seriously as if it had just been thought of. Indeed, for them it had.

---

[27] ROGÉRIO PEREZ, in his article «Biografia esquecida — Mário de Sá-Carneiro — O poeta na rua e na intimidade», in the *Diário de Lisboa,* October, 13, 1938, comments that «seu grande orgulho foram sempre as mãos que fazia tratar em 'manicures', então raras em Lisboa». He says, too, that when he first knew Sá-Carneiro, in 1905, «era Mário de Sá-Carneiro um menino que vestia muito bem, como aliás sempre vestiu».
[28] M. *de Phocas. Astarté*, p. 181.
[29] JULLIAN, *Oscar Wilde*, p. 101.
[30] RUDORFF, pp. 230-1.

COLOURS, SOUNDS, SCENTS

Sá-Carneiro resembles the Romantic dramatists in his concern with the creation of atmosphere. In the same way that the Romantics sacrificed verisimilitude and equilibrium for the sake of the emotional stimulus provided by the tricks of their trade, so Sá-Carneiro emphasises those facets of his writings that will create an emotional reaction in the reader. Colours, sounds and scents are all-important in this process, for in their appreciation we are invited to share the narrator's sensory experiences, whether pleasant or unpleasant.

It is probably true to say that colour is the most important of the factors that contribute towards the setting of a scene and by extension, the setting of an emotion. Sá-Carneiro uses colour in three ways: in straightforward descriptions of objects or people, in an allusive metaphorical way, and in actual metaphors. The simple descriptions —«enormes olhos *azuis*» (P, p. 11), «Um quarto de hospital, higiénico, todo *branco*, moderno e tranquilo» («Caranguejola», Po, p. 159), «um grande automóvel *cinzento*» (CF, p. 119), for example— are not without significance, but slightly more unconventionally, there are many phrases where colour is used to describe a state, attitude or emotion or sometimes, as in Baudelaire's *Correspondances,* «les parfums, les couleurs, et les sons se répondent»,[31] and there is synaesthesia. An exhaustive list would be excessively long, but some examples are: «ascetismo *amarelo*» (CL, p. 19), «a ânsia *flava* do Mistério» (CF, p. 68), «*áureos* sonhos» (CL, p. 53), «medo raiado de *azul*» (CL, p. 101); «apoteose *branca*» (CL, p. 99), «*cinzentas* realidades» (CL, p. 53), «amores *cor-de-rosa*» (P, p. 319), «arrepios *violeta*» (CF, p. 79), «um despeito *lilá*» (CF, p. 319), «êxtases *doirados*» («Como eu não possuo», Po, p. 71), «misticismo *escarlate*» (CL, p. 42), «enlevo *granate*» (CF, p. 286), «a idéia *rubra*» (CL, p. 138), «a vitória *fulva*» («Escavação», Po, p. 55), «ternura *loura*» (CL, p. 62), «insinuações *magentas*» (CF, p. 79), «essa ideia *negra*» (CF, p. 282), «abstenções *roxas*» (CL, p. 19), «sortilégio *roxo*» (CF, p. 98), «*ruivo* sortilégio» (CL, p. 38), and «*ruivos* amplexos» (CF, p. 285). Synaesthesia, or something approaching it, is found in: «sons perdidos de *azul*» (CF, p. 89), «num retinir *cendrado*» (CF, p. 89), «O beijo [...] tivera a mesma *cor*» (CL, p. 109), «Sinto as *cores*» (CF, p. 220), «A *cor* já não é *cor* — é som e aroma!» («Partida», Po, p. 54), «vertigens de *cor*» (CF, p. 188), «O aroma endoideceu, upou-se em *cor*» («Salomé», Po, p. 86), «Em sons *cor de amaranto,* às noites de incerteza» («Certa Voz na Noite Ruivante...», Po, p. 92), «os meus sentidos eram *cores*» («Distante Melodia», Po, p. 98) and «Sinto as *cores* noutras direcções» (CF, p. 220). Again, a full list would be endless. Actual

---

[31] *Les Fleurs du Mal* (1857).

metaphors include «o castelo / *Amarelo do medo*» («Não», Po, p. 89), «um véu *áureo* de mistério» (CF, p. 226) and «*Áureos* Templos de ritos de cetim» («Distante Melodia», Po, p. 99). The important, even crucial point about Sá-Carneiro's writings is that the actual metaphors are no more revealing, no more allusive, indeed, no more metaphorical, than the «real» elements of narrative or description. All his *mots obsédants,* motifs and locutions are equally significant. In the realm of colour, there are further areas of special interest: the frequent references to colour in general, the author's preoccupation with *o azul* and the field of precious metals — gold, silver and bronze. Colour itself is thrilling and alive: for example, the American woman in *A Confissão de Lúcio* includes «as cores» in the list of elements which would acquire «novos sensualismos» in the hands of «aquele que fosse um grande artista e que, para matéria-prima, tomasse a voluptuosidade» (CL, p. 26), and there are hundreds of examples of the use of unspecified but intense colours. As for the Symbolists' favourite *azul,* there is no shortage of examples here either: «Um pouco mais de *azul* — eu era além», says Sá-Carneiro in the poem «Quase» (Po, p. 68). In real life, in a letter to Pessoa dated January 21, 1913, Sá-Carneiro writes about a planned short story, «O Homem do Ar», in which the protagonist «Morrerá de amor e de piedade pela atmosfera e ascenderá no *azul*» (C I, p. 59), and indeed, he even considers the possibility of calling this story «Tragédia *Azul*». Gold, silver and bronze are of great importance in Sá-Carneiro too: although the images might be classified as jewellery, we are most often aware of them because of their colour. *Ouro* is one of the commonest images of all: all the fields of inspiration that we have already considered, carnal or spiritual, can be golden, which is to say touched by the Unknown. We find an «orgia de carne espiritualizada *em ouro*» (CL, p. 36), «lábios *de ouro*» (CL, p. 63), «corpos *áureos*» (CF, p. 257), a «mulher *dourada*» (CF, p. 289) and «um corpo divino, branco e *dourado*» (P, p. 206), all of which refer to the golden qualities of the flesh itself. The carnal experiences may occasionally reach this level: «êxtases fluidos, perversos *de oiro*» (CF, p. 49) for example, or «já me sentia entrelaçado *d'Ouro*» (CF, p. 298 — at the moment of orgasm in «Além»). And spiritual experiences, relationships or attitudes may provide a glimpse of glory: in «Distante Melodia» is a «sonho de íris morto *a oiro* e brasa», and the poet says: «Caía *Oiro* se pensava Estrelas» (Po, p. 98). Negatively, in the seventh «Canção de Declínio», the poet realises the inevitability of disaster: «Meu alvoroço de *oiro* e lua / Tinha por fim que transbordar...» (Po, p. 129) while in «Cinco Horas», too, we have the awareness of failure: «Que história de *Oiro* tão bela / Na minha vida abortou» (Po, p. 135). All this presupposes the existence of an autonomous entity, *o Ouro*: in the same way that earthly mysteries represent the ultimate Mystery, the occasional «espasmos dourados» or «glória dourada» of this life provide a glimpse of an absolute. There are countless references to this: though the attitude is one of despair, the lines «Se acaso em minhas mãos fica um pedaço de *oiro,* / Volve-se logo falso», from «A Queda», confirm its existence (Po, p. 79); the very title of the collection of poems, «Indícios de *Oiro*» does so too, while at the moment of climax in the poem «Apoteose», the poet says: «singro num mar de *Ouro*» (Po, p. 97). Silver, bronze and platinum are also found, though less frequently; they serve the same purpose as gold, though sometimes with extended connotations.

Sounds, too, are important. The *Confissão de Lúcio* «orgy» makes use of music to help create atmosphere as well as in accompaniment to the dancing; in «Mistério», the happy protagonist looks forward to a future of «aromas novos, novos *sons*» (CF, p. 150); Zagoriansky, in «Asas», says: «escrevo com *sons*» (CF, p. 186) and one of his poems contains a «fogo de artifícios de *sons*» (CF, p. 188); the dancing in «Bailado» evokes «Cisnes de brasa, em mar de *Som*» (CF, p. 201) and the *fixador de instantes,* in his moment of triumph, says: «Ó estátua da hora! ó minha cor, ó meu *som,* ó meu aroma — sempre te hei-de sentir» (CF, p. 270); one of the instructions for the «novo ataque» in the poem «Escala» is «mistura *os sons* com os perfumes» (Po, p. 118); in «Inter-sonho», the poet says «Vivo em roxo e morro em *som*» (Po, p. 57); in «Partida», «a cor já não é cor — é *som* e aroma!» (Po, p. 54); in «Rodopio», «Listas de *som* enveredam» (Po, p. 76); in «Nossa Senhora de Paris», «Listas de *som* avançam para mim a fustigar-me» (Po, p. 84) and in «Salomé», «Ergo-me em *som,* oscilo, e parto» (Po, p. 87). Sounds in general form part of the chain of *correspondances,* but particular sounds create particular effects. The sound of the human voice is often sexual: the poem «Certa Voz na Noite Ruivante...» refers to the «Esquivo sortilégio o dessa voz, opiada» (Po, p. 92) and likens it to «a voz duma Princesa / Bailando meia nua entre clarões de espada». The last two tercets of the sonnet are revealing:

> Entanto nunca a vi mesmo em visão. Sòmente
> A sua voz a fulcra ao meu lembrar-me. Assim
> Não lhe desejo a carne — a carne inexistente...
>
> É só de voz-em-cio a bailadeira astral —
> E nessa voz-Estátua, ah! nessa voz-total,
> É que eu sonho esvair-me em vícios de marfim... (Po, p. 93)

In *A Confissão de Lúcio,* Ricardo admits that he could love a woman for the «timbre subtil da sua *voz*» and refers to his «*ânsia sexual* de possuir vozes» (CL, p. 63, author's italics). Inácio, in «Ressurreição», wonders if he will ever possess «essa carne, essa *voz*, essa luz» (CF, p. 264). Exciting, too, are those sounds that suggest mystery, even menace: rustling, swishing and whistling. Some are good: «o brilho *roçagante*» of

141

the magic queen's dress (CF, p. 47), for example, or the «*farfalhar* dos vidrilhos» (CF, p. 176), when «uma dançarina multicolor volteia». But, like mystery itself, these sounds can be unpleasantly disturbing: there may be «figuras de medo [...] *farfalhantes*» (CF, pp. 105-6) or «turbilhões *silvantes*» may create «pavor sem nome» (CF, p. 198). Closely connected to mysterious sounds are echoes. «Os *ecos*», claims the protagonist of «A Grande Sombra», «[...] não me deixam, por afago, ouvir a vida» (CF, p. 86), while side by side with the «*sons* perdidos de azul» which form part of his landscape are «*ecos* de marfim» (CF, p. 89). In «Mistério», «a lua de dezembro incidia *ecos* de platina» (CF, p. 128), and the hero can half-see *o além,* «*ecoando* timbres esguios de aromas ritmizados» (CF, p. 147). Sometimes, though, the implication is of the solitary, painful isolation of the *persona,* a far cry, in fact, from the «tudo *ecoa* glória» of «A Grande Sombra» (CF, p. 60). The echoes of footsteps ring out in silence, and silence itself may be used as a cold, unpleasant, sterile image: «uma sensação de frio — um frio ácido, crispante, *silencioso*...» (CF, p. 95, author's italics), «É desolador como sabemos pouco de nós. Tudo é *silên-cio* em nossa volta» (CF, p. 237) or «*Silêncio,* luz fria...» («Não», Po, p. 90). Conversely, noise can be cheerful and gay and can represent what is normal and healthy: «os cafés de *ruído*» (CF, p. 49) for example, the «baía de festa, cheia de sol, embandeirada, *ruidosa*» (CF, p. 150), the line: «Quermesse — eia! — e *ruído!*» of the third «Canção de Declínio» (Po, p. 121), and the «Fitas de cor, *vozearia*» of the third «Cançao» (Po, p. 122). Finally, mysterious sounds are represented by the verb *ranger,* while *tilintar* and *retinir* are more cheerful.

Scents are often erotic: «de toda a sua carne», says Lúcio of the American woman «em penumbra azul, emanava um *aroma* denso a crime» (CL, p. 35); her ingredients for a demonstration of *voluptuosidade-arte* include «aromas» (CL, p. 36), and he admits that their flesh «era sensível aos espasmos, *aos aromas,* às melodias!» (CL, p. 38); later, Ricardo's «ânsia sexual» is directed towards «aromas» as well as voices, gestures, smiles and colours (CL, p. 63), and Marta's body is described as «*aromá-tico* e lustral» (CL, p. 101). In the stories of *Céu em Fogo* we find «*aro-mas* ritmizados» (CF, p. 147), «um aroma *com crosta*» (CF, p. 179, author's italics), «uma realização *em aromas*» (CF, p. 187), «o *aroma* rutilante da hora que fugia» (CF, p. 263), and «fogos de artifício de *aromas*» (CF, p. 74) among many other examples, all of which suggest mystery of one sort or another — direct contact with the Beyond, the transcendental nature of art, the ecstasy associated with sex, the intoxicating unknown of sumptuous opulence and the incomprehensible realm of metaphysics.

We have already seen how many images are interchangeable. It is not going too far to assert that virtually all Sá-Carneiro's images «correspond» in the Baudelairean sense; colours, sounds and scents are the most obvious examples of this, with their interchangeability explicitly pointed out. We can consider them in two ways: by seeing them as the first, sensory, step on the mystical journey of Symbolism, and by investigating their specific connotations in this world.

Colour, sound and perfumes constitute an area of life from which it is possible to be sure —or so it seems— that a greater reality does in fact exist. Jung has defined four methods «by which consciousness obtains its orientation to experience. *Sensation* (i.e. sense-perception) tells you that something exists; *thinking* tells you what it is; *feeling* tells you whether it is agreeable or not; and *intuition* tells you whence it comes and where it is going».[32] Colour, for example, is perceived by the senses and points to something absolute: there should be «novas cores» somewhere, the artist's heightened sensibility tells him. For the artist, colours are in constant evidence in life; they are intense and bright and their rôle is accorded its rightful importance by means of the attention he pays to them. This means each piece of writing will be a sensory *composition* as if it were partly a painting or, more accurate in this case, a theatrical production. Colours, patterns (for example, stripes), lustre, layout, background and foreground sound, even perfumes, all mean a lot in Sá-Carneiro. And as in theatrical productions in that period, these features are glamorous and artificial, and the director makes a pattern with them and creates a design. In a way, he plays God, reshaping life, recreating it in a new image: even human sounds are somewhat dehumanised, while those of Nature are removed from their original context; smells are invariably beautiful and colours are laid out by man.

The artist is in control. But colours, sounds and scents do have a certain autonomy, based both on their reflective powers and on a kind of internal consistency of connotations. For the Symbolists, colour was of profound importance. Rimbaud's poem «Voyelles» («A noir, E blanc, I rouge, U vert, O bleu»)[33] is a famous example of the extension of the Baudelairean principle, and even though Verlaine, in his «Art Poétique», wrote: «nous voulons la Nuance encor, / Pas la Couleur»,[34] many of his contemporaries and successors were incorporating striking colour into art as if it had been discovered only recently. Pierre Louÿs, in *Les Chansons de Bilitis,* describes a «danse des fleurs»:

> Elle déroule le voile jaune, sa chevelure noire se répand. Le voile rose glisse de sa bouche. Le voile blanc tombé laisse voir ses bras nus.
> Elle dégage ses petits seins du voile rouge qui se dénoue. Elle abaisse le voile vert de sa croupe double et ronde. Elle tire le voile bleu de ses épaules...[35]

[32] JUNG, p. 61 (author's italics).
[33] In *Poésies Éternelles.*
[34] In *Jadis et Naguère.*
[35] PIERRE LOUŸS, *Les Chansons de Bilitis* (1894).

The Decadents echoed the spangled, jewelled colour that Moreau inherited from Chassériau, and their inclusion of this aspect of the visual arts in literature is just one example of the blurring of the boundaries. Moreau himself has been considered a «literary» painter and the successor of Flaubert. Huysmans was enthusiastic about Moreau and admired, too, Odilon Redon and Rodolphe Bresdin. Authors in general became more aware of painters, and painters became more concerned with the literary import of their work. Because they were writing for the theatre, writers and composers took an ever-greater interest in décor and colour: Jullian reminds us of Maeterlinck's instructions to Pugné-Poë for the *Pelléas et Mélisande* costumes: [36]

> Ne crois-tu pas que, pour Mélisande, plutôt que le vert, mieux vaudrait peut-être quelque mauve à trouver chez Liberty? Pelléas, lui, serait en vert — une robe très simple dégageant le corps, très longue, ceinture orfévrée, rubans violets tressés dans les cheveux...

while Wagner's influence in creating a new approach towards a kind of complete art cannot be overestimated. Thus artists were more aware of each other as the century ended, and this led to fashions in art and fashionable preoccupations, techniques and materials. Indeed, with colours, there was a kind of code, with purples and violets frequently representing the mystical as well as forming part of the gold and purple décor of the Byzantine twilight. But most of all it was the *attitude* towards colour that was vital, the awareness of its powers and its rôle, and it is this that Sá-Carneiro has inherited from his predecessors rather than any fixed code. Nevertheless, he does show signs of the influence of his literary-artistic background. The most obvious examples of this are in his use of purples, blue and gold. Mauve, of course, was the typical colour of the *fin de siècle* — indeed, the *belle époque* was often referred to as «the mauve nineties». As for blue, is was Mallarmé above all others who brought the concept of *l'azur* into fashion, «l'éternel azur»: «*Je suis hanté. L'Azur! l'Azur! l'Azur! l'Azur!* » [37] taking the obvious connotations of sky, heaven and the Beyond one stage further. For Sá-Carneiro, the colour blue has one extra quality: it is the colour of the eyes of the people he most admires, the «raças louras do norte» (CF, p. 260), and throughout both the prose and the poetry the adjective *louro/loiro* is used for attractive elements and for people for whom blue eyes are natural. Like everything that is desirable, blue eyes represent something different from Sá-Carneiro himself. As John Parker has pointed out,[38] it was largely via Eugénio de Castro that colours were rediscovered

[36] *Esthètes et Magiciens*, p. 74.
[37] STÉPHANE MALLARMÉ, «L'Azur», in *Vers et Prose* (1893).
[38] PARKER, p. 155.

and «translated into Portuguese»,[39] but Sá-Carneiro's experience of the ambiance of Paris leads him to add dimensions of his own to his legacy. In addition to the influence of nineteenth-century and *fin de siècle* art, he would have found it hard to escape the contagion of the enormous popularity of the Ballets Russes, for example, which came to Paris for the first time in 1909. Lucie-Smith tells us that the production of *Schéhérazade* in 1910 «took the Parisian audience by storm, and had a profound effect on fashionable clothes and fashionable styles of interior decoration».[40] One of the features of Bakst's décor for this production was exotic colour, with a great deal of gold. This helps to account for the gold in the works of Sá-Carneiro; if its qualities in representing the supreme transcendental glory make it a favourite image for him as a post-Symbolist, then its fashionable qualities in theatrical design certainly add to his love for it as a theatre-goer. In addition to *ouro/oiro, dourado* and *áureo,* his writings are liberally spattered with other «golden» words — *fulvo, ruivo, flavo* and the verb *mordourar* (originally found in Eugénio de Castro).[41] Parker claims that these tawny words suggest the lion or tiger and contain the implication of animal strength;[42] this may well be so, but they are also variations on Sá-Carneiro's favourite gold. His use of other colours is more or less conventional: red, for example, indicating passion and violence, and white conveying youth, innocence and tenderness. Yet, as with blue, there are aspects of his manipulation of colours which are peculiar to him. Yellow, for instance, seems to suggest incompleteness in life, if not the absence of it (as well it might, since it is but a pale version of gold): abstention, renunciation, asceticism and boredom are all described as yellow. Then, whiteness it not always innocent: in *A Confissão de Lúcio* (p. 99), the hero enjoys the white heat of the «contínuo deslumbramento de uma apoteose branca de carne...». Silver, gold and bronze bring with them extra connotations: escape to the past in «prata velha» and «bronzes medievais», the spangled, sequinned surfaces of the Music Hall and the carnival with their flashy movement, and Nature made artificial with electric light: for example, the «grande esfinge platinada» in «Bailado» (CF, p. 201).

Scent and sound may be slightly less in evidence in Sá-Carneiro, but he is obsessed by strange and lovely aromas that represent the distant unknown, the past, or inaccessible (and unreal) sex. Sounds, too, are fascinating if they are mysterious or menacing. The most marvellous thing is the hint, the glimpse, of something and somewhere else, and this is often afforded by an echo. The tragedy is that sometimes the echo is not

---

[39] See too JOSÉ CARLOS SEABRA PEREIRA, *Decadentismo e Simbolismo na Poesia Portuguesa* (Coimbra, 1975).
[40] LUCIE-SMITH, p. 148.
[41] See PARKER, p. 495; it is an adaptation of the French *mordorer.*
[42] PARKER, p. 483.

of some unseen realm but only of one man alone in the silence; as Rodenbach put it: «Silence où toute l'âme assombrie est encline / À se sentir de plus en plus comme orpheline»;[43] or worse, it can be intolerable, for it proves that, after all, there is nothing there.

DÉCOR

Sá-Carneiro's interest in décor and design is already evident from our investigation of materials, costume, colour and even the four elements, but there are other areas which are worth considering. There is, of course, much straightforward description of décor, plus an unsurprising emphasis on opulence, luxury and high fashion and scenarios with an air of mystery, often suggesting a fairy story.

We find opulence in «lambrizes de incrustações exóticas» (CF, p. 64), «degraus de mármore rosa» (CL, p. 34), «ânforas de Oiro» («Vislumbre», Po, p. 105), «tapeçarias espessas» (CF, p. 48), «Reposteiros de veludo, arrastados, roçagantes — a brilhos espessos. Tapeçarias majestosas, profundas, que abafassem os passos — candelabros, serpentinas e lustres brazonados» (CF, p. 64); «pesados reposteiros de veludo dourado» (P, p. 120), a «grande poltrona magenta» (CF, p. 186), «grandes lustres» (CF, p. 48), «candelabros d'oiro» (CF, p. 268), «lustres de cristal — as velas de oiro, acesas» («O Resgate», Po, p. 103) and so on. In many cases, the categories overlap and luxury and mystery go hand in hand: «um estranho palco erguido sobre esfinges bronzeadas» (CL, p. 34), for example, or «assentos de azulejo» (for the «príncipes e rainhas encantadas», CF, p. 43), a «Cofre de Imperatriz» («Sete Canções de Declínio», V, Po, p. 124), and «salas secretas» (CF, p. 92).

Sá-Carneiro uses four more images which might be included under the heading of interior decoration: *reposteiros, serapilheiras, janelas* and *espelhos,* and clearly, they all suggest something mysterious. In the first two cases, there is something hidden, and the child in «A Grande Sombra» confesses: «vinham-me calafrios defronte dos *reposteiros* pesados» (CF, p. 48), adding «ainda hoje não perdi o medo *do que pode haver para lá de um reposteiro*» (CF, p. 48, author's italics). The «grande salto» into the Unknown, involves the same image: «se abatem tapeçarias... se desvendam *reposteiros*» (CF, p. 123). *Serapilheiras,* too, cover things, but these things have been discarded, they are no longer in use. The artist in «Mistério» suffers greatly: «A sua alma era uma casa enorme, no inverno, com a mobília atravancada, forrada de *serapilheiras*» (CF, p. 129), but when he finds love, «as *serapilheiras* tinham voado, descobrindo móveis de marfim e prata» (CF, p. 149). In «Eu-próprio o Outro», images

---

[43] In *Petits Poèmes de Bruges.*

of destruction and disuse include «a grande escadaria de mármore atape-
tada de *serapilheiras!*» (CF, p. 211). Closed windows indicate the absence
of life too; in the same short story, the narrator laments: «As *janelas
abertas* continuam cerradas...» (CF, p. 209) and «as janelas abertas, sempre... sempre fechadas...» (CF, p. 210), but later, at the moment in
which he realises that *o Outro* is «belo», «todo intensidade», «todo fogo»
and «grande», he says, «As *janelas* abertas, abriram-se-me nele» (CF,
p. 215). In the poem «Crise Lamentável», the poet includes among his
desires: «À minha Torre ebúrnea abrir *janelas*» (Po, p. 160). An opened
window may be the means of escape. Finally, mirrors are a key image.
Ricardo de Loureiro refers to a «bizarra alucinação»: «Por acaso olhei
para o espelho do guarda-vestidos *e não me vi reflectido nele!*» (CL,
p. 96, author's italics). In «A Grande Sombra», the child fears «os *espelhos*
mortos, nos paços antigos» (CF, p. 48), but his exciting «domínio de
Mistério» can be glimpsed «em *espelhos* duvidosos» (CF, p. 65). The past
is still in evidence in Venice: «Permaneceram nos *espelhos,* ali, sorrisos
doutrora...» (CF, p. 91), but the fascination turns into horror as the narrator becomes increasingly aware of his own disintegration: «À direita,
um grande armário de *espelho*. Mas estremeço... ranjo de presságios...
O *espelho* está partido...» (CF, p. 120). Mirrors are sometimes frightening,
especially when they fail to reflect the image they should, but sometimes
afford a glimpse of something far away — either the past of the Unknown.
The lines: «um *espelho* reproduz, / Em treva, todo o esplendor» («Rodopio», Po, p. 76) certainly contain excitement, and so do «Ao fundo,
em maior excesso, há *espelhos* que reflectem / Tudo quanto oscila pelo
Ar» («Apoteose», Po, p. 182), «A atmosfera: un *espelho* de Fantasmas»
(CF, p. 174), «o crepúsculo é um *espelho*» (CF, p. 203) and the line from
«Escala», «É tempo ainda de realçar-me a *espelhos*» (Po, p. 117). It is
interesting, too, that in «O Resgate», «A última ilusão foi partir os
espelhos» (Po, p. 103). But again, mystery is the source of fear, and Sá-
Carneiro's character Professor Antena points this out: «Em pequeno»,
he says, «colocando-me em face dum *espelho,* estremecia» (CF, p. 251).
Earlier he has stated categorically: «diante dum *espelho,* devíamos sempre ter medo!» (CF, p. 237). The narrator of «Eu-próprio o Outro»
records his first shock as he realises that *o Outro* is absorbing him:
«Venho para casa cheio de medo. Olho-me a um *espelho*... Horror! Des-
cubro no meu rosto, caricaturizado, o rictus de desdém do *seu* rosto»
(CF, pp. 216-17, «seu» italicised in text). In the poem «Dispersão», the
poet complains:

> Não sinto o espaço que encerro
> Nem as linhas que projecto:
> Se me olho a um *espelho,* erro —
> Não me acho no que projecto. (Po, p. 63)

The Narcissistic habit of kissing a mirror image may also have to do with mystery and fear: in «Asas», for example, the strange artist Zagoriansky recounts his fear «de ver estiolar o seu génio à força de intensidade», adding «acarinhava-o beijando-se nos *espelhos* —falava a sós com ele— dizia-lhe 'meu amor'» (CF, p. 191).

Serapilheiras, reposteiros and closed windows all act as barriers, but *serapilheiras* are very different in that they cover the old, the disused and the discarded. This, though sad or even tragic, is not frightening. On the other hand, *reposteiros,* once they are drawn aside, and open windows can lead to terror and to the Unknown itself. As in any adventure, there is danger, but any fear involved appears to be a fear of *failure*: if the connotations are superficially sexual, the venture may result in humiliation; if we are concerned explicitly with the search for the transcendental, the most terrible possibility is that there is, after all, nothing there: «Se tudo quanto é doirado / Fosse sempre um cemitério? («Não», Po, p. 89).

By far the most intriguing image in this section is that of the mirror. Traditionally, man's reflection in a mirror, his shadow and the echo of his voice lie in that mysterious area between the finite and the infinite, and although —as we have seen— Sá-Carneiro is not concerned with the primitive belief in the shadow as a manifestation of the human soul,[44] he does make use of the old idea that the reflection is. This, of course, makes it important, since human duality is mysterious, and the ramifications of the belief lead us into the realms of the great mysteries of life — personality, love, sex, death and eternity. One example of the frightening qualities of mirrors is their ability to suck in the soul. The belief that to look in a pool or glass is to risk losing it to the evil spirits who live there is widespread among many primitive peoples. It is common to cover mirrors in a sick-room, so Frazer tells us, since «in time of sickness, when the soul might take flight so easily, it is particularly dangerous to project it out of the body, and there is always a risk that it may not return».[45] Since the soul survives the body, mirrors may well reveal the image of those long since dead, like Sá-Carneiro's «grande Espelho de fantasmas» («Manucure», Po, p. 170), the «espelho de Fantasmas» of «Asas» (CF, p. 174) and the «espelhos mortos» feared by the child in «A Grande Sombra» (CF, p. 48). As Cirlot says, one function of the mirror is «anular distancias reflejando lo que un día estuvo frente a él y ahora se halla en la lejanía».[46] Yet what is even more horrifying is the possibility of seeing nothing at all in the glass: if there is nobody there, the soul has been

[44] See «The Soul as a Shadow and a Reflection» in the chapter «The Perils of the Soul», in J. G. FRAZER, *The Golden Bough* (p. 250 in the London, 1957 edition).
[45] FRAZER, p. 254.
[46] CIRLOT, p. 205.

lost, and death is inevitable. A mirror, says Cirlot, is a «puerta por la cual el alma puede disociarse y 'pasar' al otro lado».[47] In *A Confissão de Lúcio,* Ricardo's reflection has dissociated itself from him: if his reflection is his soul, it is quite logical that Ricardo should see nothing in the looking-glass when it has materialised and become «sexualised» (CL, pp. 153 and 150). Furthermore, this strange experience comes immediately after Marta and Lúcio have made love for the first time — that is, immediately after Ricardo's soul, or reflection, has proved itself in an independent existence. There are, of course, countless examples of shadows, portraits or reflections that gain independence in literature, especially in Romantic and post-Romantic writings. In the German film we have already referred to, *Der Student von Prag,* for example, in Hans Andersen's «The Shadow»,[48] in Edgar Allan Poe, Oscar Wilde, Hoffmann, Chamisso, Goethe, Frankl, Robert Louis Stevenson and Strindberg. Dr Otto Rank claims that «Presque tous les romantiques ont traité le motif du Double d'une façon ou de l'autre».[49] Ricardo, then, like the hero of Guy de Maupassant's «Le Horla» («On y voyait comme en plein jour... et je ne me vis pas dans la glace»),[50] cannot see his own reflection any more, and death is inevitable from the moment he is aware of this «bizarra alucinação». In both *Der Student von Prag* and Poe's «William Wilson», the other half of the psyche is distinguishable by being the good half, the conscience. In *A Confissão de Lúcio,* it is the feminine half, the *anima.* But in all these cases it is what Rank has called «un Moi devenu indépendant»,[51] and in all of them there is conflict. If you can no longer see your reflection, there is no hope of avoiding conflict, and if a mirror is broken, it bodes ill since it suggests that soon the reflection will no longer be visible. When a reflection «gets away» there is invariably an attempt to kill it, and this suicide —for that is what it is— amounts to complete annihilation since the soul is supposed to survive the body. (If the dead are shadows or reflections, then they cannot possess a shadow or reflection themselves. Conversely, anyone who has no shadow or reflection must be dead.) It has often been claimed that suicide is the result of the conflict between the two halves of the human psyche; many of these stories of doubles, reflections and shadows that materialise demonstrate this incompatibility. In *A Confissão de Lúcio,* though, there are *three* characters, and this would appear to confuse the issue. Yet the principle is the same. Ricardo and Lúcio may be seen as two halves of the same psyche. At the same time, in order that the two halves may

[47] CIRLOT, p. 205.
[48] In *The Complete Fairy Tales and Stories,* trans. Erik Haugaard (London, 1974), pp. 334-5.
[49] RANK, p. 32.
[50] In *Contes Fantastiques complets* (Verviers, 1973), p. 277.
[51] RANK, p. 22.

a Roma, a Petersburgo...» (P, p. 284). Two cities in particular interest him: Venice and, of course, Paris. The narrator of «A Grande Sombra», after his triumph, goes to Italy: «É que me encontro em *Veneza*» (CF, p. 90), he says, and his impressions of this city occupy more than a page and a half in the story: «Veneza! Ó cidade sagrada de fantasia, capital brocado de inter-sonho [...] Veneza surgiu-me sempre, toda ela, através dum grande vidro polido, em perspectiva, como um panorama de artifício [...] filho louco de Doge, talvez — comando préstitos de emigrantes mortos em disfarces de pompa [...] Campanários e cúpulas irrealizaram-se ao longe... [...] —Veneza! Ó cidade-Princesa [...] —*Quem sabe se eu já fui a tua alma?...*» (CF, pp. 91-2, author's italics). In «Escala» there is something similar, while in the sixth «Canção de Declínio» we find the image of «Uma *Veneza* de capricho» (Po, p. 128). But it is Paris that he loves above all. «Cada vez», he writes to Pessoa from Barcelona (August 29, 1914), «me convenço mais de que não posso passar sem Paris», and he looks back on his early days there: «Paris enfim, meu amigo, era as mãos louras, a ternura enlevada que não teve nunca a minha vida» (C II, p. 8). Sá-Carneiro's love for Paris remained inviolate until his death. One of Paris's attractions was the number of foreigners found there and its connections with the rest of the world — in fact, its cosmopolitanism. Things and places that are far away are automatically good (since they are the converse of the accessible and the familiar). Therefore distance itself is important, journeys are frequent and the image of departure is often found: «Sei a *distância*», he claims in the significantly entitled «Partida» (Po, p. 53). The «distante melodia» of the poem of the same name is beautiful and nostalgic (Po, p. 98): «Havia na minha alma Outras *distâncias*», says the poet, «*Distâncias* que o segui-las era flores...» (Po, p. 98). In «Nossa Senhora de Paris» there are «Mirtos e tamarindos» that «Odoram *a lonjura*» (Po, p. 84); in «Rodopio» are «Perfumes de *longes* ilhas» (Po, p. 78); in «Álcool», the poet says: «Respiro-me no ar que *ao longe* vem» (Po, p. 58); in «Partida», «O bando das quimeras *longe* assoma...» (Po, p. 54) and in «Não», «*Longes* se aglomeram / Em torno aos meus sentidos» (Po, p. 88). Sometimes the faraway place is specified as the North of fatal attraction: «Minha dispersão total — / Existe lá *longe, ao norte*» («Dispersão», Po, p. 64), while the Romantic appeal of the Orient has not been entirely lost either: for the hero of «Mistério», *o além* is envisaged «*de Oriente,* ecoando timbres esguios de aromas ritmizados» (CF, p. 147). Travelling itself is important, with departure the most crucial moment. The fantasy world of the child in «A Grande Sombra» is reached «nocturnamente, numa *viagem* maravilhosa» (CF, p. 43), and he includes «as longas *viagens*» among his list of sexually-exciting images later on (CF, p. 50). The whole point of Professor Antena's experiments (in «A Estranha Morte do Professor Antena») is to discover some method whereby we can move in *other* worlds; the person who achieves it «poderia [...] *viajar* nessa outra [existência]» (CF, p. 250). In «Partida», we find: «*Viajar* outros sentidos, outras vidas» (Po, p. 52), and the amount of travelling undertaken by the various fictional characters is itself of interest. But decision and departure may involve difficulty. Even in the happiest of all Sá-Carneiro's poems, «Partida» (Po, p. 51), we are aware of danger: «É partir *sem temor* contra a montanha» (Po, p. 52); in «A Queda», success eludes the poet: «... giro até *partir*... Mas tudo me resvala / Em bruma e sonolência» (Po, p. 79). The journey is unsuccessful in «Alem-Tédio» too: «*Parti*. Mas logo regressei à dor» (Po, p. 74), while in «Desquite» we hear about «O cavaleiro que *partiu*, / E não voltou nem deu notícias» (Po, p. 152), and all the connotations are of disappointment. In the fourth «Canção de Declínio», the poet addresses himself to superior beings: «Os Grandes, *partam*», he enjoins (Po, p. 123), and adds, «dominem / Sua sorte em suas mãos». In «Salomé», he says: «Ergo-me em som, oscilo e *parto*» (Po, p. 87), while the beginning of «Não» is also promising: «Cinjo-me de cor, / E *parto* a demandar. Tudo é Oiro em meu rastro» (Po, p. 88).

One of the attractions of Paris is the theatre — it is a means of escape, a form of art and, at the same time, a manifestation of all that is cosmopolitan and new, open to cultural progress and innovation from all quarters of the globe. What is more fascinating than the glamour of «os *teatros* rutilantes, atapetados a roxo» (CF, p. 49)? Or a «grande *teatro* cosmopolita» (CF, p. 264)? In fact, we find theatrically in all sorts of unexpected places, and it is looked on with approval: «Ó mágica *teatral* da atmosfera», says a line in the poem «Apoteose» (Po, p. 177); Venice is reminiscent of a «panorama de artifício — a iluminações *teatrais*» (CF, p. 91); the American woman's house, in *A Confissão de Lúcio*, looked like an «opulento, fantástico *teatro*» (CL, p. 34). Furthermore, the characters and *persona* even talk in theatrical images: «sumiu-se por alçapões *teatrais*», says the narrator of «A Grande Sombra» about the unknown woman (CF, p. 88); «Num *programa de teatro* / Sucede-se a minha vida», we find in the second of the «Sete Canções de Declínio» (Po, p. 121); «Meu *teatro* de papel», says the poet to his beloved Paris in «Abrigo» (Po, p. 131); the child in «A Grande Sombra» is excited by «*alçapões*» and «*subterrâneos*» (CF, p. 41), and in his imagined palace there would be «*alçapões* de despropósito» (CF, p. 66). The most stimulating aspect of the theatre is, of course, the dance, and in a letter to Pessoa dated March 10, 1913, Sá-Carneiro describes his delight when, for the first time, he finds he is moved and excited by it, the «dança admirável duma dançarina 'Mado Minty'» (C I, p. 84); he goes on to say: «pela primeira vez anteontem eu vi uma *dança* de arte pura [...] pela primeira vez, via uma dança-Arte» (C I, p. 85, author's italics). After this he

153

wrote «Bailado». Dancing is aesthetically stimulating, but it is also sexually exciting, and it is often associated with nudity. The American dancer in the *Confissão de Lúcio* «orgy» is referred to as the «fera *nua*» (CL, p. 42); Salome's flesh is «álcool de *nua*» (Po, p. 86); there are «apoteoses de corpos *nus*» (CL, p. 40), and three dancers finish their dance with «seios, ventres e sexos *descobertos*» (CL, p. 40). This is life and this is Paris; «na Lisboa medíocre não circulavam mulheres luxuosas na audácia *semi-nua* dos últimos figurinos [...] e não havia [...] *corpos nus* nas apoteoses dos teatros» (CF, p. 283).

In his desire to be as cosmopolitan as possible, Sá-Carneiro reveals three basic temperamental needs: for the distant, for the different and for the ultra-fashionable. Anything that has its origins in some unfamiliar region is, to him, bound to be better than the familiar, his contempt for which he makes no attempt to conceal. The familiar, the everyday, the pedestrian, are all *lepidóptero* and unsatisfactory; life itself is unsatisfactory too, and a preoccupation with travel and faraway places is a clear sign of dissatisfaction with the *status quo*. Foreigners are charged with mystery and represent an inaccessible region of which they are the only manifestation. Like many other images, they prove the existence of something and somewhere else, while at the same time being present in the immediate surroundings of a sensitive but unfulfilled artist who, in his alienated state, feels nearer to what is far away than he does to what is near. Distance itself, whether spatial or temporal, means change; for the artist living in a hostile environment, any change must be an improvement. Travel is a form of escape both from and to something; fictional emphasis on travel is indulging in fantasy. Cirlot[1] reminds us that Jung saw travelling as an «imagen de la aspiración, del anhelo nunca saciado, que en parte alguna encuentra su objeto». A further psychological explanation for Sá-Carneiro's love of the exotic is provided by Mario Praz: «the exotic and the erotic ideals go hand in hand», he says, and he adds, as we have seen before: «a love of the exotic is usually an imaginative projection of a sexual desire».[2] He is referring to Gautier and Flaubert, and he says that their dreams:

> carry them to an atmosphere of barbaric and Oriental antiquity, where all the most unbridled desires can be indulged and the cruellest fantasies can take concrete form.

It would be an exaggeration to assert that this was equally true of Sá-Carneiro. And yet it is not entirely inappropriate. In foreign places (usually Paris), a great many «unbridled desires» are indulged, and the stories and the poems are not without their quota of «cruel fantasies»

[1] CIRLOT, p. 472.
[2] PRAZ, p. 223.

which would certainly be out of place in Lisbon. Part of the author's preoccupation with distant places lies, too, in his awareness of his own mortality, his constant concern with his own death. And the inexorable image of the North, the polar pull, is associated with death. In the poem «Dispersão», we read the ominous lines:

> E sinto que a minha morte —
> Minha dispersão total —
> Existe lá longe, ao norte,
> Numa grande capital. (Po, p. 64)

The finite unknown represents the dangers of the infinite. Distance is as frightening as it is fascinating, and like the theatrical *alçapões* and secret doors from Sá-Carneiro's store of favourite images, it may be deceiving.

But to be different is important too. Foreigners are interesting for this reason, and so is exoticism in general. Sá-Carneiro and his Portuguese friends saw Paris as the centre of all that was modern, the centre, in fact, of progress. They saw themselves as progressives, waging a kind of war, and acting as a fifth column for the invasion of Portugal by «Europe». For Sá-Carneiro, as for all idealists, there was a possibility of changing the world, but the means were found not in politics, but in art. And Paris was the artistic capital of the world. For Sá-Carneiro personally, this had always been the case. Rogério Perez[3] tells us how his father indulged his every whim, taking him to Paris every year and «permitindo-lhe estar 'à la page' com a literatura francesa, cujos 'vient de paraître' adquiria na Livraria Ferreira [etc.] quando os não recebia directamente». For the inhabitants of Lisbon around the turn of the century, French influence was very great and had been for some time. François Castex gives an example of French vocabulary in the theatre, for instance,[4] which leaves us in no doubt as to the orientation of Lisbon in that period. Sá-Carneiro finds Paris preferable to Lisbon because he is an artist in search of better things, and this is commendable. But he is also a would-be aristocrat in search of better things, and this is much less appealing. There is a third reason why no praise is too high for the French capital, why foreigners are attractive and why exoticism is the order of the day, and that is because Sá-Carneiro, in spite of his Narcissism and even megalomania, feels inferior and insecure. He is making an attempt to be someone different, an attitude like that found in someone who habitually feels wrongly dressed when he discovers what other people are wearing. He wants to be everywhere at once, partly for reasons of snobbery; only the rich and aristocratic travel and are acquainted with glamorous, mysterious people and places.

---

[3] PEREZ, «Biografia».
[4] *Mário de Sá-Carneiro e a Génese de «Amizade»*, p. 47.

Sá-Carneiro's *provincianismo* reveals a real need to be part of fashion. His personality was such that he had to be at the centre of things, and the most typical features of Parisian life at that time involved all the aspects of life that he held most dear. The theatre, for example (which found itself in a lamentable state in Portugal in that period), was fashionable: it was also cosmopolitan, fantastic, artistic, colourful, erotic and forward-looking. Dancing had reached a peak of popularity, with Loie Fuller, the *Folies,* the *Ballets russes,* the *chahut* and the *can-can* — every kind of dancing, in fact. Arthur Symons felt as strongly about it as Sá-Carneiro:

> A ballet is simply a picture in movement. It is a picture where the imitation of nature is given by nature itself; where the figures of the composition are real, and yet, by a very paradox of travesty, have a delightful, deliberate air of unreality. It is a picture where the colours change, recombine, before one's eyes; where the outlines melt into one another, emerge, and are again lost, in the kaleidoscopic movement of the dance. [...] [It is a] spectacle which professes to be no more than merely beautiful; which gives us, in accomplished dancing, the most beautiful human sight; which provides, in short, the one escape into fairyland which is permitted by that tyranny of the real which is the worst tyranny of modern life...[5]

Thousands of others felt the pull of the capital of civilisation, the centre of excellence in the arts. Paris was the Mecca of artists from all over the world, the adopted home of painters, musicians, sculptors and writers (there were a great many Russians there, in particular), and many of them shared common attitudes towards life and art, used the same images,[6] longed for the same perfection. It was the most wonderful place to be. Sá-Carneiro needed this atmosphere.

Yet he was not happy. And ultimately he was so desperately unhappy that he committed suicide. Many things failed him or failed *in* him before he reached that point. We have considered several possible areas of disillusion, and now we find yet another. This, despite everything he said about it, is Paris. Sá-Carneiro looked on Paris as some kind of salvation in his life, but of course it did not save him because it could not. It may have been «different», and far from the contemptibly familiar but it failed. The failure, though, was in him. All journeys involve a certain amount of danger and effort. It is easier to «ficar sempre na cama, nunca mexer, criar bolor» («Caranguejola», Po, p. 158). There may be disappointment. If the «journey» entails converting life into a work of art, it is doomed to failure; if ambitions are transcendental, they may well be destroyed by reality. Paris failed for Sá-Carneiro because no earthly city could live up to the rôle he created for it. Andrée Crabbé Rocha has

[5] *Selected Writings,* p. 91.
[6] One common image that has come to the surface in this particular section is the Symbolists's favourite Venice.

made the vital and perceptive point that in fact, Sá-Carneiro was lonely and homesick in Paris. Although he loved the city passionately, he felt more and more isolated there as time went by, «o que sucede a quase todos os artistas portugueses expatriados».[7] In spite of all the fascinating foreigners there at that time, he moved almost exclusively in Portuguese circles; he wrote to friends in Portugal, particularly Pessoa, with astonishing frequency; he never, in fact, relinquished his Portuguese nationality *enough* to become part of Paris life. And yet Lisbon was intolerable, both artistically and emotionally. All his problems —and they were many, possibly including some we have no knowledge of— are based on internal incompatibilities, the conflict between, for example, male and female, artist and man. With the study of cosmopolitanism, we find a further area of incompatibility, between Mário de Sá-Carneiro the Portuguese and Mário de Sá-Carneiro the Parisian man-about-town and cosmopolitan artist.

TECHNOLOGY AND MODERN LIFE

Whereas Sá-Carneiro finds it easy to join in most contemporary fashions in the arts, he is faced with a dilemma when it comes to the appreciation of technology and some other features of modern urban life. He wants to be iconoclastic, but those preoccupations in art and life based on industrialisation are set in an area of reality in which aesthetic beauty is not immediately apparent. Indeed, it was the very perversity of the Futurists, singing the praises of the machine, seeing beauty «in energy and boldness», extolling «the beauty of speed», strife, aggressiveness, war, militarism, patriotism, «great crowds in the excitement of labour», «the nocturnal vibrations of arsenals and workshops», «factories suspended from the clouds», «broad-chested locomotives» and the «flight of aeroplanes»[8] which made them so interesting. Sá-Carneiro professes the desire for change, but his writings belie this and the new art he envisages is based on the same foundations as the old. The result is that he pays lipservice to the beautiful qualities of technical images, but it is little more than that.

Almost the only current movement he mentions is Futurism; he refers to it in letters to Pessoa and in two of his poems, «Apoteose» and «Manucure»: in the latter, we find the line: «Ó beleza *futurista* das mercadorias!» (Po, p, 172), and later he says:

---

[7] CRABBÉ ROCHA, p. 410.
[8] FILIPPO TOMASSO MARINETTI, «Foundation Manifesto of Futurism», in *Le Figaro*, February 20, 1909. Reproduced in JANE RYE, *Futurism* (London, 1972), pp. 7 and 9.

no difficulty in selecting freely from both sides. His eclecticism results, for example, in passages like that in the short story «Asas» in which Zagoriansky draws on both types of image in order to communicate his idea of the «fonte inesgotável de beleza» which is the atmosphere. Together such elements as «rodas das oficinas» and «braços dos guindastes» are «basílicas, memórias» and «ruínas do Egipto» (CF, p. 175). Sá-Carneiro feels no real sympathy for the *avant-garde* values of the period, and indeed, it is unlikely that someone whose obsessive concern is with the transcendental and the Unknown should feel sympathy for movements like Futurism, with imagery taken from the realm of machinery and technological advance and with heroes who are figures from contemporary life. It is equally unlikely that an artist with a marked sense of his own superiority would find inspiration in «great crowds in the excitement of labour» or «the applause of an enthusiastic crowd» [10] —he has always despised his fellow man, or at least, has affected to. The actual quantity of «modern» images in his writings is small— for every factory chimney there are thirty references to gold, or shadow, or the soul or the dance. He is scathing about Santa Rita Pintor's aspirations to be a Futurist and he expresses his disapproval of his Futurism in the same breath as his anger at his being considered the leader of the *Orpheu* group (C II, p. 111): this suggests that Sá-Carneiro's temperament would make it impossible for him to be a *follower* of any literary movement. Santa Rita wants to be a Futurist «servilmente» says Sá-Carneiro; his own idea is to create *new* art, and he and Pessoa were happy to be leaders and creators in areas such as *Paùlismo, Interseccionismo* and *Sensacionismo,* however derivative some of these may have been. (Pessoa wrote Futurist poetry, of course, but under the heteronym of Álvaro de Campos.) Another reason why Sá-Carneiro would be unlikely to form part of any iconoclastic movement is that, if his approach to Futurism is anything to go by, he did not really understand their aims. There is no evidence that he studied their ideas carefully: he merely took what appealed to him in recent writings and he reshaped it to serve the purpose he wanted. He had probably read the first Futurist Manifesto, which was published in Paris in 1909 (though we have no knowledge that he did), but it was not until mid-August, 1915, eight months before his death, that he discovered *I Poeti Futuristi,* though this had been in print for three years. In the meantime, he reveals the extent of his own understanding of the matter by referring to Cesário Verde as a Futurist (April 13, 1914, in the *República inquérito:* «O Mais Belo Livro», C I, p. 190). That Cesário Verde was largely an urban poet is undeniable; he was also original, concerned with the real, interested in the working man, the *povo,* and in life rather than literature. But he was a futurist only in the very loosest sense of the word. Sá-Carneiro,

[10] MARINETTI, p. 7.

despite the occasional burst of admiration for the industrial, sometimes unwittingly reveals his true tastes: for example, when he wants an unpleasant image, he chooses the «nevoeiro negro de cidade fabril» (C II, p. 144). It may be argued that anyone would find this repellent and ugly. But in the *Technical Manifesto of Futurist Literature* (1912), we find that Marinetti says:

> Let us not be afraid of ugliness in literature, and let us kill solemnity everywhere. [...] we must spit on the *Altar of Art!* [11]

Nothing could be further from Sá-Carneiro's attitude.

Although Sá-Carneiro has little of the Futurist in him, this is not to say that there are no aspects of modern life that appeal to him. In fact, urban living is his ideal existence, but those images of progress, industry and city life that he does use are never ugly or shocking, and those most frequently found are closely connected with areas that hold a special interest for him. With industrial imagery, it is the excitement of sound, line and colour that appeals to him, with movement seen as hypnotic, like some piece of kinetic art; everything is ordered — the artificial made even more artificial. There is beauty in machines, but the Futurists' criteria for judging this beauty are new, while his are those of the past. With the images of modern living, it is, as always, their glamour that appeals to him. He likes trains because they have to do with travel; he likes cafés since they are typical of cosmopolitan Paris, suggesting leisure hours and exciting people; he likes busy *praças* for their bustle and colour and movement; boulevards for their luxury and sophistication; typography for the way it links pictures and writing, constituting something fashionable on the edge of art.

The conflict, in the end, is one which exists more for the reader than for the author. We cannot see how he can reconcile his taste for the Symbolist ethos and his need to be in the vanguard of European art in the second decade of the twentieth century, but he himself is unaware of the problem. He can choose areas of technical progress that correspond to his ideology and ignore those that do not. He can experiment, with poems like «Manucure» and «Apoteose» (both of which have a certain tongue-in-cheek air, even though it was only «Manucure» that Pessoa classified as parodic in his *Presença* article). He can see himself as an innovator, sharing with the Futurists the task of *épater le bourgeois* (in which he succeeded in Portugal), while actually having more in common with d'Annunzio, whom the Futurists despised, than he did with them, or with «Europa progresso».

---

[11] Reproduced in the catalogue for *Futurismo 1909-1919. Exhibition of Italian Futurism* (Royal Scottish Academy, Edinburgh, December 16, 1972-January 14, 1973), p. 69, author's italics.

CHAPTER 7

ART

It was François Castex who made the assertion that art and literature are the «únicos domínios que de verdade apaixonavam Sá-Carneiro».[1] In addition to the metaphors, images and *mots obsédants* supporting this argument that we have already seen, we may now add that almost all Sá-Carneiro's fictional characters *are* artists, with their preoccupations often centred on the problems of artistic creation. Joel Serrão points out that in the first book of short stories, *Princípio,* all the protagonists are «*artistas* e adolescentes»;[2] the pattern is repeated in *A Confissão de Lúcio* and in *Céu em Fogo.* In *Princípio,* there is a «grande *escultor*», a «primoroso *contista*», an «estranho e sombrio *poeta*», a «grande *dramaturgo*» and so on. In *A Confissão de Lúcio,* Ricardo de Loureiro is «um *poeta* — um *artista*» (CL, p. 16); Vila-Nova has the personality of a «grande *artista* falido» (CL, p. 19) — he is, in fact, a sculptor; the circles in which they move in Paris consist of «*Literatos, pintores, músicos,* de todos os países» (CL, p. 21); they meet the American woman through a «*pintor* americano» (CL, p. 22); Fonseca is «um pobre *pintorzinho*» (CL, p. 25); Lúcio Vaz himself is an «*escritor*» (CL, p. 32). In *Céu em Fogo,* the suicide in «A Grande Sombra» is a playwright, the hero of «Mistério» is an «*artista*», his mad neighbour is a poet. Zagoriansky, in «Asas», is a poet, Inácio, in «Ressurreição», is a «*romancista*» (CF, p. 273), his acquaintance Manuel Lopes is a «*pintor*» (CF, p. 298), another —Robert Lagrange— is a «*dramaturgo*» (CF, p. 300), Horácio de Viveiros is a «*músico* português» (CF, p. 300), Étienne Dalembert is a «*comediógrafo*» (CF, p. 300) and Fernando Passos a poet and «genial *Artista*» (CF, p. 322). And they talk about art and worry about it: «a voluptuosidade na arte» (CL, p. 25) for example, and how to achieve «uma Arte que interseccione ideias» (CF, p. 174) or «uma Arte sem articulações» (CF, p. 189). They are striving after beauty: the «vago calafrio de beleza» (CL, p. 26), the «desejos espiritualizados de beleza» (CL, p. 27) are part of their everyday lives. Like the Symbolists,

---

[1] CASTEX, *A Genese,* p. 397.
[2] SERRÃO, p. 128.

they believe that «Belo é tudo quanto nos provoca a sensação do invisível» (C II, p. 128), and their aim is to «fixar toda a riqueza» (CF, p. 191).

PAINTING, SCULPTURE

One means of achieving a «beleza nova» (CF, p. 128) is painting, and we find many painters; the author is interested in them and their problems, and his own prose and poetry are put together as if they were paintings or tableaux. And yet he never mentions paintings themselves, with the exception of *retratos,* which have more psychological than artistic interest. It is true that paintings are dutifully included when characters talk about art — the thrill «que nos pode proporcionar uma *tela* genial» (CL, p. 26), for example — and that there is the very occasional reference to Cubism —«um amigo, jovem pintor *cubista*» (CF, p. 282)— but there is nothing else. In fact, the only other explicit references to painting in all his writings are constituted by the metaphorical use of the terminology.

Sá-Carneiro is far more fascinated by sculpture. Apart from making many of his characters sculptors, he echoes the Decadents' interest in statues in general. The hostess in *A Confissão de Lúcio* is «A *estátua* inquietadora do desejo contorcido» (CL, p. 35), while Marta is «escultural» (CL, p. 74); the legs of a dancer are described as «*talhadas* em aurora loura» (CL, p. 39); we find «*Talhei*-me em Exílio» (CF, p. 86), «[um lindo rapaz] todo *esculpido* em manteiga» (CL, p. 123), «aquele Segredo *escultural*» (CF, p. 84), «meu cioso alheamento-*Estátua*» (CF, p. 98), «Volvem-se *estátuas* de ferro os momentos» (CF, p. 120), «lábios que foram *esculpidos* para ferir» (CF, p. 164), «sombra-*Estátua*» (CF, p. 201), «deliro das minhas *estátuas*» (CF, p. 264), «Ó *estátua* da hora!» (CF, p. 270), «paredes de *esculturas*» (CF, p. 91), «Ruínas cinzentas de *estátuas* douradas» (CF, p. 211), «*Estátua,* ascensão do que não sou» («Desquite», Po, p. 151), «*Estátua* falsa ainda erguido ao ar...» (Po, p. 67), «Upam-se *estátuas* de heróis» («Rodopio», Po, p. 75) and in the sixth of the «Sete Canções de Declínio», the poet sarcastically refers to himself as «a estátua 'que nunca tombará'» (Po, p. 128).

At first glance, it appears strange that Sá-Carneiro should be so unconcerned with painting, especially as his heritage in the world of the visual arts, its themes and patterns, its colours and motifs, has become apparent in the course of this study. And yet his interest —not to say his knowledge— seems limited, and his correspondence shows little sign of any great love of pictures. Even the metaphorical usage of such terms as *esboçar* and *pintar* is largely conventional. The explanation is, firstly, that in all forms of art, his preoccupation is more with the relationship of the artist to what he is creating, with the act of creation and with the psychology of the man himself, than with the finished work. Secondly, if it is true that Sá-Carneiro converts real life into works of art, he does this *unconsciously,* and in any case, the finished «pictures» are tableaux or theatrical settings rather than paintings. In this way he achieves a balance between the real and the unreal, as the American woman herself did in *A Confissão de Lúcio* with her «quadros admiráveis» (CL, p. 40). And a further area in which this balance is achieved is that of sculpture.

His concern with the rôle of the artist was, of course, egocentrically orientated. His characters all suffer from problems which may well reflect, at least in part, his own. It is significant, too, that they are all geniuses, misunderstood by the crass characters with whom they have to deal. Of all the Sá-Carneiro protagonists, Inácio, in «Ressurreição», bears the closest resemblance to the author and, in fact, in a letter to Pessoa dated July 13, 1914, Sá-Carneiro says: «Nas páginas psicológicas da 'Ressurreição' está bem descrito o meu estado de alma actual» (C I, p. 174). (Other characters, incidentally, are called Fernando Passos —Pessoa?— Vitorino Bragança —Vitoriano Braga?— and Jorge Pacheco — José Pacheco?) All of them are unable to communicate with the everyday world and do not, in a way, form part of it. They are extraordinary and interesting as they search for beauty and try to order their personalities into a coherent, adult whole. And yet it must be admitted that they are slightly less interesting than they think they are; in 1890 they would have been fascinating but in 1914 they are out of touch with the real *avant-garde.* When we compare the lives and work of those really iconoclastic artists who were in Paris at the time —Apollinaire, for example, or Jarry, Gris, Matisse or Picasso— the gulf is striking. It may well be true, in fact, that the very thing pioneering artists were *not* seeking in that period was orthodox beauty; the Futurists certainly despised the convention, and the sort of ideal sought by the young members of the *avant-garde* was something quite different from that sighed after by Sá-Carneiro. It is unlikely that he knew any of the international group of painters in Paris at that time anyway. Santa Rita knew Picasso, but there is no evidence that Sá-Carneiro did. In any case, it is improbable that he would feel a great deal of affinity with them. He is fascinated by the artist's lot, but only if the artist is indistinguishable from himself.

Nevertheless, we do learn something from Sá-Carneiro's infrequent use of painting terminology. His preoccupation with portraits reveals his concern with personality loss and at the same time his aristocratic orientation. Portraits seem to have the same function as mirror reflections. They can be lost or absorbed into another personality, which becomes the dominant, if not the only one. As for their decorative function, they invariably form part of palaces, castles and ancestral homes. The disappearance of the portrait from the elegant frame is, too, a sign of the destruction of the security, beauty and romance of the past, a break with tradition and continuity. Then the metaphorical use of terms such as *pintar, esboçar* and so on constitutes further examples of the interchangeability of imagery. Emotions can be represented by colour, form, music, words, sounds and scents, and this way all the facets of art can replace each other. To, say, «*pintar* angústia» suggests this — the description itself becomes a work of art. And in this way we become conscious of a very modern aspect of Sá-Carneiro's writings, for it was in this period that abstract art was born,[3] and its original ideology was one which Sá-Carneiro shared:

> Beginning in 1905 the great goal was an art that would express human inwardness without recourse to metaphors drawn from the outside world. The essential was no longer to reproduce objects, but to make the picture itself into an object which, through the resonance inherent in its construction, would awaken a feeling similar to that aroused by the things and processes of visible nature.[4]

His interest in statues shows less *Zeitgeist,* since he is reflecting a preoccupation found largely among the Decadents and, of course, the Aesthetes. Burne-Jones painted four pictures on the Pygmalion theme between 1868 and 1878;[5] Olive Custance (Lady Alfred Douglas) wrote three poems on the same subject;[6] Pierre Louÿs wrote a popular novel called *Aphrodite*[7] in which the hero, Demetrios, makes love to the statue of Aphrodite before robbing it of a pearl necklace; one of M. de Phocas' interests in *M. de Phocas. Astarté* is in statues, especially those of Antinous; in Péladan's *Le Vice suprême,* the Princess learns about male anatomy from statues. It is a continuation of this tradition when the sculptor in «O Incesto» caresses the breasts of a statue of a Greek dancer, and that the projected story in «Ressurreição» should contain an erotic encounter with the statue of Christ. Statues as an image have a great many features of interest: like fictional characters, they are the creation of an artist, and the sculptor, like the author, is a kind of god, creating life — again, a balance between the real and the unreal. They are nature made artificial, like Sá-Carneiro's characters. They are a manifestation of beauty, with the statues of Ancient Greece seen as the most perfect examples of this: as people bcome art, so flesh becomes beauty,

---

[3] WERNER HAFTMANN, in *Painting in the Twentieth Century* (London, 1961), says: «abstract painting can be said to have been born in 1910/11» (vol. I, p. 135).

[4] HAFTMANN, vol. I, pp. 134-5.

[5] In the City Museum and Art Gallery, Birmingham.

[6] See BROCARD SEWELL, *Olive Custance: Her Life and Work* (London, 1975). The first poem dates from 1901.

[7] 1896.

most important facet of art is the written word, but there are relatively few references to literature (though more to literature than to painting), and even fewer images drawn from literary terminology. If we were to undertake a frequency study of *mots obsédants,* we should find that the incidence of what we have called «natural» images is far greater than that of «artificial» ones. And we should run the risk of jumping to the wrong conclusion. There is a trap in the works of Sá-Carneiro of seeing his preoccupation with sex, light, shadow, water, stars, the sky, fire and so on as symptoms of an attitude which is not, in fact, his. The key to the situation is found in the confession made by Ricardo de Loureiro in *A Confissão de Lúcio* that his emotions come to him *already reshaped into literature.* For Sá-Carneiro, everything comes to him in the form of art, that is in the form of literature and, because of the kind of literature that he writes, painting and theatrical settings and scenarios. He appears to write about nature, but in fact he is writing about art. This is the only way he can capture ephemerality and try, at least, to make it permanent; he does it, of course, for himself, to ensure survival for himself. It is almost a form of religion, especially as it is, in a way, a secondary form of Demiurgic creation. As we saw with Inácio in «Ressurreição», the author re-creates himself making —almost— another person. Sá-Carneiro was convinced of the incompatibility between enjoying «amor e família banalmente» and being aware of beauty. The obvious implications and interpretations of this mutual exclusivity have been mentioned throughout the course of this study, but one further interpretation is based on the theory that artistic creation is a substitute for procreation, even sometimes a panacea for homosexual frustration. An extension to this would be to see the act of creation, especially when it is the *re*-creation of the psyche of the author, as a substitute for the family life of which he is deprived, not necessarily because of a homosexual condition, but by virtue of his condition as an artist. We might even add that there is an element of glamorisation in the process that converts a certain abnormality into a triumph over what is usually seen as normal. It is a false glamour that is added, by and large, and Sá-Carneiro himself is sporadically aware of this. It was Francisco Sardo who called Sá-Carneiro the «poeta da incompletude»,[8] and it is by supplying the ingredient of glamorous art that any deficiencies he was aware of were made up for. It is a method of trying to make life what it ought to be and, of course, is doomed to failure. A. de Castro Gil[9] claims that Sá-Carneiro never really lived, if

---

[8] FRANCISCO SARDO, «Mário de Sá-Carneiro, poeta da incompletude», in *Vértice,* no. 285 (June, 1960). ADOLFO CASAIS MONTEIRO, in «Mário de Sá-Carneiro», in *Presença,* no. 21 (June-August, 1929), also sees incompleteness as Sá-Carneiro's most tragic condition.

[9] A. DE CASTRO GIL, *Sá-Carneiro, Miguel Torga, José Régio, três atitudes perante a vida* (Coimbra, 1949).

«a vida é encontrar a forma à vida.[10] He may well be right, since art and life cannot be the same thing, and the former, however enthralling, cannot be a substitute for the latter. It may, in theory, provide a framework for life, but if there is basic conflict, this too will be useless.

As for music, Sá-Carneiro's references to the art itself and to musicians are, of course, less important than the images using musical terminology, in which he reveals so much more of himself. And yet, his real-life attitude is not without its significance, for the listener's musical knowledge and talent are bound to affect his reactions; it is vital for any analysis of Sá-Carneiro's use of musical terminology to know how much he was merely following fashion or doing and saying what was expected of a sensitive artist. He always gives the impression that he loves music. He is greatly moved by it and sees it as one of the facets of art that can help «rasgar véus sobre o Além». Yet, as with painting, he seems to know little about it, and have little interest in it. His Parisian group of friends and acquaintances contained very few musicians and certainly none from the first rank. He seems to be more interested in what he sees as the *newness* of certain pieces, seeing them as manifestations of the ineffable. This suggests that he approached music in a sentimental, un-informed way and that his attitude is Neoromantic and undisciplined. What he wants to show is how receptive he is, an attitude again inherited from the Romantics and the Symbolists. Music as the means of reaching a transcendental state is a concept as old as the art itself, but the idea came back into fashion with Wagner, whose cult produced a new wave of enthusiastic musical mysticism from artists as seminal as Mallarmé, Verlaine, Villiers de l'Isle-Adam and Odilon Redon, as well as the ado-ration of a king, Ludwig II of Bavaria.[11] There was great emphasis on listening to music in the *fin de siècle* period, and some paintings —often showing listeners with their heads in their hands— became popular. One in particular was Balestreri's *Beethoven;* then there were Khnopff's *Listen-ing to Schumann* and *Schubert am Klavier* by Gustav Klimt of the Vienna *Sezession,* Ernest Laurent's *Au Concert Colonne* and countless others (by Henri de Croux, Lévy-Dhurmer, Maurice Denis, Klinger and so on). Artists of all sorts felt themselves close to and influenced by music. Jullian quotes Odilon Redon on the subject:

> The young people of today, moved more deeply than before by the supreme waves of music, necessarily open themselves up too to the spiritual fictions and dreams of plastic art,[12]

[10] CASTRO GIL, p. 35. Castro Gil quotes A. CORREIA DE OLIVEIRA, *Tentações de S. Frei Gil.*
[11] See WILFRID BLUNT, *The Dream King* (Harmondsworth, 1973). (First edi-tion: 1970.)
[12] *Dreamers of Decadence,* p. 124.

and the young people referred to include the group of Portuguese artists whose ethos varied so little from that of the Symbolists. So to listen to music and to regard this as a mystical exercise *was* fashionable, and the use of musical terminology in literature was fashionable too. In Spain, Ramón del Valle-Inclán wrote four *Sonatas*,[13] Rubén Darío wrote a poem called «*Sinfonía* en gris mayor»,[14] and there are countless *chansons* and *chants* (Verlaine's «*Chanson* d'Automne», Theuriet's «La *Chanson* du vannier», etc.); Paul Fort entitles one of his poems «*Hymne* dans la nuit»,[15] and as late as 1918, Gide called a novel *La Symphonie pastorale*. All these expressions owe a great deal to Baudelairean *correspondances,* of course, and Baudelaire himself wrote a poem called «*Harmonie* du Soir». A further fashionable element was the delight in oriental music, Asiatic orchestras, etc., so revealing of current trends —or, more accurately, the trends of half a dozen years earlier— in Paris. *Chinoiserie, japonisme* and the *Ballets russes* were the last word in high fashion in the Paris of the first decade of this century; composers like Satie showed the influence of orientalism as early as 1890,[16] the Asiatic pavilions in the 1900 Exhibition were disturbing and exotic, and the Exhibition also boasted Japanese waitresses, Javanese dancing girls, an Indo-Chinese theatre, Sinhalese jugglers, a Cambodian temple and a Hindu pagoda. Claude Debussy, apparently, used to «spend evenings in the oriental theatres to study new harmonies» (the *Jardins sous la pluie* was composed at this period),[17] and the Chinese pavilion was a source of wonder and fascination for all. But obviously, fashion alone is not enough: there must be some basic appeal for the artist, as well as a sense of being up-to-the-minute. For Sá-Carneiro, the appreciation of music was also part of his inner life. Although music's attraction is difficult to rationalise, it has one facet which would be sure to appeal to him, and that is the order and equilibrium brought about by rhythm and harmony. (Atonal and non-rhythmic music would not, of course, fulfil the same function.) For a writer whose aim is to find harmony of some sort (within himself since the state seems impossible vis-à-vis his fellow-man), and who in so doing re-creates existence in a new and more agreeable pattern, music will be an art almost as exciting as literature.

[13] 1902-1905.
[14] In *Prosas profanas* (1896).
[15] In *Ballades françaises* (1897).
[16] The *3 Gnossiennes,* for example.
[17] JULLIAN, *The Triumph of Art Nouveau,* p. 168.

ARCHITECTURE, GEOMETRY

Sá-Carneiro is fond of ambitious architectural imagery, and there are virtually no references to the pedestrian, only to the elaborate and the exotic, the ecclesiastical and the aristocratic. There are frequent instances of words like *abóbada, nave, campanário, catedral, basílica, cúpula, igreja, templo, mausoléu, ogiva, acastelar, emoldurar, castelo, arcaria, ameia, zimbório, escadaria, galerias, palácios (reais), paços, colunas,* and *pórtico.* There is, too, emphasis on urban architecture, with images such as *teatro, ponte, muros, telhados, obelisco, monumento, torre* and *edifício.*

True to the aesthetic orientation of his interest in religion, we find images such as: «*campanários das igrejas*» (CF, p. 48), «*cúpulas* dos *templos*» (CF, p. 65), «*mausoléus* de mentira» (CF, p. 65), «*ogivas* das *catedrais*» (CL, p. 52), «o Mistério *ogivou*-me[18] longos aquedutos» (CF, p. 86), «*ruínas ogivais*» (CF, p. 65), «*cúpulas* maravilhosas» (CF, p. 64), «grandes *catedrais!*» (CF, p. 174), «*basílicas*, memórias» (CF, p. 174), «colunas e *abóbadas*» (CF, p. 65), «Lá dentro *abóbadas, naves* de pasmo» (CF, p. 280), «*naves* partidos» («Manucure», Po, p. 171), all unconnected with faith or devotion.

Again, it comes as no surprise to note that the emphasis in the field of architecture is on the splendid: «*Palácios reais, escadarias, arcos*» (CF, p. 281), «*palácios* rutilantes» (P, p. 225), «*Paços reais* de mistérios» («Não», Po, p. 88), «*galerias* infindáveis» (CF, p. 264), «as sombras de altas *colunas*» (CL, p. 52), «uma *escadaria* muito larga, de mármore» (CF, p. 119), «Ascendo a *Escadaria*» («Não», Po, p. 90), «*ameias* a marfim e oiro» (CF, p. 40), «*castelos* de miragem» (CF, p. 201), and «*altos relevos, ornamentação*» («Apoteose», Po, p. 181). But many of these visions of splendour are not what they appear to be, and in fact, many of them are in ruins. The castle in Spain is *vendido* («Pied-de-nez», Po, p. 146); there are «*castelos* de cartas» (P, p. 280), «*Castelos* desmantelados» («Dispersão», Po, p. 65), a «sala do *castelo*» which is «deserta» («Epígrafe», Po, p. 83), «o *castelo* / Amarelo do medo» («Não», Po, p. 89), «*ruínas* ogivais de arcos partidos» (CF, p. 65) and even «grandes incêndios em *ruínas*» (CF, p. 113). But although the loss of a castle in Spain is tragic, ruins themselves are often mysterious and positive: «quando a [a Atmosfera] entalham basílicas, memórias, *ruínas* do Egipto», we have beauty, according to Zagoriansky in «Asas» (CF, p. 175), and another example is in the relationship of a beautiful naked body with the atmosphere — ultimately, «o corpo é já um montão de *ruínas*» (CF, p. 176). Even with the disappointment at the inevitable end of the beauty of the «Além» episode in «Asas», when everything «ruía em sortilégio, *noutras ruínas*: o oiro,

---

[18] JOHN PARKER, p. 497, refers to the «considerable sensuous effect» of the neologism *ogivar.*

em seios perdidos; a prata, em glória abandonada» (CF, p. 199), there is a certain Decadent pleasure. The joy of the protagonist of «Mistério» was indicated when a «montão de coisas cinzentas se desmoronara em *ruínas de azul*» (CF, p. 149), while in «Rodopio», there are «*Ruínas* de melodias» among the whirling elements (Po, p. 77), and in «Manucure», «calotes suspensas entre ogivas de *ruínas*» (Po, p. 171). Unfortunately, all ruins are not attractive, and part of the protagonist's torture in «Eu-próprio o Outro» is caused by his realisation that he has been absorbed by *o Outro:* «Absorveu-me. / Já não existo. / Desapareci da vida. / Enquistei-me dentro dele. / *Ruínas!*» (CF, p. 221). How much more intriguing and revealing is the claim of the protagonist in «A Grande Sombra» after the moment of great triumph and complete victory: «Vou sempre como através de *ruínas*» (CF, p. 87).

We have already seen the many references to theatres that form part of urban architecture of Sá-Carneiro's settings, but other common city features are also mentioned with frequency. The bridge is a favourite image; walls and roofs are sometimes in evidence, and other aspects of the author's view of the city are used in descriptions or entirely metaphorically, especially towers and houses. Then we have references to cities in general — «*Cidades! Cidades!*» (CF, p. 210), the «ruas das grandes *cidades*» (P, p. 325), «Minha *cidade*-figura, / Minha *cidade* com rosto» («Abrigo», Po, p. 131), «Ó *cidade*-Princesa» (CF, p. 92) —and to buildings in general— «um formigueiro de *edifícios*» (CF, p. 57), «o *edificamento* perdurável» (CF, p. 262) and «*edifícios* sumptuosos» (CF, p. 283). Finally, there is the occasional mention of architecture itself: for example, «alguma coisa da tua *arquitectura*» (CF, p. 92).

Sá-Carneiro's interest in *Interseccionismo* and his fascination for interlocking planes, together with his concern, however slight, for Futurism and Cubism, are all evident in his frequent geometrical images. We find, for example, verbs such as *enclavinhar-se, emaranhar-se, entrelaçar* and *enroscar, ondular, raiar* and *zigue-zaguear* as well as nouns like *espaço, área, volume, dimensão, hélice, espiral, parábola, esfera, voluta, linha, curva, circunferência, convergência, traço, planos, intersecções, ponto, disco, triângulo, crescente, losango, globo, círculo, ângulo* and *vértice.* In addition, there are adjectives from some of these, and there are others like *paralelo, oval, quadrado, cónico* and *redondo.* Finally, connected with *pattern,* if not really connected with geometry, are words such as *mancha, mosquear* and *laivo.* There are innumerable examples of the imagery of geometry and pattern, so many that it would be tedious to list them: «torsos *contorcidos, enclavinhados*» (CL, p. 46), «*espaços* vazios emoldurados por arcos» (CL, p. 53), «mágicas *volutas*» (CL, p. 34), «o seu corpo de *linhas quebradas*» (CL, p. 19), «*manchas* de luz podre» (CL, p. 92), «*laivos* de roxidão» (CL, p. 119), «largos *losangos*» (CL, p. 93),

«Planos, quebras e *espaços* / Vertiginam em segredo» («Rodopio», Po, p. 76), an *«espira* aérea» («Partida», Po, p. 175), «hélices, rastros» («Rodopio», Po, p. 75), *«curvas* pederastas» («Apoteose», Po, p. 178), *«Laivos* sonoros» («Apoteose», Po, p. 175), «séries instantâneas de *quadrados»* («Manucure», Po, p. 173), *«planos* de aço» («Bárbaro», Po, p. 107), «Um *disco* de oiro» («Álcool», Po, p. 59), «Cibório *triangular»* («Taciturno», Po, p. 101), *«triângulos* sólidos» «Manucure», Po, p. 171), *«Planos* [...] que *se enclavinham»* (CF, p. 174), «uma Arte-*geometria* no *espaço»* (CF, p. 175), «movimientos de *hélice»* (CF, p. 89), etc.

Despite the splendour of the architectural images and the modernity of the kinetic geometrical terminology, disillusion, confusion, and suffering are what they project. An architect is an artist and a building is a work of art, often —as in the case of cathedrals— combining splendour and mystery, often —as with castles and palaces— evoking the past and the marvellous world of childhood. And yet a large proportion of these images are negative, qualified so as to point to the frustration experienced by one who is conscious of glory but aware of its inacessibility. *Abóbadas* are frightening, *arcos* are broken, *castelos* are part of a mirage, made of playing cards, have crumbled or are deserted; archways are horrifying, ivory towers are unreal, church towers are ominous, houses are dull, suburban and *lepidópteras;* cathedrals are unconsecrated and made of mist; tall columns cause terror, stately staircases are covered with dust-sheets, a golden stairway is «descida / Aos pinotes, quatro a quatro!» («Sete Canções de Declínio», II, Po, p. 121), or «suspeita e perigosa» («O Fantasma», Po, p. 163); it is hard not to lose one's way in galleries, altarless temples crumble; obelisks and the pointed archways of churches are frightening; provincial red roofs are repellent, bridges may be sinister or false, doors are often closed, and in the end, even the *torre maravilhosa* (P, p. 347) will not quite reach heaven. Ruins may provide a sense of the past and mystery, and their form is not obvious and immediately visible. But ruins cannot be rebuilt, and it is only in those few moments when the author is most divorced from life's reality that ruins are seen as pleasant; when suffering takes over, they represent a state of decay from which nothing can be salvaged. Even bridges, which have so many positive connotations (their pictorial qualities make them aesthetically pleasing, they are typical of Paris, they represent a means to a goal, the bridging of the gulf between individuals, and man's passage through this world) are not free from danger: they can collapse, they often bear the traveller over dangerous terrain and, at the very least, some sort of fall is risked and some sort of new and perilous territory penetrated if they are crossed. There is almost always a sense of the author's shattered illusions and of fear (sometimes, it seems, with a sexual basis) in the architectural imagery; like an architect, the author-artist designs and

173

elmos principescos» («Desquite», Po, p. 152), «Pequenos *timbres* d'oiro» («Apoteose», Po, p. 176), «sou *licorne* e *acanto*» («Partida», Po, p. 53), «nostalgias-*Docel*» (CF, p. 204), «*Arnezes, lanças, Rogério!*» (CF, p. 294), «a *espada fulva e medieval*» («Partida», Po, p. 52) and «o *bergantim real*» (CF, p. 202) are some examples. There is much use of adjectives such as *heráldico, lendário, ancestral, medieval* and *feudal* too, and there are many references to royalty: «esmola de *rainha*» (CL, p. 116), «uma figuração de *príncipes e rainhas*» (CF, p. 43), «certa *rainha* de brocado» (CF, p. 46), «*princesas* nuas» (CF, p. 48), «Cofre de *Imperatriz*» («Sete Canções de Declínio», V, Po, p. 124) and «eu sou *Rei* exilado» («Distante Melodia», Po, p. 99), for example. Then the Court is mentioned, its décor, ceremonies and its personnel: «*tronos* de marfim» (CF, p. 84), «que *pompa* ao meu redor» (CF, p. 88), «Festivais de *coroação*» (CF, p. 203), and «ser *pagem* na vida» (CL, p. 64).

If not royal, Sá-Carneiro's leanings are often aristocratic, concerned with power and control: «Sou *hierarquias* em Bizâncio», we find (CF, p. 88), and there is a «*domínio* do Mistério» (CF, p. 64), a «*domínio* de Erro» (CF, p. 65), an *Império* and a *Principado* (CF, p. 66). The choice of this imagery suggests two areas of quest: for the Ideal and, perhaps even more important, and inextricably linked with this, for himself. The choice is the more natural when we remember how popular the images were with the Symbolists.

The search for the Ideal will obviously lead into the realms of fantasy, and fantasy-escape may well go back to the far-distant past and, just as important, to the more recent past of childhood, when folk tales and fairy stories set in the Middle Ages were so real and comforting. All —except for evil, which was always defeated— was beautiful; all was shining, bejewelled, colourful, different (and yet recognisable), aristocratic, ordered, clean, special and laced with pomp and ceremony. All was, in a word, artistic, and the imagery of the idealised mediaeval world invariably represents something to be striven after or returned to. Princesses, for example, are ideal women: they are hypersensitive, as all who know Hans Andersen's «The Princess on the Pea» [24] recognise. Iona and Peter Opie, writing about this story, point out that Andersen's tale enshrines «our secret knowledge that princesses are different from the rest of us»; they add that in the East «the sensivity of those of royal or distinguished blood has been appreciated, or at least made the subject of fable, for many centuries».[25] It goes without saying that they are beautiful, and they are potential queens, with whom a prince or king may find fulfilment. What is even more important for Sá-Carneiro is that

[24] HANS ANDERSEN, «Prindsessen paa Ærten», in *Eventyr fortalte for Børn* (Copenhagen, 1885).
[25] OPIE, p. 216.

they are sexually defused; they are aesthetically attractive and marriage-able, but dehumanised. Thus expressions like «princesas nuas, lindas e debochadas» somehow manage to capture the best of both worlds for the author, encapsulating the «artistic» sex which he longs for. If the princess represents the sexual goal, the seeker must be a prince or king, a young hero or an archetypal, possibly immortal, figure of power and ideal aristocratic perfection, always in command. Their coronation will be a moment of climax and fulfilment, as it is in the «Bailado» section of «Asas», and life will have become art.

The search for identity is part of the search for the Ideal; tragedy lies in the incompatibility between the need to solve this mystery and the fact that mystery is essential to life. For hope to survive, no clear-cut solution must be found, and the ultimate catastrophe is not unconnected with Sá-Carneiro's arrival at an answer to at least some of the mysteries that filled his life. His version of the Sleeping Beauty story, the poem «Não», is a good example of the quest for self, although the author, in a letter to Fernando Pessoa dated August 31, 1915, refers to it as «fraca» (C II, p. 78). He penetrates the castle in search of something, he wants to become the king himself («Quero depor o Rei / Para lá me coroar», Po, p. 90), and at the same time he is seeking his own hidden centre. Cirlot tells us that palaces may be the symbol «del centro recóndito del 'motor inmóvil'», and he goes on:

> La idea de centro refunde el corazón y la mente, por esto el palacio del anciano rey de las leyendas y cuentos folklóricos tiene cámaras secretas (inconsciente) que guardan tesoros (verdades espirituales).[26]

According to Loeffler-Delachau,[27] mirrored castles are symbols of man-kind's ancestral memory, of the primitive knowledge of the Golden Age. So we have ignorance, but at the same time, a certain vague nostalgia for paradise lost, for lost childhood and, in true Sá-Carneiro fashion, for the present and future, for what he is and must be. He starts off as a heroic youth («Cinjo-me de cor, / E parto a demandar. / Tudo é Oiro em meu rastro — / Poeira de amor...», Po, p. 88), for despite his insecurity, he is confident of success, with that intuition reserved for princes.[28] But he does not find it, and confidence is followed by disillusion. He reaches the «hidden centre» and all is revealed, fear has become empty awareness that the throne —the centre of the centre— has crumbled, the sources of light are broken, the queen is crippled, dried out and old, colour is dead and even to defeat dragons leads nowhere. If they represent the carnal aspect of life and the queen is the *alma* (as Sá-Carneiro explicitly

---

[26] CIRLOT, p. 364.
[27] LOEFFLER-DELACHAU, *Le Symbolisme des contes de fées* (Paris, 1949).
[28] CIRLOT, p. 385: the virtue of princes is intuition.

states, thereby adding a somewhat clumsy and unnecessary epilogue to a poem which is, thus far, a successful one), then the implication is of thorough disillusionment with the goal that has always preoccupied him. He was almost king. When still unsure of his rank there was hope, but with the mystery solved, there is nothing but despair. All is spoiled or unfulfilled, not just inaccessible but non-existent. Jullian tells us that Schuré's preface to *Les Grands initiés* includes the observation that the human soul has never «aspiré plus ardemment à l'invisible au-delà sans parvenir à y croire»;[29] he was, of course, referring to the Symbolists, but the judgment applies equally to Sá-Carneiro. He could not really have meant it when he wrote to Pessoa on January 8, 1916: «se me fosse possível, apagaria o *oiro*...» (C II, p. 142, author's italics), for when mystery, shadow, gold —whatever interchangeable image is used— is removed, there is absolutely nothing left.

The difference between the Symbolists and Sá-Carneiro may well be one of scale, since they are investigating the collective unconscious in the hope of finding out about man, while he treads more or less the same path, but his goal is individual salvation. The irony of the situation is that self-knowledge was a major contribution to his disillusion and to the images of the quest had been used before — Maeterlinck's princesses for instance, or the mediaeval women of the Pre-Raphaelites. Like others, he echoes painters and illustrators such as Arthur Rackham, Walter Crane, Henry A. Payne, Edmund Dulac, Armand Point, Carlos Schwabe, Rochegrosse and Burne-Jones. Then there was the opera and the theatre, with the influence of Wagner and productions such as Andhré des Gachons' *Le Prince naïf* in 1893 (with tableaux with such titles as «Le Château sanglant», «La Fuite vers les ailleurs» and «La Vierge aux cheveux clairs»),[30] and, significantly, Henri Bataille and Robert d'Humières' *La Belle au bois dormant,* given in Paris in 1982 with settings by Burne-Jones and Rochegrosse. The material was all there, ready for Sá-Carneiro to use in his own way.

[29] *Esthètes*, p. 334.
[30] Referred to in JULLIAN, *Dreamers of Decadence*, p. 63.

CONCLUSION

The aim of this study was to understand Sá-Carneiro's work better, firstly by making a thorough investigation of it in order to see if it would grant us some kind of insight into Sá-Carneiro the man, and then by looking at it again in the light of what we had learned in this way. In other words, Sá-Carneiro himself would act as a bridge (to use one of his favourite metaphors) between our first reactions and our later judgment of them. As a largely confessional writer, everything this author wrote was autobiographical to a certain extent, and this method of studying him and his writings could almost be said to have chosen itself: it is my contention that favourite descriptive elements and repeated narrative actions and events are themselves metaphors that represent the author's life, emotions and attitudes.

Needless to say, the question that has to be asked now is if in fact we do understand the author better than we did — whether the dissection of his literary and epistolary output has shed any light on the man. And the answer would seem to be that we do now have a relatively clear picture of Sá-Carneiro. This is not to say that all mysteries have been solved: there is undoubtedly a great deal more that could be said on the subject. Nevertheless, our various conclusions in the course of the study do come together in such a way that we can be fairly confident about the author's social, psychological and artistic orientation, and the combination of hindsight and the insight gained from our investigation of virtually everything he wrote makes so much of what happened to him seem almost inevitable: his internal conflicts were surely bound to lead to unhappiness, and even his suicide has a certain ineluctable quality about it. The pull of male against female, Portugal against what he called «Europe», the past against the unsatisfactory present, artistic hypersensibility against the desire for love and tranquillity, the flesh against the spirit, and —in my opinion, the most important of all— life against art (for these two were certainly incompatible in his vision of the world) made everything intolerable. There is one other important feature of his work that has come to light; it incorporates yet another area of what might be supposed would be incompatibility — the difference between the author's emotional immaturity and his artistic maturity. Unlike other mutually hostile elements that we have considered, these have come together in an elegant and often original manner, especially in the poetry.

When a creative artist dies young, there is the temptation to speculate as to what he might have done had he lived: which way would his work have developed, given the new artistic movements and influences that would have accompanied its progress and the artist's own changing outlook on life and himself? In the case of Sá-Carneiro it is impossible even to hazard a guess at what might have been, since what he wrote was so representative of his life and emotions at a given period. His work, to quote Ricardo de Loureiro, was his short life *literalizada*.

SELECT BIBLIOGRAPHY

ANON., «'Casa de Comédia'— Mário de Sá-Carneiro e José Régio», in *Diário de Notícias,* October 17, 1969.
— *Delacroix et le Fantastique.* Catalogue to exhibition, Musée Delacroix, 6 Place Furstenberg, Paris: May-November, 1972.
ABRAMS, M. H., *Natural Supernaturalism.* London, 1971.
AGUIRRE, J. M., *Antonio Machado, poeta simbolista.* Madrid, 1973.
ALLEN, Donald (ed.), *The New American Poetry 1945-1960.* New York, 1960.
ALLEN, Rupert C., *The Symbolic World of Federico García Lorca.* Albuquerque, 1972.
— *Psyche and Symbol in the Theater of Federico García Lorca.* Austin, 1974.
ANDERSEN, Hans, *The Complete Fairy Tales and Stories,* trans. Erik Haugaard. London, 1974.
ALVAREZ, A., *The Savage God. A Study of Suicide.* London, 1971.
ALVES, João, *O Génio de Vila-Moura.* Oporto, 1937.
— «Os modernistas», *Lusíada,* III (July 1959), 261-3.
ANDRADE, Ione de, «Realismo fantástico e simbolismo dos trajes na *Confissão de Lúcio*», in *Bulletin des Études Portugaises,* XXVIII-XXIX (1967-1968), 337-354.
ANDRADE, João Pedro de, *A Poesia da Moderníssima Geração.* Oporto, 1943.
D'ANNUNZIO, Gabriele, *La Nave* (1908).
ANSELMO, Manuel, *Soluções Críticas.* Coimbra, 1934.
— *Antologia Moderna.* Lisbon, 1937.
— *Caminhos e ansiedades da poesia portuguesa contemporânea.* Lisbon, 1941.
ANTUNES, M. A., «A poesia modernista. De *Orpheu* a *Altitude*», *Brotéria,* XXXI [Lisbon] (October, 1940), 300-20.
AZEVEDO, F. Alves de, *Figuras Contemporâneas.* Lisbon, 1933.

BALDICK, Robert, *The Life of J.-K. Huysmans.* Oxford, 1955.
BANVILLE, Théodore de, *Occidentales, Rimes dorées, Rondels.* Paris, 1875.
BARBEY D'AURÉVILLY, Jules Amédée, *Les Diaboliques* (1874). Paris, 1963.
BARRETO, Moniz, *Estudos Dispersos.* Lisbon, 1963.
BARROS, João de, *Pequena História da Poesia Portuguesa.* Lisbon, 1941.
BARZUN, Jacques, *Classic Romantic and Modern* (second, revised edition of *Romanticism and the Modern Ego,* 1943). New York, 1961.
BATESON, F. W., *The Scholar-Critic.* London, 1972.
BATTERSBY, Martin, *Art Nouveau.* Feltham, 1969.
BAUDELAIRE, Charles, *Les Fleurs du mal,* 2nd edition. Paris, 1861.
— *Curiosités. L'Art romantique.* Paris, 1962.
— *Le Peintre de la vie moderne,* in *Oeuvres Complètes.* Paris, 1963.
BÉCQUER, Gustavo Adolfo, *Obras,* vol. I. Madrid, 1915.
— *Rimas.* Madrid, 1963.

GAUTHIER, Xavière, *Surréalisme et sexualité*. Paris, 1970.
GAUTIER, Théophile, *Mademoiselle de Maupin* (1835). Paris, 1966.
— *Émaux et Camées* (1852). Paris, 1854.
— *Contes Fantastiques*. Paris, 1973.
GIL, A. de Castro, «Sá-Carneiro — o rastro duma alma que se queimou», *Novidades — Letras e Artes*, no. 43 [Lisbon] (November 2, 1947), 1-3.
— *Sá-Carneiro, Miguel Torga, José Régio, três atitudes perante a vida*. Coimbra, 1949.
GIL, Ildefonso Manuel, *Ensayos sobre poesía portuguesa*. Saragossa, 1948.
GOMBRICH, E. H., *Symbolic Images* (1972). London, 1975.
GOURMONT, Remy de, *Le Livre des masques*. Paris, 1896-1898.
— *Histoires Magiques*. Paris, s/d.
GRIMM, The Brothers, *The Juniper Tree and Other Tales*, trans. Lore Segal and Randall Jarrell. London, 1974.
GUILLÉN, Claudio, *Literature as System*. Princeton, 1971.
GUILLÉN, Jorge, *Lenguaje y poesía* (1961). Madrid, 1962.
GUIMARÃES, Fernando, «Simbolismo, saudosismo, modernismo...», in *Diário de Lisboa*, August 8, 1966, September 8, 1966 and September 22, 1966.
GUIMARÃES, Luís de Oliveira; SANTOS, José Ribeiro dos, *Memória dos Outros*. Lisbon, 1944.
GUISADO, Alfredo Pedro, «Ainda os 35 anos do *Orpheu*. Como apareceu Álvaro de Campos», in *República*, Lisbon, May 12, 1950.
— «A história do *Orpheu*», *Boletim da Sociedade de Escritores e Compositores Teatrais Portugueses*, no. 10 (Autumn, 1960).
— «Comentário: Ainda o *Orpheu*», in *República*, Lisbon, April 23, 1965.
— *Tempo de Orfeu*. Lisbon, 1970.
GULLÓN, Ricardo, *Direcciones del modernismo*. Madrid, 1963.

HAFTMANN, Werner, *Painting in the Twentieth Century*. London, 1961.
HAMBURGER, Michael, *The Truth of Poetry*. London, 1969.
HAMENACHEM, Miriam S., *Charles Nodier. Essai sur l'Imagination mythique*. Paris, 1972.
HAYTER, Alethea, *Opium and the Romantic Imagination* (1968). London, 1971.
HERCULANO, Alexandre, *Lendas e Narrativas*. Lisbon, s/d.
HOFFMANN, E. T. A., *Contes Fantastiques*. Paris, 1964.
HOURCADE, Pierre, «Panorama du Modernisme littéraire en Portugal», *Bulletin des Études Portugaises*, 1 (1931), 69-78.
— «Defesa e ilustração da poesia portuguesa viva», trans. J. G. S. [João Gaspar Simões?], in *Presença*, vol. II, no. 30, January-February, 1931.
— «Cartas a Fernando Pessoa (de Mário de Sá-Carneiro)», in *Bulletin des Études Portugaises*, XXII (1959-1960), 326-31.
HUBER, Egon, «Zur Lyrik Mário de Sá-Carneiros», in *Studia Iberica. Festschrift für Hans Flasche* (Berne, 1973), pp. 282-94.
HUYSMANS, J.-K., *À Rebours* (1884). Paris, 1968.

ILHARCO, João, *Libelo contra a Poesia Modernista*. Coimbra, 1955.

JAFFÉ, H. L. C., *Twentieth-Century Painting*. London, 1963.
JENNINGS, Hargrave, *The Rosicrucians — their Rites and Mysteries*. London, s/d.
JOHNSON, R. V., *Aestheticism*. London, 1969.
JUIN, Hubert, *Écrivains de l'Avant-siècle*. Paris, 1972.
JULLIAN, Philippe, *Robert de Montesquiou*. Paris, 1965.

— *Esthètes et Magiciens* (Paris, 1969), translated as: *Dreamers of Decadence.* London, 1971.
— *Oscar Wilde* (London, 1969), trans. Violet Wyndham. London, 1971.
— *D'Annunzio.* Paris, 1971.
— *French Symbolist Painters.* Catalogue to exhibition, Hayward Gallery, London, June 7-July 23, 1972.
— *Jean Lorrain ou le satiricon 1900.* Paris, 1974.
— *The Triumph of Art Nouveau. Paris Exhibition 1900,* trans. Stephen Hardman. London, 1974.
JUNG, Carl Gustav, *Man and his Symbols.* London, 1964.

KAYSER, Wolfgang, *Interpretación y análisis de la obra literaria.* Madrid, 1954.

LAFORGUE, Jules, *Moralités légendaires,* 1887.
LAING, R. D., *The Divided Self* (1960). Harmondsworth, 1972.
LALOU, René, *Histoire de la Littérature française contemporaine.* Paris, 1928.
LANGER, Susanne K., *Philosophical Sketches* (1962). Chicago, 1964.
LAVER, James, *The First Decadent.* London, s/d.
LEAL, Raul, «Trinta anos de *Orpheu*», in *República,* Lisbon, May 20, 1945.
— «As tendências orfaicas e o saudosismo», in *Tempo Presente,* no. 5, September, 1959, 17-24.
LEBESGUE, Philéas, «Lettres Portugaises», in *Le Mercure de France,* April 1, 1913.
LE GENTIL, Georges, *Abrégé de Littérature portugaise.* Paris, 1935.
— *La Littérature portugaise.* Paris, 1951.
LÉVI, Éliphas, *Dogme et Rituel de la haute magie.* Paris, 1972.
LIMA, Ângelo de, *Poesias completas.* Oporto, 1971.
LIMA, Duarte, «Breve ensaio sobre o modernismo», in *Síntese,* vol. II, no. 14, 615, Coimbra, October-December, 1941.
LIND, Georg Rudolf, «Acerca de uma tese alemã sobre a lírica de Mário de Sá-Carneiro», *Ocidente,* LXIV (1963), 169-70.
LISBOA, Eugénio, *O Segundo Modernismo em Portugal,* 9th ed. Lisbon, 1977.
LOEFFLER-DELACHAUX, M., *Le Symbolisme des contes de fées.* Paris, 1949.
LOPES, Óscar, «A dialéctica do espaço-tempo nas novelas de Mário de Sá-Carneiro», in *Seara Nova,* no. 1, 464, Lisbon, September, 1967, 329-30.
LOPES, Teresa Rita, «Pessoa, Sá-Carneiro e as três dimensões do Sensacionismo», in *Colóquio. Letras,* no. 4, Lisbon, December, 1971.
LORRAIN, Jean (pseudonym of Paul A. M. Duval), *La Forêt bleue* (1883).
— *L'Ombre ardente* (1897).
— *Monsieur de Bougrelon* (1897).
— *Histoires de masques* (1900).
— *Monsieur de Phocas. Astarté* (1901).
— *Le Vice errant* (1901).
— *Princesses d'Ivoire de d'ivresse* (1902).
— *Le Mandragore* (1903).
— *Fards et Poisons* (1904).
— *La Maison Philibert* (1904).
LOURENÇO, Eduardo, «*Orpheu* ou a poesia como realidade», in *Tetracórnio,* Lisbon, February, 1955, 27-39.
LUCAS, F. L., *The Decline and Fall of the Romantic Ideal* (1936). Cambridge, 1963.
LUCIE-SMITH, Edward, *Symbolist Art.* London, 1972.
— *Eroticism in Western Art.* London, 1972.

185

MADSEN, S. Tschudi, *Art nouveau*, trans. R. I. Christopherson. London, 1967.

MAETERLINCK, Maurice, *Poésies Complètes*. Brussels, 1965.

MARQUES, Manuel Correia, «Mário de Sá-Carneiro — alguns inéditos do poeta», in *Diário Popular*, Lisbon, February 13, 1958.

— «Novos Aspectos de Mário de Sá-Carneiro», in *Panorama*, no. 16, 3rd series, Lisbon, December, 1959.

MATORÉ, Georges, *La Méthode en lexicologie. Domaine française*. Paris, 1953.

MATOS, Lígia-Maria da Câmara de Almeida, «A poesia modernista em Portugal», in *Estudos*, Ano XXV, fascículos 6, 7, nos. 258-59 [Coimbra] (June-July, 1947), 280-316.

MAUL, Carlos, *A Concepção da Alegria em alguns Poetas Contemporâneos*. Lisbon, 1914.

MAUPASSANT, Guy de, *Le Horla* (1886). Paris, 1909.

— *Contes du Jour et de la nuit*. Paris, 1922.

— *Les Soeurs Rondoli. Le Baiser*. Paris, 1924.

MAURON, Charles, *Des Métaphores obsédantes au mythe personnel*. Paris, 1962.

MEIER, Harri, *Ensaios de Filologia Românica*. Lisbon, 1948.

MEIRELES, Cecília, *Poetas Novos de Portugal*. Rio de Janeiro, 1944.

MELO E CASTRO, E. M. de (ed.), *Antologia do Conto Fantástico Português* (1965), Lisbon, 1974.

MENDES, João R., «Crítica a *Indicios de Ouro*», *Brotéria*, XXVI (January 1938), 111-12.

— «Sá-Carneiro, Poeta da Soledade», *Brotéria*, XXXII, fascículo 5 (May, 1941), 507-19.

MENDES, Maria Paula Canas, «Contribuição para o estudo do motivo do 'tédio' nas obras poéticas de Fernando Pessoa (ortónimo) e de Mário de Sá-Carneiro», Lisbon, 1955 (tese de licenciatura).

MÉRIMÉE, Prosper, *La Double méprise. La Guzla* (1833, 1840). Paris, 1908.

MIGUEL, António Dias, «Algumas notas a respeito da poesia de Mário de Sá-Carneiro», *Afinidades*, no. 17 (April, 1946), 46-55.

— «A sinceridade na poesia de Mário de Sá-Carneiro», in *O Comércio do Porto*, August 11, 1953. Reproduced in *Estrada Larga*, vol. I, p. 225.

MILOSZ, Oscar, *Le Poème des décadences*. Paris, 1899.

MIRBEAU, Octave, *Le Jardin des supplices* (1899). Paris, 1957.

MITCHELL, Bonner, *Les Manifestations littéraires de la Belle Époque*. Paris, 1966.

MOISÉS, Massaud, *A Literatura Portuguesa através dos Textos*. São Paulo, 1960.

MONTALVOR, Luís de, «Rapazes de ontem, homens de hoje... os 30 anos de *Orpheu* ou a revolução literária de 1915», in *República*, Lisbon, May 20, 1945.

— *Poemas*. Oporto, s/d.

MONTEIRO, Adolfo Casais, «Mário de Sá-Carneiro», in *Presença*, no. 21, June-August, 1929.

— *Considerações Pessoais*. Coimbra, 1933.

— «La poesia portoghese d'avanguardia», in *Augustea*, Rome, October 28, 1935, November 4, 1935, May 15, 1936, January 1, 1937.

— *Le Moderne et l'éternel dans la poésie portugaise contemporaine*. Lisbon, 1939.

— «*Orpheu*-Orfeu», in *República*, Lisbon, April 28, 1950.

— «La Génération de l'*Orpheu*: Fernando Pessoa, Mário de Sá-Carneiro, Almada Negreiros», in *Courrier du Centre International d'Études Poétiques*, no. 35-36 [Brussels] (December, 1961).

MONTENEGRO, Federico, «A ficção portuguesa como estética e como cultura», in *Diário de Lisboa*, November 3, 1966.

SELECT BIBLIOGRAPHY

MORAES, Maria da Ascensão Ferreira Custódio de, «Aspectos estilísticos da poesia de Mário de Sá-Carneiro», Lisbon, 1947 (tese de licenciatura).
MORAIS, Manuel, «Mário de Sá-Carneiro», Lisbon, 1940 (tese de licenciatura).

NASCIMENTO, Cabral do, «Do Simbolismo ao *Orpheu*», *Aleo*, ano V, no. 48, série 4 [Lisbon] (January 1, 1947).
NEGREIROS, José de Almada, *Manifesto anti-Dantas e por extenso*. Lisbon, 1916.
— «Mário de Sá-Carneiro morreu há 41 anos — Notas breves sobre o poeta», in *Diário Ilustrado*, Lisbon, May 14, 1957.
— *Obras Completas*. Lisbon, 1970.
— *Nome de Guerra*. Lisbon, 1972.
NEMÉSIO, Vitorino, «Crítica a *Indícios de Oiro*», *Revista de Portugal*, I, fascículo 2 [Coimbra] (January, 1938).
— «La poésie portugaise moderne et la France», *Revue de Littérature Comparée* (January-March, 1938), 218-22.
— *Études Portugaises, Gil Vicente, Herculano, Antero de Quental. Le symbolisme*. Lisbon, 1938.
— «A geração de *Orpheu*», in *Diário Popular*, Lisbon, April 25, 1950.
— *Conhecimento da Poesia*. Salvador, 1958.
— *Destino de Gomes Leal*. Lisbon, s/d.
NERVAL, Gérard de, *Les Filles du Feu. Aurélia*. Paris, 1961.
— *Les Chimères*. London, 1973.
NEVES, João Alves das (ed.), *Mário de Sá-Carneiro*. São Paulo, s/d (1962?).
— *O Movimento Futurista em Portugal*. Oporto-Lisbon-Viana do Castelo, 1966.
— *Poetas Portugueses Modernos*. Rio de Janeiro, 1967.
NODIER, Charles, *Les Tristes ou Mélanges tirés des tablettes d'un suicide*. Paris, 1806.
— *Smarra ou les Démons de la nuit*. Paris, 1821.
— *Contes*. Paris, 1961.
NOGUEIRA, Albano, *Imagens em Espelho Côncavo*. Coimbra, 1940.
NORONHA, Mário, «Soltas considerações sobre literatura contemporânea», in *Seara Nova*, Lisbon, August 29, 1935.

OLIVEIRA, José Manuel Cardoso de, *Poetas e Prosadores Portugueses*. Lisbon, 1923.
OLIVEIRA, José Osório de, *Panorama da Literatura Portuguesa*. Lisbon, 1947.
OPIE, Iona and Peter, *The Classic Fairy Tales*. Oxford, 1974.
ORTEGA Y GASSET, José, *Caracteres y circunstancias*. Madrid, 1957.
— *El espectador*, I. Madrid, 1968.

PARKER, John M., «The Life and Works of Mário de Sá-Carneiro», Cambridge, 1959 (unpublished thesis).
— *Three Twentieth-Century Portuguese Poets*. Johannesburg, 1960.
PASCOAES, Teixeira de, *Antologia Poética*. Lisbon, 1962.
PATER, Walter, *The Renaissance* (1873). London, 1961.
PAYEN-PAYNE, V.; CLARKE, Isabelle H. (eds.), *French Poems of Today*. London, 1930.
PAZ, Octavio, *Los hijos del limo*. Barcelona, 1974.
PEILLEX, Georges, *Nineteenth Century Painting*. London, 1964.
PEIXOTO, Jorge, «Mário de Sá-Carneiro escolar de lei em Coimbra», in *O Comércio do Porto*, May 9, 1967.
PÉLADAN, Joséphin (Sâr), *Le Vice suprême*. Paris, 1884.
— *À Coeur perdu*. Paris, 1888.

— «Mário de Sá-Carneiro ou a Ilusão da Personalidade», in *O Mistério da Poesia,* Coimbra, 1931, pp. 123-68.
— «'Indícios de Ouro' por Mário de Sá-Carneiro», in *Diário de Lisboa,* December 30, 1937.
— *Novos Temas.* Lisbon, 1938.
— *António Nobre. Precursor da Poesia Moderna.* Lisbon, 1939.
— «A propósito da *Dispersão* de Mário de Sá-Carneiro», *Cadernos de Poesia,* no. 1 [Lisbon] (1940), 11-15.
— «Interpretação e juízos» (a confissão de Mário de Sá-Carneiro), in *Mundo Literário,* no. 9, July 6, 1946.
— «Alguns poetas e uma sua intérprete», in *Afinidades,* 19-20, October-November, 1946.
— «Evocação de Mário de Sá-Carneiro em Paris», in *Diário Popular,* Lisbon, December 12, 1946.
— *Liberdade de Espírito.* Oporto, 1948.
— *Natureza e Função da Literatura.* Lisbon, 1948.
— «O mistério da correspondência de Mário de Sá-Carneiro e Fernando Pessoa», in *Diário Popular,* Lisbon, March 13, 1949.
— *Historia da Poesia Portuguesa do Século XX.* Lisbon, 1955, 1956 and 1959.
— «Mário de Sá-Carneiro, *Orpheu* e o Surrealismo», in *O Estudo de São Paulo,* November 15, 1958.
— *História do Movimento da Presença.* Coimbra, 1958.
— «Crítica literária», in *Diário de Notícias,* March 16, 1961.
— *Itinerário Histórico da Poesia Portuguesa.* Lisbon, 1964.
— *Literatura, Literatura, Literatura.* Lisbon, 1964.
— «Crítica literária», in *Diário de Notícias,* Lisbon, October 22, 1964.
— «*Céu em Fogo* por Mário de Sá-Carneiro», in *Diário de Notícias,* Lisbon, January 12, 1967.
— «Alguns precursores da poesia modernista», in *O Primeiro de Janeiro,* Oporto, September 18, 1967.
— *50 Anos de Poesia Portuguesa do Simbolismo ao Surrealismo.* Lisbon, 1968.
SPENCER, Robin, *The Aesthetic Movement.* London, 1972.
STANFORD, Derek (ed.), *Writing of the 'Nineties.* London, 1971.
STENDHAL, *Mémoires d'un Touriste.* Paris, 1927.
STENGEL, Erwin, *Suicide and Attempted Suicide.* Harmondsworth, 1971.
STORR, Anthony, *Sexual Deviation* (1964). Harmondsworth, 1968.
SYMONS, Arthur, *The Symbolist Movement in Literature* (1899).
— *Studies in Prose and Verse* (1904).
— *Cities and Sea-Coasts and Islands* (1918).
— *Wanderings* (1931).
SZASZ, Thomas S., *The Myth of Mental Illness* (1961). St. Albans, 1975.

THORNTON, R. K. R. (ed.), *Poetry of the Nineties.* Harmondsworth, 1970.
TILLICH, P., *The Courage to Be.* London, 1952.
TORRE, Guillermo de, *Literaturas europeas de vanguardia.* Madrid, 1925.

VALÉRY, Paul, *Introduction à la Poétique.* Paris, 1938.
VARIOUS, *Futurismo 1909-1919.* Catalogue of exhibition of Italian Futurism, Royal Scottish Academy, Edinburgh, December 16, 1972-January 14, 1973.
VARIOUS, *Kinetics.* Catalogue of exhibition, Hayward Gallery, London, September 25-November 22, 1970.
VASCONCELOS, Mário Cesariny de, «*Orpheu* e literatura de vanguarda», in *Contraponto,* Lisbon, 1950.

VERLAINE, Paul, *Poèmes Saturniens* (1866).
— *Jadis et Naguère* (1884).
VEIGA, Pedro, *O Sr. Adolfo Casais Monteiro e os Modernistas Portugueses.* Oporto, s/d.
VILA-MOURA, Visconde de, *A Vida Mental Portuguesa* (1909).
— *Nova Safo* (1912).
— *Doentes de Beleza* (1913).
— *Obstinados* (1921).
— *Novela Mensal* (1924).
— *Dor Errante* (1933).
— *Novos Mitos* (1934).
VILHENA, Henrique de, *Ensaios de Crítica e Estética.* Lisbon, 1922.
VILLIERS DE L'ISLE-ADAM, *Contes Fantastiques.* Paris, 1965.

WHEELWRIGHT, P., *Metaphor and Reality.* Bloomington, 1962.
WILSON, Colin, *The Outsider* (1956). London, 1970.
WOLL, Dieter, «A lírica de Mário de Sá-Carneiro vista por um alemão», *Colóquio,* nos. 5-6 [Lisbon] (November, 1959), 91-3.
— *Realidade e Idealidade na Lírica de Sá-Carneiro.* Lisbon, 1968.
— «Decifrando 'A Confissão de Lúcio'», in *Miscelânea de Estudos em honra do Prof. Vitorino Nemésio* (Lisbon, 1971), pp. 425-38.
WILDE, Oscar, *Complete Works.* London, 1970.

YEATS, W. B., *Ideas of Good and Evil.* London, 1903.
YOUNG, Wayland, *Eros Denied* (1965). London, 1969.